Contents

Abbreviations

A.B.M. Anti-ballistic missile.
A.N.C. African National Congress.
A.N.Z.U.S. Australia, New Zealand, United States Pact 1951.
B.O.S.S. Bureau of State Security (Republic of South Africa).
C.P.P. Convention People's Party (Ghana).
D.M.Z. Demilitarized Zone.
E.E.C. European Economic Community (Common Market).
E.F.T.A. European Free Trade Association.
F.A.O. Food and Agriculture Organization (United Nations).
F.L.N. National Liberation Front (Algeria).
G.D.R. German Democratic Republic (East Germany).
I.C.B.M. Intercontinental ballistic missile.
I.G.Y. International Geophysical Year.
I.R.B.M. Intermediate range ballistic missile.
M.I.R.V. Multiple Independently-targeted Re-entry Vehicle.
N.A.S.A. National Aeronautics and Space Administration (USA).
N.A.T.O. North Atlantic Treaty Organization (founded 1949).
N.L.F. National Liberation Front (a) militant Aden political party, (b) title preferred by the Viet Cong.
O.E.E.C. Organization for European Economic Co-operation.
P.K.I. Indonesian Communist Party.
P.L.O. Palestine Liberation Organization.
P.N.I. Indonesian Nationalist Party.
S.A.L.T. Strategic Arms Limitation Treaty.
S.D.I. Strategic Defence Initiative.
S.E.T. Selective Employment Tax.
S.W.A.P.O. South West African People's Organization.
T.V.A. Tennessee Valley Authority (United States).
U-2 Lockheed U-2 'spy-plane' (United States).
U.D.I. Unilateral Declaration of Independence.
U.S.I.S. United States Information Service.
U.S.S.R. Union of Soviet Socialist Republics.
U.N.I.C.E.F. United Nations International Children's Emergency Fund.
U.N.R.R.A. United Nations Relief and Rehabilitation Administration.
V.1; V.2 'Vergeltungswaffen', reprisal weapons, V.1 was the 'doodle-bug' or flying bomb. V.2 was a supersonic rocket.
V.S.O. Voluntary Service Overseas.
W.H.O. World Health Organization.
Z.A.P.U. Zimbabwe African People's Union.

A MAP HISTORY OF THE MODERN WORLD

1890 to the Present Day

Third Edition

Brian Catchpole

Maps and drawings by Regmarad

HEINEMANN EDUCATIONAL BOOKS LTD
OUTH

Heinemann Educational Books Ltd
22 Bedford Square, London WC1B 3HH

Heinemann Educational Books Inc
70 Court Street, Portsmouth, NH 03801, USA

LONDON   EDINBURGH   MELBOURNE   AUCKLAND
HONG KONG   SINGAPORE   KUALA LUMPUR
NEW DELHI   IBADAN   NAIROBI   JOHANNESBURG
PORTSMOUTH (NH)   KINGSTON

Other books by Brian Catchpole

ISBN 0 435 31098 4
© Brian Catchpole 1968, 1974, 1982
First published 1968
Reprinted 1969
Reprinted with corrections 1970
Reprinted 1971
Second Edition 1974
Reprinted with corrections 1976, 1978
Reprinted with additions 1980
Third Edition 1982
Reprinted with additions 1985
Reprinted with additions 1986

COVER PHOTOGRAPHS (left to right):
*President Sadat, President Carter and Prime Minister
    Begin after signing the Egyptian–Israeli Peace Treaty
    in March 1979* (Keystone).
Lech Walesa meets Pope John Paul II (Keystone).
*US troops climb down in Viet Nam to look for Viet Cong
    guerrillas* (Popperfoto).

Photoset in Malta by Interprint (Malta) Ltd
Reprinted in Great Britain by
Fletcher & Son Ltd, Norwich

Preface

The aim of this world history is to tell the story of the Twentieth Century by means of maps which are directly related to the text. Each self-contained page of narrative faces maps which are designed to contribute to the understanding and amplification of the topic under consideration. Topics have been chosen to meet the needs and interests of students and to lend themselves both to class teaching and to private study assignments. Themes such as *World War II* or *The Internal Problems of Modern States* offer opportunities for 'patch' or 'centre of interest' studies in depth; while the use of several *related* topics (such as Nos. 8; 16; 29; 34; 36; 45 on aspects of communism) will provide rapid guidance in the development of project work.

INTRODUCTION

The rise of the modern states

'A man who is ignorant of the society in which he lives, who knows nothing of its place in the world and who has not thought about his place in it, is not a free man even though he has a vote. He is easy game for the "hidden persuaders" ....'

The Newsom Report Page 163

(Half our Future – a report of the Central Advisory Council for Education)

1 : The rise of the modern states 1890–1980
Political Development

Today we define a modern state as one which can organize its political and economic resources on a national scale. Before 1890, few nations measured up to this definition, although by that date four major industrial nations had emerged. Well in the lead were *America, Germany* and *Britain*, while a fourth, *Japan*, was striving to catch up with the others. These modern states based their wealth on manufactured goods and commerce. They had also introduced systems of state education and possessed vigorous populations with a strong sense of national pride. They were the world leaders.

Other great countries were falling behind because they based their economies on agriculture rather than on industry. They had large peasant populations who represented problems so great that in most cases their rulers were unable to solve them peacefully. For example:

Italy was a newly united country, but poor in industrial resources.

France in 1890 was still mainly an agricultural country and had been defeated by Germany in 1871 when she had lost Alsace and Lorraine, two important industrial provinces.

The *Austro-Hungarian Empire* embraced peasants of many nationalities and seethed with discontent.

The *Ottoman Empire* was ruled by the Muslim Sultan of Turkey. His dominions covered much of the Arab Middle East as well as parts of the Christian Balkan areas of South East Europe.

The *Chinese Empire* was peopled by 400 million poor, inarticulate peasants governed by an alien Manchu Emperor. Foreign nations controlled his country's trade.

The *Russian Empire* was a vast, sprawling state ruled over by a despotic Czar. There were few industrial areas and most Russian peasants lived a life that had not changed much since the Middle Ages.

So although this was the age of the rising modern state, many old empires survived and were joined by new colonial empires. The greatest of these was the *British Empire* whose Queen 'Victoria' was Empress of India, Queen of Australia, New Zealand, Canada and South Africa, ruler of many colonies in East and West Africa, as well as numerous islands and naval bases in the seas and oceans of the world.

The Pace of Change

Within the span of a single lifetime, a man would see fantastic changes. By 1980, after two World Wars, the old empires had vanished. There were no more important Czars, Sultans or Emperors. Instead, scores of modern states had emerged. The Commonwealth of Nations had replaced the British Empire. The most powerful states of all were the two greatest industrial nations or 'superpowers', Russia and the United States.

By 1980 the whole world had been explored. The first men had landed on the Moon and returned safely to their own planet. The world's population had almost doubled since 1890—yet most people were still under-nourished. And for the first time in his history, because of the development of thermo-nuclear weapons, man was capable of his self-destruction.

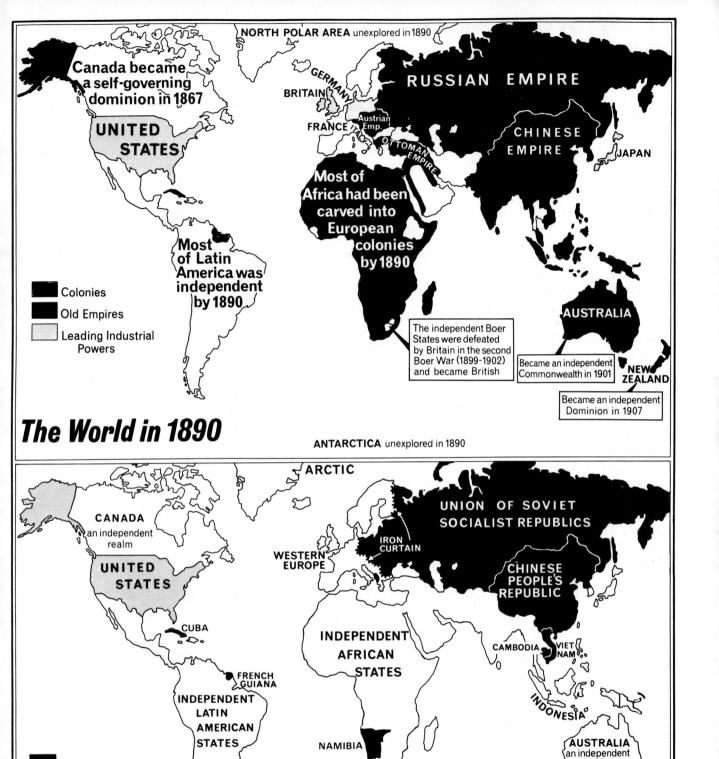

NORTH POLAR AREA unexplored in 1890

Canada became a self-governing dominion in 1867

UNITED STATES

GERMANY
BRITAIN
FRANCE
Austrian Emp.
OTTOMAN EMPIRE

RUSSIAN EMPIRE

CHINESE EMPIRE

JAPAN

Most of Africa had been carved into European colonies by 1890

Most of Latin America was independent by 1890

■ Colonies
■ Old Empires
▨ Leading Industrial Powers

The independent Boer States were defeated by Britain in the second Boer War (1899-1902) and became British

AUSTRALIA

Became an independent Commonwealth in 1901

NEW ZEALAND

Became an independent Dominion in 1907

The World in 1890

ANTARCTICA unexplored in 1890

ARCTIC

CANADA
an independent realm

UNITED STATES

WESTERN EUROPE

IRON CURTAIN

UNION OF SOVIET SOCIALIST REPUBLICS

CHINESE PEOPLE'S REPUBLIC

CUBA

FRENCH GUIANA

INDEPENDENT LATIN AMERICAN STATES

INDEPENDENT AFRICAN STATES

CAMBODIA
VIET NAM

INDONESIA

NAMIBIA

AUSTRALIA
an independent realm

■ Communist countries
■ Large areas awaiting independence

NEW ZEALAND
an independent realm

The World in 1980

ANTARCTIC

2: The rise of the modern states 1890–1980
Economic Development

How had it all happened?

The maps and information in this book will help you to find some of the answers. But the main reason for all these changes was that man had discovered how to exploit the economic wealth of his world and to concentrate on technical progress and labour-saving devices. He had invented the petrol and diesel internal combustion engines, put electrical power and nuclear energy to his use. He had produced high grade steels, discovered new minerals and new sources of fuel such as oil and natural gas. He had invented the aeroplane, which revolutionized war and peace. He had changed the face of the earth, carving out his airfields, altering the course of rivers and constructing monster dams to increase his wealth and his standard of living. All of this had taken less than 80 years and during the process he had decided on two main ways in which he would organize and pay for these projects—two ways which now divide the world:

(1) The CAPITALIST system: some nations favour private enterprise and encourage the individual first to accumulate wealth and then to invest it in commercial enterprises. Owners and managers pay their employees agreed wages and salaries, but share most of the profits among the investors—or shareholders—who put up the money in the first place. The number of investors varies enormously from one capitalist country to another; but in most the individual is able to risk a few pounds on the stock market in the hope that his shares, as opposed to his own efforts, will bring him a profit. This system has led to the growth of huge industrial companies, employing thousands of workers.

(2) The COMMUNIST system: other nations have evolved a system during the 20th century whereby their governments own ALL the means of production—i.e. the factories, farms and offices. The 'state' then rewards the workers according to their efforts and their needs. The individual is not permitted to engage in investment or in any form of currency deal. For such a crime people were executed in the Soviet Union during the 1960s. Such countries have adopted the teachings of Karl Marx, who preached a world *revolution against capitalism*, and Lenin, who carried out such a revolution in Russia. Nations known as communist states are, for example, the Soviet Union and the Chinese Peoples' Republic.

Significantly, in the seventies the measure of a country's success was still its ability to produce wealth and happiness for its people by means of its raw materials and manufactured goods.

World Steel Production

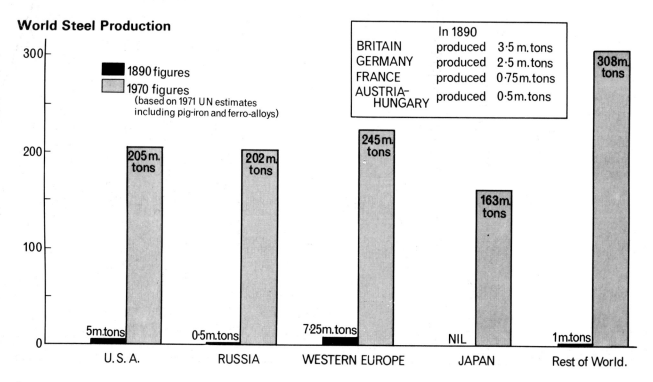

■ 1890 figures

▨ 1970 figures
(based on 1971 UN estimates
including pig-iron and ferro-alloys)

In 1890
BRITAIN produced 3·5 m.tons
GERMANY produced 2·5 m.tons
FRANCE produced 0·75 m.tons
AUSTRIA-HUNGARY produced 0·5 m.tons

	U.S.A.	RUSSIA	WESTERN EUROPE	JAPAN	Rest of World.
1890	5m.tons	0·5m.tons	7·25m.tons	NIL	1m.tons
1970	205m. tons	202m. tons	245m. tons	163m. tons	308m. tons

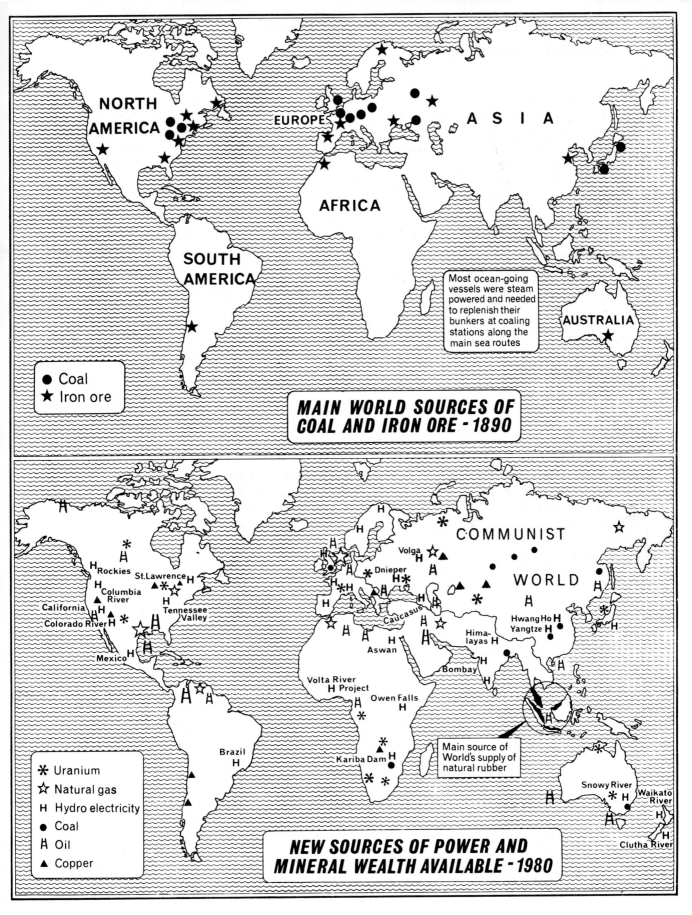

Map 1 (top)

NORTH AMERICA

EUROPE

A S I A

AFRICA

SOUTH AMERICA

Most ocean-going vessels were steam powered and needed to replenish their bunkers at coaling stations along the main sea routes

AUSTRALIA

● Coal
★ Iron ore

MAIN WORLD SOURCES OF COAL AND IRON ORE - 1890

Map 2 (bottom)

Rockies
St. Lawrence
H
Columbia River
California
Colorado River
Tennessee Valley
Mexico

Volga
Dnieper
Caucasus
COMMUNIST WORLD
Hwang Ho
Yangtze
Himalayas
Aswan
Bombay

Volta River Project
Owen Falls

Brazil

Kariba Dam

Main source of World's supply of natural rubber

Snowy River
Waikato River
Clutha River

✳ Uranium
☆ Natural gas
H Hydro electricity
● Coal
Ħ Oil
▲ Copper

NEW SOURCES OF POWER AND MINERAL WEALTH AVAILABLE - 1980

LAUNCHED 1890, BLOWN UP IN HAVANA HARBOR AT 9.40 P.M.
DIMENSIONS:- LENGTH OVERALL 324 FT 4½ INCHES, BREADTH EXTREME 57 FT.
MEAN DRAUGHT 21 FEET 6 INCHES; DISPLACEMENT 6682 TONS, SPEED 17 KNOTS
AN HOUR. 9293 HORSE POWER; TURRET ARMOUR 8½ INCHES THICK; COST $ 3,000,000.

DESTRUCTION OF THE U.S. BATTLESHIP MAINE
IN HAVANA HARBOR FEB'Y 15TH 1898.

ARMAMENT:- 4-10 INCH BREECH-LOADING RIFLES; 16 RAPID FIRE GUNS.
4 REVOLVING CANNONS, 4 GATLINGS, 7 TORPEDO TUBES, THE SIDE BELT WAS
12 INCHES THICK & 180 FEET LONG. OFFICERS & CREW 450, KILLED & DROWNED 266

REMEMBER THE MAINE! This lithograph depicts the scene which spurred on the ambitions of one modern state. Many Americans were only too delighted to exploit the destruction of the USS Maine in Havana harbour (15 February 1898). It provided them with an opportunity to declare war on Spain, acquire the Philippines, Guam, Puerto Rico as well as commercial control of Cuba – despite the fact that an appalled Spanish government made every effort to avoid war. (*Chicago Historical Society*)

PART I

The ambitions and fears of the modern states 1890–1919

During the years before 1914 the modern states, as well as the old empires, were straining to increase their wealth, size and security. They were prepared to use force to protect their interests; they built new weapons and conscripted huge armies. Their rivalries came to a head in the First World War, 1914–1918. The war destroyed the Czarist Empire and saw the birth of the first communist state in Russia in 1917. In 1918 the Austro-Hungarian Empire disintegrated into a mass of nation states. In 1918 Imperial Germany vanished, leaving behind it millions of resentful, defeated Germans about to experiment with a democratic way of life. The British and French Empires survived, whilst both America and Japan made some profit out of their participation in a world war. Finally, an international organisation called the League of Nations came into existence—designed to promote peace on earth and to prevent a repetition of the holocaust that had killed millions of men.

3: Colonial and trade rivalries

German Empire

In 1890 Germany was the most restless power in Europe. Her young Kaiser Wilhelm II, who had become Emperor in 1888, envied the far-flung empires of Britain and France and decided that Germany too would have colonies abroad. Plenty of Germans supported this idea—in fact most men at that time believed that a large colonial empire meant increased trade and overseas investment profits for the mother country. By 1900, the Kaiser ruled over a million square miles of colonial territory; Germany had, he said, her 'place in the sun'.

Germans forge ahead

By 1900 Germany was also the most advanced industrial power in Europe. She had outstripped Britain, so long the 'workshop of the world'. Britain was beginning to pay the price for having been the first in the industrial field, for by 1900 her long established railways and manufacturing plant were becoming obsolete at the precise moment when German and American competition was increasing. The British people had plenty of new ideas to meet this situation, but the industrialists were not always prepared to adopt them. For example, a British amateur chemist named Sidney Gilchrist-Thomas invented a technique for producing quality grade steel from iron ore with a high phosphorus content. But the British steel factories had already been built and were geared to the import of foreign ore with low phosphorus content. Rapid conversion to the new method would mean increasing the factory-owners' costs, so Britain was slow to adapt. But in Germany the new industrial plants in the Ruhr immediately introduced the Gilchrist-Thomas process and by 1900 they were producing $1\frac{1}{2}$ million tons of steel above the British figures. Similarly, the Germans forged ahead in their new chemical and electrical industries. So although Britain was still enormously wealthy, she was no longer the leading industrial power in Europe in 1900—let alone the world. But her colonial and industrial rivalry with Germany did not lead to excessive hostility between the two countries because in the years after 1900 Germany was selling most of her manufactured goods in Europe, while Britain concentrated on developing trade with her empire.

Colonial rivalry leads to war

Elsewhere in the world, colonial and trade rivalries did lead to warfare. Aggressive Japan defeated China; America fought Spain. These two wars:

The Sino-Japanese War   1894–95

The Spanish-American War 1898

underlined the colonial ambitions of modern states who, by using new methods of waging war, were able to inflict rapid defeats upon backward empires such as China and Spain. As a result, Japan won Formosa and the Liaotung Peninsula* and America gained control over Cuba, Puerto Rico, Guam and the Philippines. The sudden rise of Japan was a real threat to the Far Eastern ambitions of the Russian Czar. It was only a matter of time before Russia and Japan would clash in the Far East.

*The great powers insisted that Japan should return the Liaotung Peninsula to China. In 1905, Japan regained the Peninsula.

Japanese troops defeat Chinese in 1895. This is an example of 19th century propaganda; Chinese troops were frequently as well equipped as their Japanese adversaries.

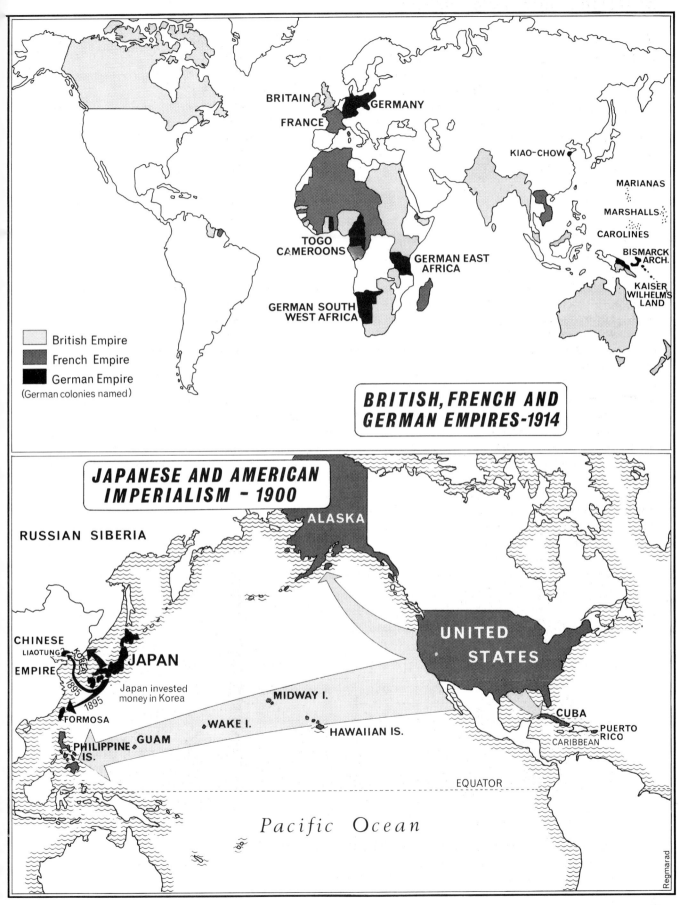

BRITISH, FRENCH AND GERMAN EMPIRES-1914

BRITAIN
GERMANY
FRANCE

KIAO-CHOW

MARIANAS

MARSHALLS

CAROLINES

TOGO
CAMEROONS

GERMAN EAST
AFRICA

BISMARCK
ARCH.

KAISER
WILHELMS
LAND

GERMAN SOUTH
WEST AFRICA

British Empire
French Empire
German Empire
(German colonies named)

JAPANESE AND AMERICAN IMPERIALISM - 1900

RUSSIAN SIBERIA

ALASKA

CHINESE
LIAOTUNG
EMPIRE

JAPAN

Japan invested
money in Korea

UNITED
STATES

MIDWAY I.

FORMOSA

WAKE I.

HAWAIIAN IS.

GUAM

PHILIPPINE
IS.

CUBA

PUERTO
RICO

CARIBBEAN

EQUATOR

Pacific Ocean

Regmarad

9

4: The increasing importance of world communications

Revolution in communications

Anyone living at the end of the last century could hardly fail to be impressed with the advances that had been made in world communications—and with the changes still taking place. Wireless linked ships with shore stations; submarine cables ran below oceans to connect continents; 13 million telephones, most of them in America, were in use before 1914. Canal building at Suez, Kiel and Panama reduced the sailing time between countries while the ships themselves were travelling faster. After 1907 a Cunarder fitted with steam turbine engines—such as the 'Lusitania'—could cross the Atlantic in 4½ days.

In Germany, Gottlieb Daimler and Carl Benz had pioneered the motor-car during the 1880s, but it fell to Henry Ford to revolutionize road transport and bring the automobile within reach of ordinary people. He invented the technique of mass-production and in 1907 the first of 15 million Model T Fords rolled off the Detroit assembly lines. Flying machines also excited the imagination. At Kitty Hawk in 1903 the Wright Brothers managed to make the first powered flight in history. Within twelve years, aircraft reached speeds of 125 mph and altitudes of nearly 20,000 feet. But the most important and universal form of communication was the railway. So important was it that it contributed to international tension and even wars. By 1890, railways were an established feature of the advanced countries where their task was to carry the freight and passengers of an expanding industrial society. It was the railways that had encouraged the settlement of the American West; even in the more backward areas such as Latin America, India, Africa and the Middle East railway projects had begun before the end of the nineteenth century.

The Trans-Siberian Railway

In one area in particular, railway projects were a cloak for national ambitions. For centuries the Russians had tried to expand into Western Europe and the Mediterranean but always their advances had been blocked. So, with an impassable Arctic in the north, Russia sought an outlet on her Pacific coastline. Here she built Vladivostock and in 1891 the Czar ordered the construction of a rail link between this port and Moscow, 4,600 miles away. Nicholas of Russia personally dug the first shovelfull of soil to mark the beginning of the Trans-Siberian Railway and for the next 13 years thousands of Russian convicts, peasants and foreign workers toiled to build the longest railway in the world. They linked it with two other Russian-built projects, the Chinese Eastern Railway and the South Manchurian Railway. The latter led to a brand new naval base at Port Arthur (ice-free throughout the year) which the Czar leased from China. To guard this railway, the Russians transfered a large number of troops to Manchuria.

Russo-Japanese War 1904–1905

In Tokyo, the Japanese interpreted these moves as a threat to their own ambitions in Manchuria and Korea, where they too were building railways. Without any warning the newly constructed Japanese fleet attacked Port Arthur in February 1904. Two Russian battleships and a cruiser were damaged. A short but furious war followed in which both sides used all the weapons that modern science could supply: machine-guns, howitzers, mines and torpedoes. Casualties were heavy. At the siege of Port Arthur in 1904 the Japanese were the victors—but they lost 60,000 men; and at the Battle of Mukden more than half a million men were in combat. Again the Japanese won—at the cost of 40,000 dead. Finally, in 1905, almost the entire Russian Baltic Fleet (a ramshackle collection of ships that had sailed halfway round the world) was sunk by the Japanese at the Battle of Tsushima.

Treaty of Portsmouth (U.S.A.) 1905.

The 1905 Treaty of Portsmouth (U.S.A.) ended the first major war of the twentieth century. Japan now gained the lease of the Liaotung peninsula, Port Arthur, Southern Sakhalin and the rail link between Changchun and Port Arthur. She forced the Russians to accept that Korea (later annexed by Japan in 1910) was a Japanese 'sphere of interest', thus ending all Russian hopes of expansion in the Far East and consequently reviving Russian dreams of expansion in the West.

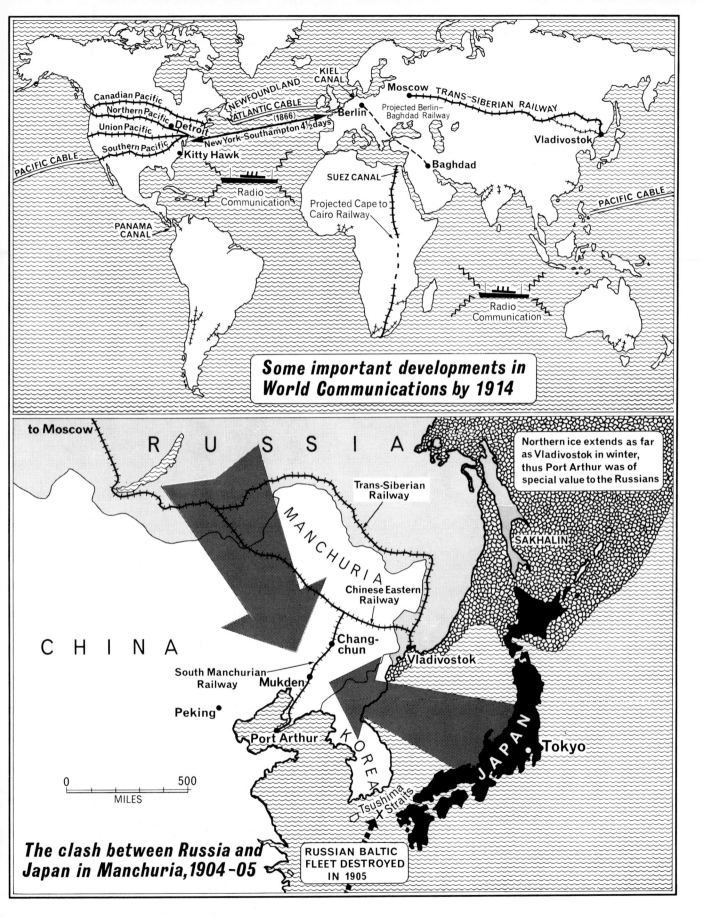

Some important developments in World Communications by 1914

Canadian Pacific
Northern Pacific
Union Pacific
Southern Pacific
Detroit
Kitty Hawk
PACIFIC CABLE
PANAMA CANAL
NEWFOUNDLAND
ATLANTIC CABLE (1866)
New York–Southampton 4½ days
KIEL CANAL
Berlin
Moscow
TRANS-SIBERIAN RAILWAY
Projected Berlin–Baghdad Railway
Vladivostok
Baghdad
SUEZ CANAL
Projected Cape to Cairo Railway
Radio Communication
PACIFIC CABLE
Radio Communication

The clash between Russia and Japan in Manchuria, 1904–05

to Moscow
R U S S I A
Trans-Siberian Railway
Northern ice extends as far as Vladivostok in winter, thus Port Arthur was of special value to the Russians
SAKHALIN
MANCHURIA
Chinese Eastern Railway
C H I N A
Chang-chun
Vladivostok
South Manchurian Railway
Mukden
Peking
KOREA
Port Arthur
JAPAN
Tokyo
0   500
MILES
Tsushima Straits
RUSSIAN BALTIC FLEET DESTROYED IN 1905

11

5: The threat of war

The alliance system before 1914

The German leader Bismarck united his country through a series of wars which reached their climax with the defeat of France in 1871. Then, to prevent a war of revenge against Germany, Chancellor Bismarck created a system of international alliances designed to debar France from finding any allies in the future. In 1879 he negotiated the Dual Alliance with Austria; in 1882, by befriending Italy, he turned it into the Triple Alliance; and in 1887 he made the 'Reinsurance Treaty' with Russia, renewable every three years. Only Britain resisted Bismarck's web of alliances and remained aloof from foreign entanglements. By 1887, Bismarck felt secure on all sides and confident that Germany need never go to war again. But in 1890 Kaiser Wilhelm II dismissed Bismarck and omitted to renew the Russian alliance. Naturally, Russia drew closer to isolated France and the two signed a military treaty during 1894–95. Then, between 1904 and 1907, the British government made cautious agreements with France and Russia, settling old differences and indicating that there was to be a friendly understanding—or 'entente'—between all three. Consequently there were two distinct international groupings in Europe by 1907:

The Triple Alliance	*The Triple Entente*
GERMANY	FRANCE
AUSTRIA	RUSSIA
ITALY	BRITAIN

Both blocs contained one of the great modern industrialized states; both were to clash in World War. Two main issues were a constant source of tension between them: one, the growing rivalry between Austria and Russia over the future of the Balkan countries; the other, an arms race in Europe.

The arms race

Ever since 1898 it had been the policy of the German government to reduce the enormous gap between British and German naval power. The British did not regard the German naval programme as a serious challenge until 1906, when the British launched a new battleship, H.M.S. 'Dreadnought'. Its armament of ten 12″ guns and a speed of over 20 knots made it the most formidable fighting ship in the world. But at the same time it made every other kind of battleship—including those of the Royal Navy—obsolete. Now the Germans were able to challenge Britain directly by building Dreadnought-type battleships for their High Seas Fleet and by constructing a number of the new Unterseebooten—the U-boats. Most European countries began to spend more on armaments so that by 1914 the generals and admirals were prepared for war, even if their governments strove to prevent it.

H.M.S. "DREADNOUGHT"

Launched 1906 it began an expensive race on the part of Britain and Germany to re-equip their navies with fighting ships of this type.

"BIG BERTHA"
Long-barrel 420mm mortar.

Both Germany and Austria secretly specialised in the production of enormous howitzers and mortars at their Krupp and Skoda arms factories. The German mortar (1916 model) had a calibre of about 17″ and fired a shell weighing over a ton. A two-gun battery needed 20 wagons for transportation purposes!

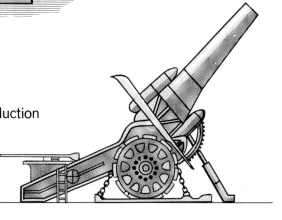

ARMIES AND ARMAMENT CENTRES, 1914

Triple Alliance
Triple Entente
Circles indicate relative sizes of armies

BRITAIN
Birmingham

B.E.F. 8 Divisions
T.A. 28 Divs.
plus Empire forces

RUSSIA

114 Infantry Divisions
36 Cavalry Divisions
Poorly trained and badly equipped

50 divisions plus 32 in reserve
Superbly trained and equipped

Essen
GERMANY
• Skoda Works

FRANCE

62 Infantry Divisions
10 Cavalry Divs.
All trained to attack in the best tradition of Napoleon
le Creusot

AUSTRIA

ITALY

54 Divisions
but efficiency reduced by numerous nationalities and languages

THE BALKANS TURKEY

Small and totally unprepared for war

One cynical Frenchman observed that the Italian army would "rush to the aid of the victors".

A comparison between different organisations of infantry divisions
BRITISH DIVISION:
18,000 men, 5,000 horses, 76 guns, 24 machine guns
GERMAN DIVISION:
17,500 men, 4,000 horses, 72 guns, 24 machine guns
FRENCH DIVISION:
15,000 men, 5,000 horses, 36 guns, 24 machine guns

NAVIES AND NAVAL BASES, 1914

✠ German naval base
▲ Allied naval base
Triple Alliance
Triple Entente
(Italy did not fight on Germany's side in 1914, and later joined the Allies)

▲ Scapa Flow
▲ Rosyth
North Sea
Heligoland ✠
✠ Kiel Konigsberg ✠
Wilhelmshaven
Baltic Sea
BRITAIN
Harwich ▲
Plymouth ▲ ▲
Portsmouth
Brest ▲
GERMANY
FRANCE
AUSTRIA
ITALY
ATLANTIC OCEAN
RUSSIA
▲ Sevastopol
Black Sea
THE BALKANS
TURKEY
Toulon ▲
Mediterranean
Gibraltar ▲
Malta ▲
Sea

TYPE	BR.	GER.
Dreadnoughts	20	13
Older Battleships	40	22
Battlecruisers	8	5
Cruisers	58	7
Light Cruisers	44	34
Destroyers & MTBs	300	144
Submarines*	78	28

*Notice that even here Britain had a marked numerical superiority

6: The coming of war

Rivalry between Austria and Russia in the Balkans

After her defeat by Japan in 1905, Russia's ambitions turned to the Balkan countries in South East Europe—at precisely the same moment that Austria was seeking to expand there also. This rivalry was complicated by a problem that had troubled the Austrians for years. Within their empire lived millions of Slavs who resented Austrian government. They wanted to break away from Austria and unite in a national Slav state. Just across the border such a state existed—Serbia. Serbia was a tough, proud little country which had distinguished herself in two wars against her Balkan neighbours, including Turkey, during 1912 and 1913. But to the Austrian leaders, the acquisition of Serbia could be the solution to their domestic problem. It might quieten their own Slav rebels and might also act as a stepping stone towards the Mediterranean.

Sarajevo 1914

Serbia had no intention of being swallowed up in the Austrian Empire and asked for protection from the biggest Slav country in the world—Russia. The Russians agreed to help Serbia if the need arose. And in 1914 the need did arise when on 28 June a young Serbian student named Gavril Princip shot the Austrian Archduke Franz Ferdinand in the Bosnian town of Sarajevo. An infuriated Austrian government made impossible demands of the Serbs and then declared war on Serbia on 28 July 1914.

The World at war

How did these events lead to world war? An attack by Austria on Serbia was likely to bring in the Russians. Russia's ally was France so, sandwiched in the middle, lay Austria's ally Germany. The Germans had anticipated this situation and had a fantastic plan ready to forestall a war on two fronts. In the event of a war with Russia, Germany would attack France! And she would send her troops through Belgium, to take the French by surprise. This scheme was known as the 'Schlieffen Plan', devised by a former Chief of the German General Staff. Schlieffen's successor, von Moltke, was confident that a short, sharp war would soon roll up the French armies so that the Germans would be free to face the badly equipped Russian millions, who would still be lumbering towards Germany's eastern frontiers. So when Russia honoured her promise to Serbia and mobilized her armies (29 July 1914), Germany declared war first upon Russia (1 August 1914) and then upon France (3 August 1914). German armies invaded Belgium on 3 August and the next day Britain, pledged since 1839 to defend Belgium's neutrality, declared war upon Germany. The First World War had begun.

The burden of responsibility

The Austrian and German generals were ready for war and believed that they had not underestimated their enemy's strength. They believed that when the crisis came, they must strike the first blow so hard that the enemy would never recover. They envisaged short, glorious campaigns; they could not foretell that four years of horrifying, unprecedented slaughter would be the result of their actions in that summer of 1914. The political leaders of Austria and Germany were easily swayed by the military arguments. They had had no major war since Bismarck's day simply because they had not wanted war; always they had contrived to find a temporary diplomatic solution to their problems. But in 1914 Austria chose to use force in order to solve the Serbian crisis. And Germany was also prepared to back her ally with force. So when the Central Powers (Germany and Austria) opted for war, the British and French governments just could not find a way of preserving peace. Therefore there was no resort to diplomacy: the mechanism of the alliance system whirred and the two 'armed camps' in Europe joined in war. Cautious Italy refused to support her allies and remained neutral; but Turkey—still smarting from her defeat at the hands of the Serbs—willingly took her place. And on the other side of the world, Japan declared war on Germany and proceeded with gusto to commandeer her colonies in the Far East.

THE BALKANS, 1914

Vienna ✪

AUSTRIAN

EMPIRE

RUSSIA

DIRECTION OF AUSTRIAN AMBITION

Belgrade ✪

RUMANIA

Sarajevo ✪

SERBIA
(A Slav nation)

MONTE-NEGRO

ALBANIA

BULGARIA

DIRECTIONS OF RUSSIAN AMBITION

Black Sea

✪ Constantinople

GREECE

TURKEY

Mediterranean Sea

**THE SCHLIEFFEN PLAN –
and its assumptions, 1914**
It shows how Germany hoped to avoid
a war on two fronts simultaneously

RUSSIA

"Britain would
probably
remain neutral."

GERMANY

STAGE 2
AUTUMN
1914

STAGE 1

SUMMER
1914

FRANCE

"Russian mobilisation
would take many weeks, so
there would be time to defeat
France first and then transport
by rail the German armies in
the west to the east."

"Two German
armies would contain the
anticipated French attack
in the Vosges while five armies advanced through Belgium to encircle the French."

"Austria would easily
defeat Serbia"

SERBIA

Regmarad

7: The First World War 1914–1918
The War in the West 1914 to the beginning of 1918

Schlieffen Plan frustrated

On 4 August 1914 the German army swept in a great curve through Belgium. The huge howitzers smashed all resistance and soon the Germans captured Brussels. 'His Majesty orders the German armies to march on Paris', ordered the Kaiser and his elated men pushed on into France. But their commander could see from his map that they were advancing too fast—they were drawing ahead of their supply wagons and mobile kitchens. The French and the B.E.F.* were fighting back—and even worse news arrived that the Russians had not only invaded East Prussia but had beaten the Germans at Gumbinnen. Little help would come from the Austrians—the gallant Serbs were blocking their advance. Despite these drawbacks, Moltke pressed on until his troops were fifteen miles from Paris. Here the German army was held at the important Battle of the Marne: the Germans lost their impetus and retreated to the Aisne to reform for another attack. Desperately, the French and British forces raced to outflank the Germans who in turn widened the field of battle to prevent this. By October 1914 both sides had dug lines of trenches from the North Sea to the Swiss frontier. The war of movement was over, the Schlieffen Plan frustrated.

Static warfare

Now the soldiers would expend their lives in the mud and misery of the Western Front as they tried in one 'Big Push' after another to smash their way through the enemy's defences with all the strength that modern technology could provide: mortars, machine-guns, shrapnel, poison gas, tanks and flame-throwers. Until the beginning of 1918 the fighting was a catalogue of horrific battles between massed infantry armies 'going over the top'—their advance announced by fantastic artillery barrages. Their generals pinned their faith on forcing a gap in the barbed wire and sandbags so that they could surge on to victory in the green country beyond the battlefields:

1914 The new German commander Falkenhayn attacked at Ypres, leaving the Allies holding a dangerous salient.
1915 Again the Germans attacked at Ypres—using poison chlorine gas for the first time.
1916 Falkenhayn planned to slaughter the French armies as they defended their great fortress at

*B.E.F.—British Expeditionary Force.

Verdun. This move failed and the German losses were almost as great as the French.

Similarly a British attack on the Somme failed with 60,000 casualties on the first day; tanks were used for the first time.

1917 Nivelle, the French commander, began the annual offensive but the Germans—now under Ludendorff's command—immediately retreated to an even stronger position, the Hindenburg Line. Nivelle poured thousands of his men against this unknown defence system and finally the French armies mutinied. This meant that the British and Imperial troops had to shoulder the main burden—fighting the battles of Arras, Vimy Ridge and Passchendaele.

Vimy Ridge and Passchendaele

Vimy Ridge was a vital objective in the Battle of Arras which raged from April to May 1917. It was also one of the toughest assignments given to infantrymen during the First World War—and it went to the four divisions of the Canadian Corps. They waited while a million shells exploded on the German positions and then attacked on 9 April 1917. They captured the crest within hours and their rapid victory—at the cost of 10,000 casualties—gave men hope that the war would soon be won. But two months later at Passchendaele, the attack was disappointing. Spearheaded by New Zealanders and Australians, the assault forces made initial advances but were then slowed down by bad weather. They attacked again during September and October and again the weather broke, turning the ground into a 'porridge of mud'. By November, the British casualties topped 244,000 with very little to show for it; and when Canadian troops finally captured the village of Passchendaele (6 November 1917) it was but a 'brick-coloured stain on a watery landscape'.

New allies

By the end of 1917, neither side had made real progress on the Western Front. It was now simply a war of attrition. Allies had come and gone. Turkey joined Germany in 1914 as did Bulgaria in 1915; Italy joined the Allies in 1915 and America followed suit in 1917. But the Serbs were overrun in 1915 while a communist revolution in November 1917 led to the withdrawal of Russia from the war.

THE WAR OF MOVEMENT:
Frustration of German Plans Aug–Sep. 1914.
She now faces a war on two fronts.

North Sea

Konigsberg

Gumbinnen

EAST PRUSSIA

RUSSIA

BRITAIN

Berlin

GERMANY

Brussels

BEL.

B.E.F.

Marne

Paris

FRANCE

Unexpected Russian attacks
threaten German naval base
at Konigsberg

Static German
armies resist
French attacks

Vienna

AUSTRIA

Neutral
Switzerland

ITALY

Belgrade RUMANIA

Italy remains
neutral in 1914

BULGARIA

Serbs hold
Austrians

SPAIN

TURKEY

Joins Germany
in 1914

North Sea

PASSCHENDAELE

Brussels

HOLLAND

Ypres
Salient

BELGIUM

VIMY RIDGE

Arras

HINDENBURG
LINE

GERMANY

British and imperial
troops held the tren-
ches from roughly
North of the Somme

R. Somme

The French armies
held the line from
the Somme through
Verdun to the Swiss
frontier

R. Aisne

Verdun

R. Rhine

R. Seine

R. Marne

Paris

FRANCE

Main areas of trench
warfare

Area occupied by Germany

Nearly all the fighting took place
outside German territory

THE STATIC WAR:
THE WESTERN FRONT
1914 to the beginning of 1918

Neutral
SWITZERLAND

8: The War in the East 1914–1918

Russian offensives 1914

'Kossacken kommen!' 'The Cossacks are coming!' was the cry of frightened German refugees in August 1914 when the Russians began their unexpected invasion of East Prussia. On the Western Front the British and French were delighted—with luck the Russians would soon be in Berlin and the war would be over by Christmas. But it was not to be. Because there were only small German forces available in the East, these initial Russian victories were deceptive. Once the Germans were reinforced and led by their new commanders, Generals Hindenburg and Ludendorff, the Russians suffered two major defeats at Tannenberg and the Masurian Lakes in 1914. Had the Austrians in Galicia been able to imitate the German example, then the Russian 'steamroller' might have been destroyed. But the Russians routed the Austrian troops at the Battle of Lemberg and forced them to retreat.

Russian defeat

Now Germany and Austria realised that the war in the East would be a prolonged commitment. And this was to be the undoing of the Russians, who simply did not have the means of waging a protracted twentieth century war. Their arms factories were inefficient—they had nothing comparable with Skoda and Krupp. Their transport system was inadequate and unable to cope with the demands of war. Soon they ran short of weapons and ammunition in the front line whilst the Germans drew on their immense industrial resources to outgun and outfight the Russian millions. For 1915 the new German Chief of Staff, General Erich von Falken-

hayn, decided that the defeat of Russia must be Germany's primary target:

Hold the solid wall in the west and let the British and French dash themselves against it; strike down Russia in the east.

To save their ally from defeat, the British and French made a desperate attempt to force the Dardanelles at Gallipoli in 1915 in an effort to get war supplies through to the Russians. But this was a costly failure and had to be called off at the beginning of 1916, by which time the German armies had driven deep into Russian territory.

Revolutions in Russia and the Peace of Brest-Litovsk

Still the Russians made courageous attempts to fight back during 1916, but when these failed they were ripe for revolution. Trouble came in March 1917 when bread riots in Petrograd led to the overthrow of Czar Nicholas II and the formation of a new government led first by Prince Lvov and then by Kerensky. But Kerensky was no more successful against the Germans than the Czar had been and in November 1917 Lenin, whom the Germans had transported back to Russia from his exile in Switzerland, overthrew Kerensky in a second revolution. Lenin's policy was 'Peace at any price' and in March 1918 the communist revolutionaries signed a harsh peace treaty at Brest-Litovsk with the German invaders. Freed from all commitments in the East, the Germans were able to bring all their strength to bear on the Western Front where General Ludendorff was planning to crush Britain and France before American armies arrived in the West in large numbers.

Russian infantry charge. The leading soldiers have already been hit. (*Ullstein Bilderdienst*)

THE EASTERN FRONT 1914 — 1917

Petrograd

Revolution 1917

Moscow *Revolution 1917*

Russian soldiers quit the firing line

R U S S I A

German naval base

Konigsberg

E. PRUSSIA

1914

1914

Tannenberg

Berlin

Masurian Lakes

G E R M A N Y

1915

Lemberg

GALICIA

Vienna

A U S T R I A

1917

Caporetto

Italian defeat in 1917

I T A L Y

Fought on Allied side 1915-1918

1915

RUMANIA

Black Sea

SERBIA (defeated)

BULGARIA

Constantinople

1915

GREECE

Gallipoli

Unsuccessful landings by British, French and ANZAC troops in the Dardanelles area 1915-1916

T U R K E Y

	Russian attacks, 1914
	Offensives by the Central Powers, 1915-1917
	Allied attempts to land on the Gallipoli peninsula
	Territory occupied by Central Powers by end of 1917

Turkey straddled the entrance to the Black Sea. Britain and France wanted to defeat the Turks, break through into the Black Sea and send war aid to Russia

SIGNIFICANCE OF BREST LITOVSK

Petrograd

Moscow

R U S S I A

Berlin

G E R M A N Y

Troops to Western Europe

★ Brest Litovsk

UKRAINE

Vienna

A U S T R I A

By the Treaty of Brest-Litovsk, Russia ceded this territory ☐ to Germany and allowed German troops to enter and occupy ▨ including the rich wheat lands of the Ukraine

① German troops harvested the crops of the Ukraine in 1918

② German front-line units were transferred to the Western front

Regmarad

9: The War at sea 1914–1918

Britannia, Rule the Waves!

In the early days of the war, the British people looked forward to a decisive naval victory over the Germans. To their consternation, easy victories did not materialize. The Royal Navy failed to sink the *Goeben* and *Breslau*, two German warships that sailed through the Mediterranean to Constantinople, a feat which encouraged the Turks to declare war on Britain. For nearly two years, the Kaiser refused to send his High Seas Fleet out into battle. Two small engagements, the Battle of Heligoland Bight (1914) and the Battle of the Dogger Bank (1915) proved indecisive. Understandably, the Kaiser would not throw his battleships against the Grand Fleet based at Scapa Flow until the numerical superiority enjoyed by Britain's Navy had been reduced—and here the German weapons were mines and submarines. Well aware of the damage that these could do, Admiral Jellicoe preferred to hold his 24 battleships in readiness for a German breakout. Thus the big ships of both sides languished for much of the war within the safety of torpedo nets at Scapa Flow, Kiel and Wilhelmshaven.

Surface raiders and U-Boats

In the early months of the war, the Royal Navy swept all German surface raiders from the seas. At the Battle of the Falkland Islands (1914) British warships virtually wiped out the German Pacific Fleet, but only after the British had sustained heavy losses at the earlier Battle of Coronel. By the end of 1914, all German surface raiders had been destroyed. The U-boats were a tougher and more elusive foe and the war against them was fought out at all times and in all weathers. In 1915 the Germans began their first full-scale submarine campaign, their best known victim being the Cunarder 'Lusitania'. 1,198 people died, including over 100 Americans. The United States, still a neutral country, protested and the Germans reduced their indiscriminate torpedoing.

Battle of Jutland, 31 May 1916

Only once did the Royal Navy have to cope with the breakout of the High Seas Fleet. At Jutland in 1916, Admiral Jellicoe fought a running action against Admiral Scheer's battleships, most of which managed to escape as a result of their superior gunnery and construction. Never again did the High Seas Fleet dare venture out into the North Sea; instead the Germans turned to a second and more intensive U-boat campaign in 1917. All ships entering the war-zone around Britain were liable to attack. This was the policy which decided the Americans: on 6 April 1917, the United States declared war on Germany.

1917–1918

The U-boat menace was never entirely beaten, although the British Prime Minister, Lloyd George, used the convoy system, echo-sounders, depth-charges and innocent-looking 'Q-ships' (merchant-ships, manned by the Royal Navy and mounting hidden guns, which tempted incautious U-boats to approach on the surface). By 1918, the shortage of food in Britain became serious enough for the government to impose rationing. But the British suffering bore no comparison with the misery of the German people. They had endured blockade since the beginning of the war and by 1916 (the year the German potato harvest failed) they were running short of food. This was one reason why the capture of the Ukrainian wheatfields was vital to Germany. So ultimate British control of the sea meant not spectacular victories in the tradition of Trafalgar, but slow starvation of the German people.

Wartime camouflage. This liner is 'dazzle painted' to avoid detection by the U-boats. (*Imperial War Museum*)

BLOCKADE AND COUNTER BLOCKADE, 1914–1918

Comparative losses at Jutland

Casualties (killed) :-
BRITISH 6000 GERMAN 2500

Ships sunk :-	BR.	GER.
Pre-Dreadnoughts		1
Battlecruisers	3	1
Cruisers	3	4
Destroyers	8	5

Scapa Flow

U-Boats penetrate mine-fields, 30 miles wide in 1918!

Grand Fleet

Br. submarines enter Baltic

Rosyth   Cruisers

Jutland 1916

High Seas Fleet

Dogger Bank 1915

Heligoland Bight 1914

Heligoland

CANAL   Kiel
Wilhelmshaven

Food rationing 1918

U-Boat Base

HOLLAND

Food crisis 1916–1918

Dover

Plymouth   Portsmouth   Zeebrugge

CONVOYS FROM NORTH AMERICA

'Lusitania' sunk 1915

U-Boats penetrate Minefields

THE WESTERN FRONT

GERMANY

FRANCE

German minefields
British minefields

Main U-Boat activity here

Scapa Flow

British control of the oceans enables overseas help to flow in

GERMANY

JAPAN
Profits from the war when her shipyards build merchantmen to replace Allied losses

CANADA   Sends troops

Newfoundland

Gibraltar   Malta

KIAO CHOW
German naval base captured 1914

U.S.A. sends goods to Britain & troops after April, 1917

INDIA

Surface raider sunk 1914

TOGOLAND 1914

Freetown

CAMEROON 1914

Surface raider sunk 1914

GERMAN E. AFRICA (Never surrendered)

Sends troops

Singapore

Surface raider sunk 1914

Surface raider sunk 1914

NEW GUINEA 1914

GERMAN PACIFIC FLEET

SAMOA 1914

S.W. AFRICA 1914

Cape Town   Durban

AUSTRALIA

NEW ZEALAND

Australia and New Zealand send 'ANZACs' (Australia and New Zealand Army Corps)

Defeated Royal Navy Squadron, Battle of Coronel, 1914

Sunk by Royal Navy, Battle of Falkland Is. 1914

German overseas possesions; all, apart from East Africa, were captured by Allies in 1914
Important British naval bases

10: The War in the air 1914–1918

Air combat begins

When the B.E.F. sailed to France in 1914 its air force of the Royal Flying Corps, then part of the army, totalled 63 machines. The French had 123 planes; the Germans 384 and 30 airships. At first all aircraft and observation balloons acted as the eyes of the armies, reporting back artillery targets and troop movements to the ground commanders. During 1914 and 1915 fighting and bomber duties were rarely carried out for the simple reason that aircraft had not been designed for such purposes. In 1916 and 1917, however, aircraft companies such as Bristol and Sopwith in Britain and Fokker and Gotha in Germany began to produce planes designed as fighting scouts and reconnaissance bombers. They were fitted with machine guns which on many fighters were synchronized to fire through the propeller blades. Soon air combats between Allied fighter squadrons and the brightly painted German Jagdstaffeln became common.

The aces

High above the shell-torn Western Front, a few fighter pilots built up impressive reputations. In the trenches the infantrymen remained anonymous; but the names of the 'fighter aces' soon became household words. Governments were quick to exploit the propaganda value of a 'war-hero'; they encouraged glamorous accounts of air combat and arranged—for the aces who survived—lecture tours to inspire arms workers and schoolboys. So the victories of young men such as Captain Albert Ball and Major 'Micky' Mannock were on everybody's lips. Even better known were the German air aces—men such as Max Immelmann and Oswald Boelcke who developed the tactics and techniques of 'the dogfight'. Undoubtedly, the most publicized ace of the First World War was Baron Manfred Von Richtofen. A brilliant flier and shot, he built up his 'circus' of skilful fighter pilots. Their favourite tactics were to sweep down on allied squadrons and, in the midst of the dog-fight, select the weakest enemy for the 'Red Baron' to kill. Richtofen's bright red Albatross fighter inspired fear and respect along the Western Front; for example, on a single day during the Battle of Arras (1917) he brought down five British aircraft.

Civilian populations suffer

For the British people, terror from the sky came first in the form of giant airships designed by Count Zeppelin. The Zeppelins began to bomb Britain in 1915 and caused 1900 civilian casualties, but these gas filled monsters were highly susceptible to bad weather and British incendiary bullets. Much more dangerous were the Gotha bombers which inflicted over 2000 casualties. They caused Londoners to shelter in the Tubes; and as a result factory production figures fell. Then the British retaliated with big bombers such as the Handley Page Type 0/400 which attacked German air bases and Rhineland towns during 1918.

Importance of air power

But aircraft were of the most use on the battlefields of Europe and the Middle East. The British used bombers and fighters in increasing numbers from the Battle of the Somme onwards. By 1918 Sopwith Camels were being used against German tanks, whilst other fighters specialized in 'ground-strafing' enemy troops huddled in the trenches. So important was the air war on the Western Front that the army's R.F.C. was replaced by the Royal Air Force in 1918 as a separate arm of the services. The R.A.F. was also stationed in Italy, where it carried out bombing missions over the Alps against Austria, and in the Middle East, where in Palestine aircraft acted as scouts for General Allenby and played a very important part in the Battle of Megiddo, which destroyed the Turkish army in 1918.

By the end of the war the importance attached to air power was apparent in the size of the Royal Air Force and the Naval squadrons—no less than 23,000 aircraft.

THE AIR WAR 1914–1918

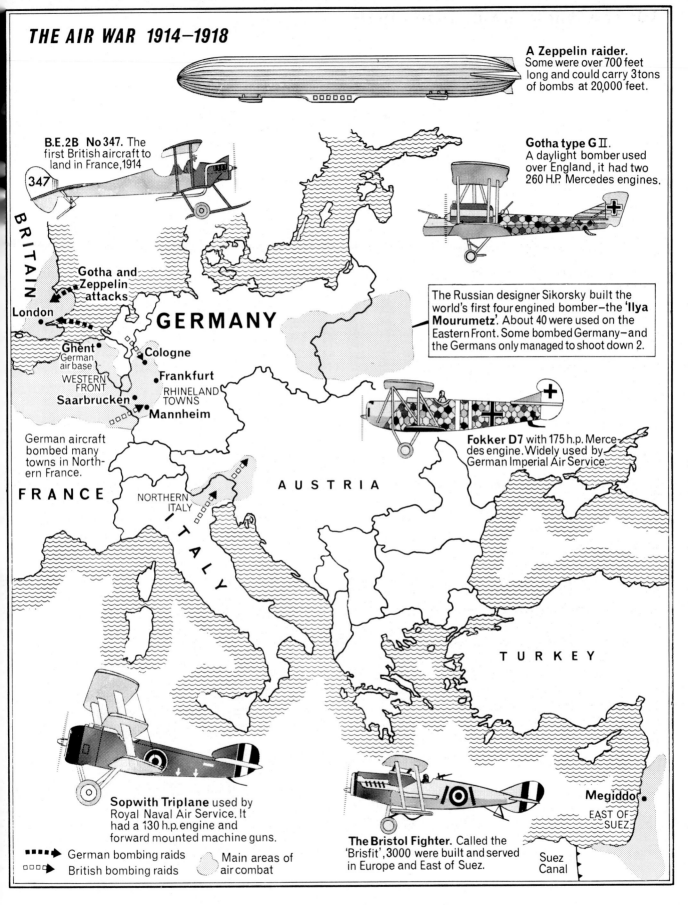

A Zeppelin raider. Some were over 700 feet long and could carry 3 tons of bombs at 20,000 feet.

B.E.2B No 347. The first British aircraft to land in France, 1914

347

Gotha type G II. A daylight bomber used over England, it had two 260 H.P. Mercedes engines.

BRITAIN

Gotha and Zeppelin attacks

London

GERMANY

Ghent German air base

Cologne

WESTERN FRONT

Frankfurt

Saarbrucken

RHINELAND TOWNS

Mannheim

The Russian designer Sikorsky built the world's first four engined bomber—the **'Ilya Mourumetz'**. About 40 were used on the Eastern Front. Some bombed Germany—and the Germans only managed to shoot down 2.

German aircraft bombed many towns in Northern France.

FRANCE

NORTHERN ITALY

AUSTRIA

ITALY

Fokker D7 with 175 h.p. Mercedes engine. Widely used by German Imperial Air Service.

TURKEY

Megiddo

EAST OF SUEZ

Sopwith Triplane used by Royal Naval Air Service. It had a 130 h.p. engine and forward mounted machine guns.

The Bristol Fighter. Called the 'Brisfit', 3000 were built and served in Europe and East of Suez.

Suez Canal

▪▪▪▶ German bombing raids
▫▫▫▫▶ British bombing raids

Main areas of air combat

11: The defeat of Germany and her allies 1918

Ludendorff's gamble

Codeword *Michael*! This was Ludendorff's plan for the destruction of the Allied armies on the Western Front in 1918. He secretly assembled 47 assault divisions whose task was to infiltrate, to probe, to tear through at the enemy's weakest points. This was to be a war of movement: 'The reserves must be put in where the attack is progressing NOT where it is being held up.' He now had plenty of men—all fit German soldiers under 35 had been transferred to the west from the now defunct Russian front. Ludendorff was gambling everything on Operation Michael; behind him Germany was starving, there had been strikes in German towns as well as demands for an end to the war, and by 1918 he was growing short of the means of waging war—essential supplies of rubber, oil and fodder. The great German war machine was giving way under the constant strain of $3\frac{1}{2}$ years of fighting. Germany could not go on much longer; certainly her fate would be sealed once the Americans had fully mobilized their vast reserves of material and manpower.

Failure of the offensive

So Ludendorff attacked on 21 March 1918. On the first day his assault troops shattered the British lines; on the second they broke into open country; on the third the Kaiser exulted:

The battle is won, the English have been utterly defeated! But they hadn't. Eventually, after a long retreat, the Germans were held and Operation Michael failed.

Ludendorff tried other offensives between April and July, but none had the power of Michael. Against him the Allies increased their strength: hundreds of light tanks appeared, fresh American divisions, numerous aircraft and above all a superb, reinforced British army spearheaded by the brilliant Australian Corps under the command of General Monash. In July and August the German armies on the Western Front suffered a series of shattering defeats. They lost all their earlier gains and in September had to abandon the Hindenburg Line. But they did not surrender because the Allies were unable to advance rapidly enough over the old, pulverized battlefields.

Collapse

Elsewhere, in the Balkans, Middle East and Italy the Allied offensives moved forward against Germany's partners. The Bulgarians surrendered in September, the Turks in October, the Austrians on 3 November. And in the West, the Allies still slogged forward in the pouring November rains, still suffering heavy casualties at the hands of the retreating Germans.

At this point, Germany collapsed. The German people had had enough; the idle sailors in the High Seas Fleet mutinied; the Kaiser, robbed of all dreams of victory, abdicated on 9 November. A German armistice delegation came forward to sign the terms the Allies offered.

Hostilities will cease at 11 hours today, November 11th.

The last shots were fired and the killing stopped. The First World War was over.

Some of Ludendorff's assault troops move into action. (*Imperial War Museum*)

Failure of the Ludendorff offensives on the Western Front, 1918

British Official History:
"The collapse of Germany began not in the Navy, not in any of the side-shows, but on the Western Front in consequence of defeat in the field."

HOLLAND

Collapse of Imperial Germany-the Kaiser abdicates and escapes to Holland

A great deal of Belgium was still occupied by the Germans when fighting stopped on November 11th.

British Attacks, September

Ypres
Apr. attacks

FRONT LINE ON ARMISTICE DAY

OPERATION "MICHAEL" March 21st

LUXEM-BOURG

R. SOMME

Anglo-French attacks, August

May attacks

R. SEINE

Foch, Allied Commander-in-Chief, began the counter attacks in July

Verdun

American attacks, Sept.

Paris

R. MARNE

■ Ground captured in Ludendorff's offensives

▨ Ground captured in Allied offensives July–Nov. 1918

Sketch of a French Renault Light Tank 1918

Hundreds of these were used in the final battles

Manned by a crew of 2, armed with an 8mm Hotchkiss MG, it could travel at 6 mph, and cross a trench 6ft wide. 13 ft 6ins in length.

THE DEFEAT OF GERMANY'S PARTNERS 1918

Kiel
Revolution in GERMANY
BERLIN

FRANCE

AUSTRIA NOV 3rd.

ITALY

BULGARIA SEP 29th.

Salonika

TURKEY OCT 31st

Aleppo

Regmarad

12: The Peace Treaties

The Peacemakers assemble

The horror of the First World War could not be eradicated from the minds of those who had survived. Many clamoured for revenge on the Germans and for the Kaiser to be hanged. Hardship and misery remained on after the war, for now a deadly influenza epidemic was harrying the undernourished populations in the countries of vanquished and victor alike. It was against this background that the Allied leaders met to discuss among themselves the sort of peace treaty that should be made with Germany. At the beginning of 1919, they assembled in the Palace of Versailles. The Frenchman, Clemenceau, sought to punish the Germans and make it impossible for them ever to start another war against France. Orlando of Italy wanted his country rewarded with Austrian territory and was less concerned with the German question. Lloyd George, re-elected Prime Minister of a Coalition Government in 1918, privately realized that harsh treatment of defeated Germany would achieve nothing except to store up trouble for the future; publicly, however, he had announced that he would 'hang the Kaiser' and 'make Germany pay'. President Wilson of the United States urged the Peace Conference to accept his formula for future peace and stability—the Fourteen Points—and pleaded for 'no annexations, no contributions, no punitive damages'.

Germany's punishment at Versailles

During the last days of the First World War, the new German Republic had been proclaimed in Berlin. Ebert, Chairman of the German Social Democrat Party, had formed a government in the city of Weimar and then sent his representatives to Versailles to receive the terms of the peace treaty. Here they discovered that the new Germany had lost West Prussia and Posen—so that the 'Polish Corridor' now separated East Prussia from the rest of Germany. Danzig, Memel, Eupen, Malmedy, parts of Silesia, Northern Schleswig, Alsace and Lorraine—all were lost. The Allies also removed every square inch of the Kaiser's colonial empire from the new German republic. These terms meant that thousands of dispossessed and embittered Germans would flock home to the Fatherland. In addition, the Allies disbanded the Imperial German Air Force, confiscated the High Seas Fleet (later in 1919 the German crews scuttled most of their warships at Scapa Flow) and limited the German Army to 100,000 men. They took most of Germany's merchant ships and much of her railway rolling stock. They told the Germans that they would also have to pay reparations to cover the cost of the war *after* they had accepted the blame for causing the war in the first place—this was the hated 'War Guilt' clause. Finally the German delegates were not allowed to discuss the terms; they were forced to accept them.

The effect of the Treaty of Versailles on the German people

They were furious with this 'Diktat'—dictated peace. For a few days the Weimar Government seriously considered refusing the terms (which, of course, would have meant the resumption of war). But on 28 June 1919 the Germans signed the Treaty of Versailles in the palace's Hall of Mirrors, where, in 1871, Bismarck had proclaimed the German Empire. Wilhelm II, the last of the Kaisers, was now safe in neutral Holland and he lived long enough to see Hitler's Panzers enter Paris in World War II. But in 1919 it was unthinkable that there should be another war; and to make sure that it would never happen .President Wilson had persuaded his colleagues to create a 'League of Nations', an international organization designed to outlaw war.

WAR DEATHS, 1914-1918

THE 'WAR GUILT' CLAUSE
Article 231 of the Treaty of Versailles:
"The Allied and Associated Governments affirm and Germany accepts the responsibilities of Germany and her allies for causing all the loss and damage to which the Allied and Associated Goverments and their nationals have been subjected as a consequence of the war imposed upon them by the aggression of Germany and her allies."

900,000 (incl. Empire)

1,750,000

1,750,000

1,500,000

1,250,000

600,000

50,000

300,000

100,000

300,000

THE PRICE OF DEFEAT
Germany's territorial losses by the 1919 Treaty of Versailles

Northern Schleswig to Denmark

MEMEL

Danzig (free city)

EAST PRUSSIA

Germany lost **all** of her colonies. Many displaced Germans returned to Germany.

WEST PRUSSIA

R. Elbe

Communist Rebellion 1918-19
Berlin

R. Oder

POSEN

POLAND

Eupen & Malmedy to Belgium

HOLLAND

Demilitarised Zone

New government met here because of the rebellion in Berlin; hence Germany became known as the Weimar Republic

Weimar

to Poland

BELGIUM

R. Rhine

SILESIA

Paris
Versailles

ALSACE & LORRAINE

Saar coalfields placed under Fr. rule for 15 years

CZECHOSLOVAKIA

to France, (which lost this territory to Germany in 1871)

R. Danube

Germany was forbidden to unite with Austria

FRANCE

AUSTRIA

Territory lost by Germany to other countries

Territory lost by Germany to the League

Displaced Germans

THE OTHER PEACE TREATIES: all were signed in French palaces a few miles from Paris

Treaty of St.Germain	1919	— with defeated Austria
Treaty of Neuilly	1919	— with defeated Bulgaria
Treaty of Sèvres	1920	— with defeated Turkey; but this treaty was not adopted and a new one was signed at Lausanne in1923
Treaty of Trianon	1920	— with defeated Hungary

Regmarad

27

Part I – Book List

General reference: *The Great War* — J. Terraine — Hutchinson

3. *Short History of Germany* — E. J. Passant — CUP — pp 98–117
4. *History of Modern Japan* — R. Storry — Pelican — pp 121–145
5. *Struggle for Mastery in Europe* — A. J. P. Taylor — OUP
6. *Good Soldier Schweik* — J. Hasek — Penguin
7. *Somme* — A. Farrar-Hockley — Pan
8. *Making of Modern Russia* — L. Kochan — Pelican
9. *Jutland* — D. McIntyre — Pan
10. *Picture History of Flight* — J. Taylor — Hulton
11. *The Sword Bearers* — C. Barnett — (see individual studies especially Ludendorff)
12. *Short History of Germany* — E. J. Passant — CUP — pp 153–158

British Infantry 1916.   (*Camera Press*)

PART 2

'The brave, new world'

The survivors of World War I were determined to build a 'brave, new world', a world safe for democracy. The allied leaders had created the League of Nations and now placed the former colonial territories of the German and Turkish Empires under its control. They had redrawn the map of Europe so that every European race could set up its own national state. They had tried to set the stage for a new era of democracy. Europe, now free and independent, had the chance of becoming a better place.

These hopes were dashed within a few years. World war had overstrained both the peoples and the resources of many European countries and their democratic governments were frequently unable to cope with the scourge of the post-war years: poverty, unemployment and violence. Other political leaders thrust themselves forward, men of unusual personality, offering alternative forms of government based on the rule of a single political party. These men argued that their beliefs, or ideologies, were superior to democracy and fanatical bands of armed supporters backed up their arguments. These men were the dictators who, when they came to power, forced their political beliefs on the people and crushed all who opposed the rule of one party.

The first of these men, Lenin, struggled with the aid of his Bolshevik Party to set up the world's first communist state in Russia. Then Mussolini and his Fascist Party took control in Italy. And in Germany, during 1933, Adolf Hitler and the Nazi Party came to power. Within six years, they had involved the world in yet another war.

13: The birth of the League of Nations 1919–1920

Wilson's idea

The League of Nations was neither the first nor the last of man's attempts in recent times to secure world peace by means of international organizations. In 1899 and 1907 international conferences at the Hague had tried to outlaw war. Now in 1919 President Wilson of the United States enthusiastically developed his idea of a World League to which all nations would bring their disputes, content to submit to the decisions of a Supreme League Council and an International Court. In Paris Wilson presided over the Commission which rapidly drafted the details of an organization capable of handling international problems. It was called the League of Nations and formally came into existence in 1920.

Organization of the League

The Covenant of the League: all nations would swear a solemn promise—or covenant—that they would stand by the League's principles of international law and order.
The Council: here the great powers, assisted by smaller, selected states, would recommend 'sanctions' or punishments that might be needed to bring to heel any nation threatening to break the Covenant. Sanctions would take three forms:

> The moral sanction—where the League would use world opinion to persuade the offending power to accept a settlement.
> The economic sanction—where the League would cut off world trade with the offending nation.

Finally, if all else failed

> The military sanction—where the League would impose its will by force.

The Assembly: once a year all member nations would send delegates to the Geneva *Assembly* to discuss world problems.
The Permanent Court of International Justice: this was the League's Court—located at the Hague. It would pass judgments on international disputes.

The League's chance of success

The League was Wilson's creation—the greatest achievement by any one man at the Paris Peace Talks after the war. But would it work? It had a fair chance if the world observed three essential conditions. First, all nations must join the League and there be treated as equal partners in the organization. Secondly, all nations would have to sacrifice some of their sovereign powers and be prepared to put the League above their kings, presidents and parliaments. And lastly, all nations would have to accept that sometimes, for the future happiness of man, they might have to back up the League's decisions with *collective military action*.

The weakness of the League

Unhappily, from the very beginning, these three essential conditions were not observed. The American people rejected both President Wilson and his ideas—so the United States never joined the League. And in 1919–1920, there was no intention of admitting Russia, still in the throes of a communist revolution. And most people agreed that before Germany could join she would have to prove that she was worthy of membership. So the League never truly had world support and rapidly degenerated into a talking shop dominated by the European victors of World War I. At times they were able to bully small countries into submission; but they were powerless to influence the other great nations.

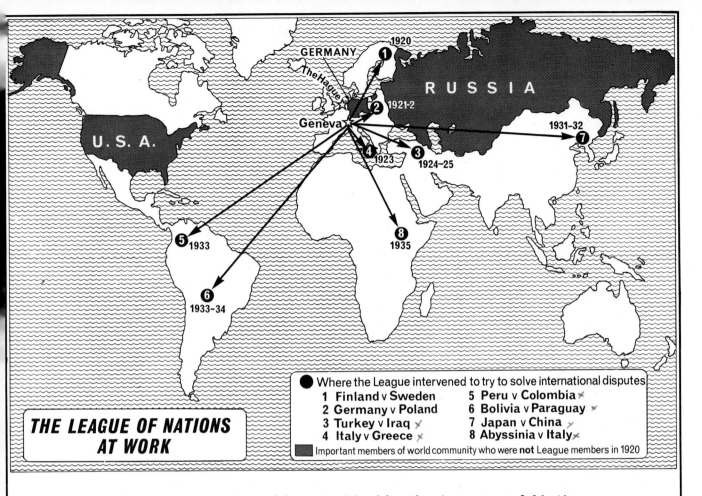

THE LEAGUE OF NATIONS AT WORK

● Where the League intervened to try to solve international disputes
1 Finland v Sweden
2 Germany v Poland
3 Turkey v Iraq ✗
4 Italy v Greece ✗
5 Peru v Colombia ✗
6 Bolivia v Paraguay ✗
7 Japan v China ✗
8 Abyssinia v Italy ✗

■ Important members of world community who were **not** League members in 1920

A typical international problem tackled by the League of Nations:

THE PROBLEM OF UPPER SILESIA
(Number 2 on above map)

The people living in Upper Silesia were mainly Poles and Germans. In 1921 they were asked to vote in a plebiscite to decide with which country to unite. When 700,000 voted for Germany and 480,000 voted for Poland the League was asked to interpret this result. It decided that the plebiscite area would be partitioned between the two nations. Though this seemed fair, the half given to Poland contained the rich industrial area of Silesia, so the Germans were embittered by this loss.

The principle of partition rarely offers a permanent solution to international disputes and there was constant bickering between Poland and Germany over Silesia for the next seventeen years.

1921–22 The plebiscite in Upper Silesia and the decision of the League of Nations ▷

— League frontier
▨ Plebiscite area
⋯ Coalfield on which wealth of Upper Silesian industry was based

14: The spoils of war: colonies change hands

Mandates

Article 22 of the Covenant of the League of Nations required all nations to help underdeveloped countries whose peoples were 'not yet able to stand up by themselves under the strenuous conditions of the modern world'. All agreed that this was to be the 'sacred task of civilization'. Thus when the peacemakers faced the task of managing the German and Turkish colonial possessions, they decided to create the 'Mandatory System'. A mandate is a command to carry out an agreed policy and the peacemakers awarded three kinds of mandate to selected nations who, in return, would be responsible to the League for the welfare of the peoples placed in their care. 'A' mandate countries were to become independent in the very near future—and on this condition Britain gained Palestine, Iraq and Transjordan. France received Syria and the Lebanon. 'B' mandate areas—the Cameroons, Togoland, Tanganyika—were less advanced regions with no immediate prospect of independence. Britain and France looked after their administration also. Belgium too received a 'B' mandate—Rwanda-Urundi, a part of German East Africa. 'C' mandate areas were sparsely populated and underdeveloped; because of their exceptional backwardness, they were handed over to the powers who had originally conquered them from the Germans. This meant that the North Pacific Islands went to Japan, New Guinea to Australia, South West Africa to the Union of South Africa and Western Samoa to New Zealand. These changes had two very important results.

International resentment

First, the British and French empires—the largest to survive the war—increased in size so that between 1919 and 1939 they were to be at the height of their powers. This seemed entirely unfair to many people; particularly to the Germans who now had nothing, and to the Italians who, after losing half a million men, had gained very little. On the other hand Japan, who had played very little part in the actual fighting in the World War, emerged richly rewarded with new sources of trade and the Mariana, Marshall, and Caroline islands which quite unlawfully she transformed into military bases.

Britain and Palestine

Secondly, nobody bothered to consult the peoples who lived in the mandated areas; some naturally objected to these new arrangements. For example, the Arabs in the Middle East had been of enormous help in fighting the Turks. Lawrence of Arabia had led them to believe that the British would reward them with new lands and he hinted that they would also receive Palestine. But in 1917 the British Foreign Secretary, Balfour, had declared that:

> His Majesty's Government view with favour the establishment in Palestine of a National Home for the Jews.

Yet over 90% of the people living in Palestine were Arabs! So when the British began to honour their promise to the Jews by permitting limited Jewish immigration into Palestine, the Arabs were understandably infuriated—and this was to lead to years of hostility between Jew and Arab in the Middle East.

Thus the Peace Settlement, designed to prevent future racial tension, actually helped to create it.

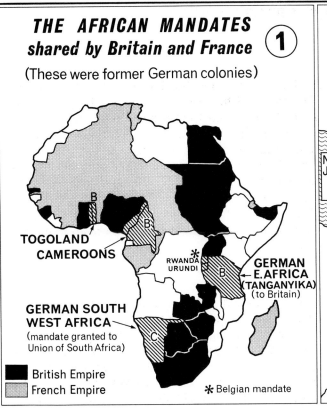

THE AFRICAN MANDATES
shared by Britain and France
①

(These were former German colonies)

TOGOLAND
CAMEROONS

RWANDA
URUNDI ∗

GERMAN
E. AFRICA
(TANGANYIKA)
(to Britain)

GERMAN SOUTH
WEST AFRICA
(mandate granted to
Union of South Africa)

■ British Empire
▨ French Empire

∗ Belgian mandate

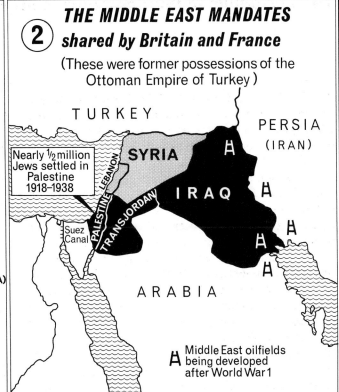

② THE MIDDLE EAST MANDATES
shared by Britain and France

(These were former possessions of the
Ottoman Empire of Turkey)

TURKEY

PERSIA
(IRAN)

SYRIA

LEBANON

Nearly ½ million
Jews settled in
Palestine
1918–1938

PALESTINE

TRANSJORDAN

IRAQ

Suez
Canal

ARABIA

Middle East oilfields
being developed
after World War 1

MANDATES

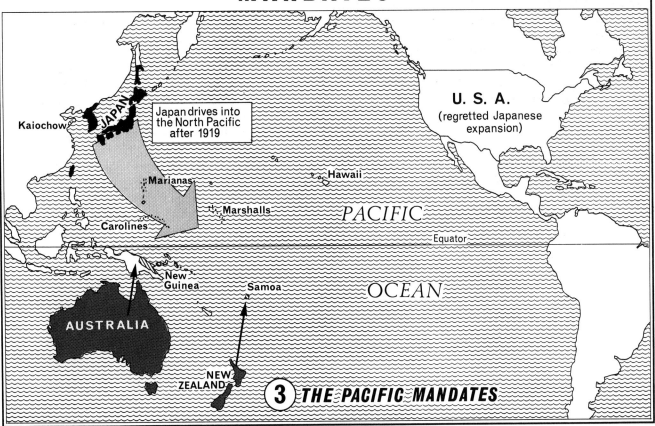

Kaiochow

JAPAN

Japan drives into
the North Pacific
after 1919

Marianas

Marshalls

U.S.A.
(regretted Japanese
expansion)

Hawaii

PACIFIC

Carolines

Equator

New
Guinea

Samoa

OCEAN

AUSTRALIA

NEW
ZEALAND

③ *THE PACIFIC MANDATES*

15: Problems arising out of the new European frontiers

The collapse of old empires

Both the Hapsburg Empire of Austria-Hungary and the Czarist Empire of Russia had disintegrated before all the fighting had stopped in 1918. Their subject peoples had seized their opportunity; they set up their own governments and proclaimed new, independent states. . . Finland, Estonia, Latvia, Lithuania, Czechoslovakia, Yugoslavia.

Self-determination

The Allied leaders saw their victory over the Central Powers in 1918 as a triumph for democracy and individual liberty, twin ideals which they hoped both these new nations and the defeated enemy would learn to cherish. They sympathized with the principle of 'self-determination' in Europe—the right of all peoples to set up their own forms of government within the security of ther own national frontiers. So an important—and very difficult—task faced the peacemakers; they had to draw the new frontiers as carefully as possible around the different European races. Of course, other factors had to be borne in mind. They created Poland as a 'buffer state' between those traditional enemies, the Germans and the Russians. They rewarded Italy with parts of the Austrian Tyrol. They gave Greece the southern part of Bulgaria as well as the Smyrna hinterland.

Dissatisfaction: war between Greece and Turkey

This complicated process involved 80 million people in a change of allegiance and was bound to breed discontent—the kind of problem which the League of Nations was designed to solve. For example, fighting flared up in Turkey between 1920 and 1922 when Mustafa Kemal, the general who had helped to defeat the Allied landings at Gallipoli in 1915, resisted the Greek occupation armies:

> We are Turks; we will never be the subjects of a people who were yesterday our slaves.

Threatening to drench every square inch of Turkey with blood, Kemal fought merciless battles against the Greeks, who had hopes of advancing as far as Ankara. In 1921 he defeated them at the Sakarya River and forced them to flee the mainland. Kemal then advanced on Constantinople, only to find his way barred by 1200 British soldiers who, at Chanak, were guarding the Straits Zone. For a time in 1922 there was a real danger that the British leaders, Lloyd George and Churchill, would choose war rather than let the Turks enter Europe. But Kemal backed down, content to see the invaders expelled from Asia Minor. He rejected the Treaty of Sèvres and in 1923 he was able to extend Turkey's frontiers by the Treaty of Lausanne. By then he had overthrown the Sultan, set up a new Turkish Republic, and was its first President.

Breakdown of democracy

Significantly, the newly established League of Nations had been powerless to prevent one strong man from breaking international law in order to get his own way by force of arms. And such actions were becoming common in post-war Europe. Unable to cope with the harsh effects of world war and jealous of their neighbours' wealth and possessions, nation after nation turned to men who promised a 'brave, new world' not by democratic processes but by appeal to national pride and material gain. These were the men who advocated revolution and the ruthless extermination of all resistance to their beliefs—a total denial of democracy. These men were the 'dictators'.

The new frontiers

Legend (top right):
- — Frontier
- Germans
- Ruthenians
- Poles
- Hungarians

The difficulty of drawing frontiers is illustrated by the location of various European races living in Czechoslovakia

Legend (middle right):
- Former German territory
- Extent of Austro-Hungarian Empire
- Former Russian territory
- Western Thrace to Greece from Bulgaria
- ••••• Frontiers in dispute

War between Greece and Turkey, 1920–1922

- Turkish territory given to Greece at Sèvres but regained by Turkey at Lausanne in 1923
- → Greek advances
- ▸▸▸ Kemal's attacks
- ∷∷∷ Straits zone

Labels on maps:
FINLAND, ESTONIA, LATVIA, LITHUANIA, DENMARK, E. PRUSSIA, GERMANY, POLAND, CZECHOSLOVAKIA, AUSTRIA, HUNGARY, TRANSYLVANIA, RUMANIA, TYROL, ITALY, YUGOSLAVIA, BULGARIA, ALBANIA, GREECE, TURKEY, Prague, CZECHS, SLOVAKS

BULGARIA, BLACK SEA, Constantinople, Chanak, Sakarya R., Ankara, GREEKS 1919, GREEKS, Smyrna, TURKEY, GREECE, Athens, MEDITERRANEAN SEA, SYRIA

35

16: Revolution in Russia and the creation of the communist state

Lenin

The first modern dictatorship of the twentieth century arose from the 1917 Bolshevik revolution in Russia. Its leader was Lenin, creator of modern Russia. Born in Simbirsk in 1870, he had seen his brother hanged for plotting against the Czar. Afterwards, Lenin took up his brother's cause, bringing to it the teachings of Karl Marx who had preached that communists should lead rebellions against the ruling classes all over the world. For years the Czar's secret police hounded Lenin, jailing him in Siberia and then sending him into exile. Abroad, Lenin founded the Bolshevik Party (later known as the Communist Party) and produced an anti-Czarist newspaper called 'Iskra'—'The Spark'. One of the couriers who smuggled it across Russia was Josef Stalin.

Revolutions in Russia

Whilst Lenin was in exile, a revolution broke out in Russia when the war with Japan ended in 1905. Though it failed, Lenin learnt a lesson: that to stage a successful rebellion the Russian people must be armed. Therefore he would have to wait until Russia was again involved in war. One may imagine his disappointment in 1914 when the Russian people rallied to support the Czar against Germany. On the Eastern Front they died in their millions until, in March 1917, they reached the limit of their endurance; a bread riot in Petrograd sparked off a successful revolution. Czar Nicholas II abdicated and Lenin's socialist rivals formed a provisional government. When Kerensky, a member of the Social Revolutionary Party, became Prime Minister in July he continued the war against Germany—a decision which was to give Lenin his chance.

The Bolshevik Revolution

From Switzerland Lenin called on Russia's war-weary soldiers to desert: 'Peace with your own legs!' The Germans, delighted to inject an anti-war revolutionary into Russia, transported Lenin across Europe in the famous 'sealed train'. Back in Petrograd, Lenin demanded Kerensky's resignation in favour of the Bolsheviks, but when elections were held the Bolsheviks lost. Lenin refused to accept this verdict and called for civil war. In November 1917 his troops, known as the Red Guard, captured key points in Petrograd and Moscow and declared that the Workers' Councils, or Soviets, were now the real rulers of Russia.

Counter-revolution

At this point other countries intervened. The Allies wanted Russia to stay in the war but Lenin, desiring 'peace at any price', ordered his lieutenant, Trotsky, to sign the Peace of Brest-Litovsk in March 1918. This made the Allies act: British, French, American, Japanese and finally Polish armies invaded Russia to help the 'counter-revolutionaries'—those who were opposed to Lenin. By the spring of 1919, when the First World War was over, the Bolshevik Red Army was hemmed in around Moscow. Most of Russia was outside Lenin's control. But Russia is a vast and inhospitable land to the invader and the Red Army, commanded by Trotsky and aided by thousands of partisans, forced the interventionists to evacuate. So successful was Trotsky that his armies pushed the Poles back to Warsaw, but the Russians had to retreat after losing the Battle of the Vistula in 1920. Nevertheless, by 1922 Russia was completely free of interventionists and counter-revolutionaries; the communists had won and in 1923 they proclaimed their new state—the Union of Soviet Socialist Republics (U.S.S.R.).

Lenin's achievement

Lenin died in 1924. He had set out to liberate the Russian people and to start a chain reaction of communist revolutions all over the world. But in fact he had isolated the Russian people from the rest of mankind under a communist dictatorship and, far from uniting the world, he had begun the process which was to divide it into two.

Civil war and interventions in Russia, 1918-22

HAMMER AND SICKLE SYMBOL OF COMMUNISM

Finland, Estonia, Latvia & Lithuania took advantage of the revolution to declare independence and attack their former rulers

British, French and American forces landed in North Russia in 1918. They hoped to link up with Admiral Kolchak who advanced from Siberia.

Admiral Kolchak (once commander of the Russian Black Sea fleet) set up a counter-revolutionary government in Siberia. He was supported by the armies landing at Vladivostok.

KOLCHAK 1919

CZECHS 1918

JAPANESE

AMERICANS 1918

TRANS-SIBERIAN RAILWAY

Many counter revolutionaries as well as the French attacked from the South

Czech prisoners of war were being shipped along the Trans-Siberian Rly. prior to evacuation from Russia. *En route*, they rebelled and advanced on Moscow but Trotsky stopped them at Kazan. The interventions then began officially to "aid the Czechs."

American forces landed here to prevent Japanese acquiring Russian territory

Murmansk

FINLAND

Warsaw

LITH.

EST.

LAT.

Petrograd

Archangel

Moscow

Kiev

Kazan

Br. & Fr. naval forces

TURKEY

SIBERIA

CHINA

KOREA

Vladivostok

PERSIA (IRAN)

Territory controlled by counter-revolutionaries and interventionists

Territory controlled by Red Army

The Creation of Communist U.S.S.R., 1923

The U.S.S.R. in 1923 was made up of four Soviet Republics

① **RUSSIAN SOVIET FEDERATED SOCIALIST REPUBLIC**

② **BYELORUSSIAN SOVIET SOCIALIST REPUBLIC**

③ **UKRAINIAN SOVIET SOCIALIST REPUBLIC**

④ **TRANSCAUCASIAN REPUBLIC**

② Leningrad (The new name for Petrograd)

● Moscow (Capital of the U.S.S.R.)

③

①

④

THIS AREA WAS LATER DIVIDED INTO OTHER SOVIET REPUBLICS

CHINA

17: Mussolini and Italian Fascism 1919–1929

Condition of Italy

Benito Mussolini, from 1922 to 1943 'Duce' or 'Leader' of Italy, became dictator as a direct result of the unhappiness and disorder experienced by his countrymen after the First World War. The cost of living had jumped 500% since 1915 and there was a general demand for higher wages. The middle classes complained they were impoverished by high taxation; ex-servicemen grumbled because of the lack of jobs; industrial workers went on strike; the peasantry wanted better conditions and a chance to improve the barren soils of the Italian hillsides. Matters were so serious that in 1920 the country came close to revolution when workers commandeered the factories and tried, unsuccessfully, to market their own products. As well as these troubles, there was general dissatisfaction with Italy's war gains. Italy had hoped to expand into the Adriatic—but all she received were the Trentino and Southern Tyrol areas, Istria and Trieste.

Fascists

Mussolini said he had an answer to these problems. In 1919 he had formed his own political force—the Fascio di Combattimento—and soon his blackshirted thugs were busy breaking up the meetings of other political parties. Mussolini explained this violence, excusing it on the grounds that Italy was on the brink of a communist revolt and that his Fascists were strong enough to prevent this even if the government was not. Plenty of discontented Italians joined the Fascist Party and in 1922 they were strong enough to march on Rome and there demand a share in the government. The king, Victor Emmanuel III, soon agreed and Mussolini became Prime Minister that year.

Il Duce

For three years he ruled Italy along semi-democratic lines, but always in the background his Fascists were eliminating opposition, resorting where necessary to torture and murder. In 1925 Mussolini accepted responsibility for such events and declared himself dictator of Italy. His talent lay in propaganda, and soon he convinced most Italians that his rule was in their interests. He controlled the press. He made emotional speeches to hysterical crowds who raised their hands in the Fascist salute and chanted 'Salutiamo il Duce!', whilst he had the uproar piped into every radio set in Italy. After 1925 he outlawed all political parties except the Fascists. Elections disappeared, to be replaced by plebiscites in which the people approved a list of hand-picked deputies. Parliament vanished, to be replaced by a mockery called the Fascist Grand Council and the Chamber of Deputies. Mussolini claimed to have created a 'corporate state' where the population, divided into 22 'corporations', would work in harmony for 'social justice'. There would be no more strikes and no more unjust dismissals from work. He promised the peasants a 'battle for wheat' in which they too would prosper. Fascist Italy was now, he said, the greatest country in the world. At least the children were brought up to believe this, for Mussolini had all school text books rewritten by Fascist propagandists.

Mussolini's impact

These despotic tactics were widely publicized and often admired by people abroad. Here was a dictator who seemed to be getting results. Wheat production increased, land reclamation schemes were launched, railways and motor roads improved. His foreign policy was flamboyant and at first fairly successful. In 1923, after some Greeks murdered an Italian general, Mussolini bombarded Corfu; in 1924 he surrendered his claims to Dalmatia, but exacted Fiume and Zara as the price of his generosity. And in 1929 Mussolini won world fame by negotiating an agreement or Concordat with the Pope who, in return for the tiny Vatican City in the heart of Rome, recognized the legality of Fascist Italy.

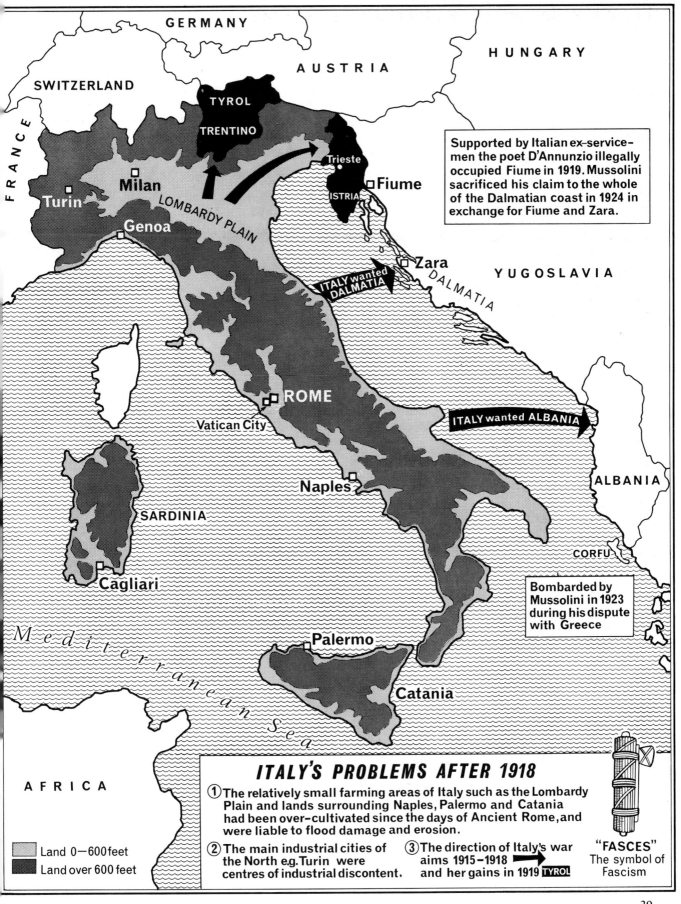

GERMANY

AUSTRIA

HUNGARY

SWITZERLAND

FRANCE

TYROL

TRENTINO

Trieste

Milan

Turin

LOMBARDY PLAIN

Genoa

Fiume

ISTRIA

Supported by Italian ex–service-
men the poet D'Annunzio illegally
occupied Fiume in 1919. Mussolini
sacrificed his claim to the whole
of the Dalmatian coast in 1924 in
exchange for Fiume and Zara.

ITALY wanted DALMATIA

Zara

DALMATIA

YUGOSLAVIA

ROME

Vatican City

ITALY wanted ALBANIA

ALBANIA

Naples

SARDINIA

CORFU

Cagliari

Bombarded by
Mussolini in 1923
during his dispute
with Greece

Mediterranean sea

Palermo

Catania

AFRICA

ITALY'S PROBLEMS AFTER 1918

① The relatively small farming areas of Italy such as the Lombardy
Plain and lands surrounding Naples, Palermo and Catania
had been over-cultivated since the days of Ancient Rome, and
were liable to flood damage and erosion.

② The main industrial cities of
the North e.g. Turin were
centres of industrial discontent.

③ The direction of Italy's war
aims 1915–1918 ➤
and her gains in 1919 TYROL

"FASCES"
The symbol of
Fascism

Land 0–600 feet
Land over 600 feet

Post-war difficulties

The task of bringing stable democratic government to Germany seemed insuperable to leaders of the various political parties who now made up the Weimar government. A killer influenza epidemic raged in Germany, jobs were scarce, prices were rising, disorder and open rebellion were commonplace. Yet the Weimar government managed to survive these trials until it was faced with inflation, the causes of which were largely outside its control. In 1921 the Allies had decided that Germany would have to pay £6,600,000,000 in reparations to compensate for all the damage in the First World War. Within a year the Germans fell behind with payments and, as a reprisal, French and Belgian troops invaded the Ruhr in 1923 and confiscated the factories and mines there. But the Ruhr workers refused to co-operate with their old enemies. They downed tools in defiance—and inadvertently increased the unemployment problem as well as causing German trade to come to a standstill. As soon as goods became scarce, prices went up. Then the workers demanded higher wages, or better unemployment benefits, so that incomes as well as prices soared. This was the process of inflation which soon made the German mark utterly worthless. A German with a million marks in the bank (worth about £50,000 in 1914) found that this wouldn't buy a loaf of bread by the end of 1923. So the middle-classes depending on their savings and the war-pensioners living on fixed incomes were ruined overnight.

Munich Putsch

In the midst of this chaos an ex-soldier named Adolf Hitler led a revolt or putsch in Munich. He accused the Weimar politicians of having betrayed Germany in 1919 by signing the hated Versailles Diktat. But the Munich police soon dispersed his National Socialist (Nazi) demonstrators and Hitler found himself jailed in Landsberg Prison for a short time. Here he began to write his autobiography *Mein Kampf* ('My Struggle') in which he outlined his plans for the expansion of Germany and for the elimination of all 'enemies of the state', which was how Hitler viewed Jews and Communists.

Aid for Germany

Now the Allies, realizing that they were partly to blame for Germany's misfortunes, came to her aid. They introduced a new German currency; American investors poured in dollars. This revitalized German industry and for a few years the nation seemed on the road to recovery. In 1925 the ever-popular Field Marshal Hindenburg became President of the Weimar Republic; in 1926 the Germans joined the League of Nations; and in 1928 they renounced war by signing the international Kellogg Pact.

Hitler comes to power

But in 1929 came a crisis from which the Weimar Republic never recovered. A world trade slump prevented the Germans from selling their exports. Once more the factories closed down and many unemployed workers joined the extremist political parties—such as the Communist Party and Nazi Party—who offered help. Between 1929 and 1931 Hitler's brownshirted storm-troopers fought their communist rivals in the streets and clamoured for political power. In the elections held during 1932, the Nazis emerged as the biggest single political party in the German Reichstag (parliament). Soon it was impossible to form a government in Germany without admitting the Nazis. Reluctantly, President Hindenburg gave way to his advisers. He agreed to let Hitler form a government and on 30 January 1933 Hitler became Chancellor of Germany.

This was how Hitler came to power and why all those Germans who had suffered during the post-war years—or who feared a communist revolution in Germany—were prepared to support him.

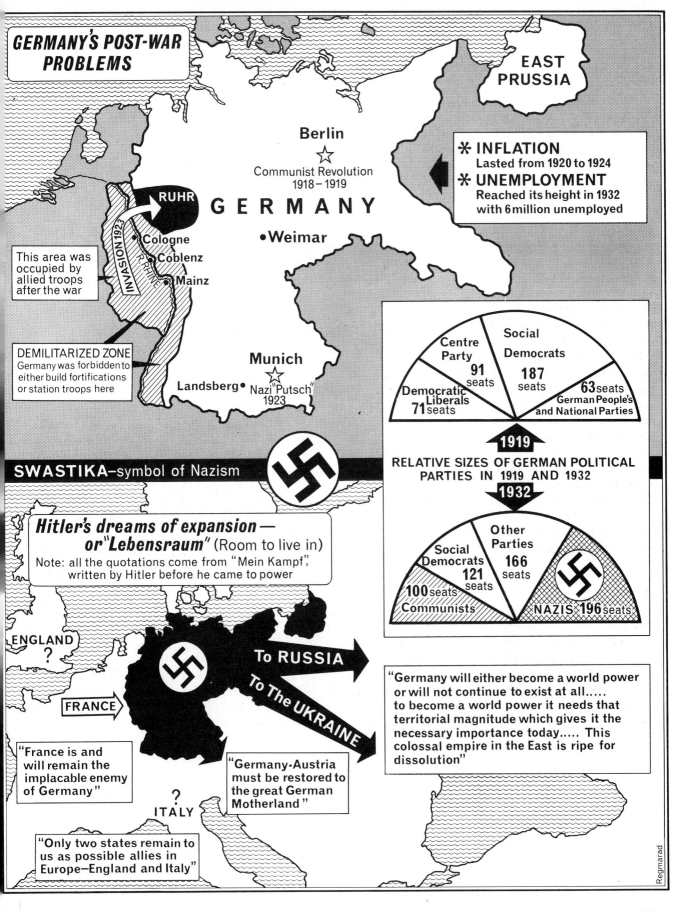

GERMANY'S POST-WAR PROBLEMS

EAST PRUSSIA

Berlin
☆
Communist Revolution
1918 – 1919

GERMANY

✳ INFLATION
Lasted from 1920 to 1924
✳ UNEMPLOYMENT
Reached its height in 1932
with 6 million unemployed

RUHR

INVASION 1923

•Cologne
•Coblenz
•Mainz

•Weimar

This area was
occupied by
allied troops
after the war

DEMILITARIZED ZONE
Germany was forbidden to
either build fortifications
or station troops here

Munich
☆
Landsberg• Nazi"Putsch"
1923

SWASTIKA–symbol of Nazism

Hitler's dreams of expansion —
or"Lebensraum" (Room to live in)
Note: all the quotations come from "Mein Kampf",
written by Hitler before he came to power

ENGLAND
?

FRANCE

To RUSSIA

To The UKRAINE

"France is and
will remain the
implacable enemy
of Germany"

"Germany-Austria
must be restored to
the great German
Motherland"

?
ITALY

"Only two states remain to
us as possible allies in
Europe–England and Italy"

"Germany will either become a world power
or will not continue to exist at all.....
to become a world power it needs that
territorial magnitude which gives it the
necessary importance today..... This
colossal empire in the East is ripe for
dissolution"

RELATIVE SIZES OF GERMAN POLITICAL PARTIES IN 1919 AND 1932

1919

Centre
Party
91
seats

Social
Democrats
187
seats

Democratic
Liberals
71 seats

63 seats
German People's
and National Parties

1932

Social
Democrats
121
seats

Other
Parties
166
seats

100 seats
Communists

NAZIS **196** seats

Regmarad

41

Part 2 – Book List

Lenin in Red Square 1919.   (*Novosti Press Agency*)

PART 3

The years of rapid change, 1919–1939

The years between 1919 and 1939 saw the destruction of so many of the hopes cherished by the survivors of World War I. For the most part Russia and America opted out of international relations so that the task of maintaining world peace fell upon the unwilling shoulders of Britain and France. At first glance, both countries appeared to be at the peak of their powers. Both forged ahead in the scientific and technical field; both ruled over empires that were bigger than ever before. Despite these factors, the depression after 1929 and the intense spirit of pacifism tended to reduce the quality of leadership that these two countries were prepared to give to the newly formed League of Nations. First Japan, then Fascist Italy and finally Nazi Germany flouted the principles of the League and committed acts of aggression which the British and French leaders were unwilling to prevent.

So the Thirties degenerated into years of excuses, years in which the British people became bemused by their private economic misery and allowed themselves to be led by political mediocrities such as Baldwin and Ramsay Macdonald who spoke so often about 'Peace' and 'Safety First' and yet did so little to make these phrases a reality.

19: The advance in science and technology 1919–1939

The twenty years which divided the two world wars saw spectacular advances in mass communication, transportation, physics and medicine which today we take for granted as part of our everyday lives. World War I had stimulated scientific developments and the next generation was to witness the application of a great deal of new scientific knowledge.

Public broadcasting

During 1917 the German Army had broadcast music and propaganda to its troops on the Western Front. This was to point the way to broadcasting radio entertainment on a national scale—although pessimistic doctors warned that radio waves might be harmful to health and would upset the weather! Within a few years many countries had broadcasting stations and the 'wireless craze' swept the world. Later the dictators were to use the radio for mass propaganda purposes. In Britain, the B.B.C. (founded 1922) became the main source of reliable news during the 1926 General Strike, whilst Stanley Baldwin was to be the first British Prime Minister to appreciate the value radio could be in winning general elections.

Television

Once man had transmitted the human voice on a national scale, he began to try to transmit pictures. John Logie Baird was the first to send a reasonably clear picture in 1925. But the cost of transmission and of TV receivers was high, so that few people enjoyed television in their homes during this period. Nevertheless, the Nazis beamed transmissions from Berlin after 1934; and both the 1936 Berlin Olympic Games and the coronation of King George VI in London during 1937 were televized.

Radar

In the Thirties, progress was made in the detection of objects by radio waves. Telefunken, the German electronics firm, developed a device that located the approach of British bombers en route to attack Wilhelmshaven in 1939, whilst the R.A.F., thanks to the pioneer work of Robert Watson-Watt, had a radio-location chain which proved indispensable in defeating the Luftwaffe during the Battle of Britain. Later, the American term for radio-location—'Radio detection and ranging'—was abbreviated into its present form: RADAR.

Aviation

After 1918 it was hoped that giant airships might be the answer to future air travel, but the disasters involving the British R.101 in 1931 and the German 'Hindenburg' in 1937 caused interest to decline. The fixed wing aircraft had already proved itself. In 1919 a Vickers 'Vimy' made the first nonstop transatlantic flight and in the same year another Vimy flew from Britain to Australia. All over the world airlines began to grow up. Their aircraft were slow and uncomfortable, but the safety record of individual airlines was remarkable. British Imperial Airways' fleet of eight Handley Page 42's flew 10,000,000 miles between 1931–39 without injury to a single passenger. All of these aircraft were powered by airscrews, but there was interest in other forms of propulsion. Rocket research was led by the Germans such as Dr. Wernher von Braun, whilst the pioneer of jet propulsion was Frank Whittle, who began his research into gas-turbines in 1929.

Medicine

Dramatic medical discoveries were to reduce human suffering in both war and peace. F. G. Banting developed insulin, the German Domagk worked on the sulphonamides, whilst in 1929 Alexander Fleming detected the 'wonder drug', penicillin.

Atomic physics

Scientists were aware that all matter contained immense reserves of energy. Rontgen had discovered the properties of X-rays in 1895; Henri Becquerel had detected radioactivity; Mme. Curie and her husband had demonstrated the powers of radium. But how was it possible to release the energy locked up inside the atoms that made up all matter? Ernest Rutherford found the answer. A New Zealander, he carried out his research at the Cavendish Institute, Cambridge and in 1919 succeeded in splitting the atom. He warned his students at the time:

We are now entering No-Man's Land.

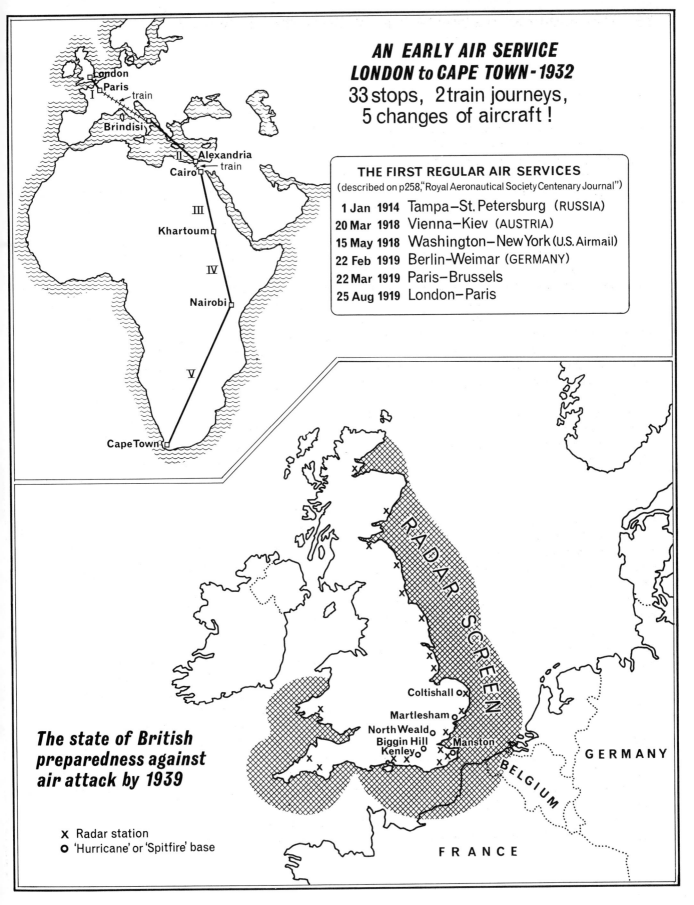

**AN EARLY AIR SERVICE
LONDON to CAPE TOWN - 1932**
33 stops, 2 train journeys,
5 changes of aircraft !

London
Paris
I
train
Brindisi
II Alexandria
Cairo — train
III
Khartoum
IV
Nairobi
V
Cape Town

THE FIRST REGULAR AIR SERVICES
(described on p258,"Royal Aeronautical Society Centenary Journal")

1 Jan	**1914**	Tampa–St. Petersburg	(RUSSIA)
20 Mar	**1918**	Vienna–Kiev	(AUSTRIA)
15 May	**1918**	Washington–New York	(U.S. Airmail)
22 Feb	**1919**	Berlin–Weimar	(GERMANY)
22 Mar	**1919**	Paris–Brussels	
25 Aug	**1919**	London–Paris	

RADAR SCREEN

Coltishall o x
Martlesham o
North Weald o
Biggin Hill o
Kenley o
Manston o

GERMANY

BELGIUM

*The state of British
preparedness against
air attack by 1939*

FRANCE

x Radar station
o 'Hurricane' or 'Spitfire' base

20: The condition of the democracies: France

'Les salles boches'

The war had devastated and depopulated much of north-eastern France and it took the French people seven years to rebuild their homes and their businesses after 1918. So it is easy to understand why the French hated the Germans after the war and French leaders such as Clemenceau and Poincaré were resolved never to give the Germans a chance of invading again. At Versailles, Clemenceau had worked to reduce not only Germany's military power but also her *industrial* capacity for waging war. He had insisted on regaining the iron-ores of Alsace-Lorraine, on controlling (for the next 15 years) the coalfields of the Saar. Two other French hopes were not realized: one was the plan to turn the French occupation zone in Germany into a 'buffer' Rhineland state; the other, the attempt to drain Germany of her wealth by imposing heavy reparations. This had proved both a failure and a disaster after Poincaré, the French Premier, had authorized the 1923 invasion of the Ruhr.

Apprehension

Nearly 1½ million Frenchmen had died in the First World War and after this catastrophe all French people desired more than anything else security against a 'German war of vengeance'. Another generation of young Frenchmen must not die in the trenches: 'Il faut conserver la jeunesse'—'We must hang on to our young people', they said. To ensure this the French built, during the Thirties, their famous Maginot Line of steel and concrete forts. It guarded the French border between Belgium and Switzerland and was strong enough, the French military experts said, to resist any German attack. Young Charles de Gaulle, then a captain in the French Army, criticized this static defence system and pointed out in 1936 that fast German tanks and bombers might one day start a war of movement that would leave the French troops, cocooned in their protective concrete, utterly helpless.

Domestic problems

But France could not pay for radical changes in her defence policy. She too had been badly hit by the world slump after 1929. Moreover, the French governments during the Thirties were notoriously weak, composed as they were of coalitions of many political parties. Sometimes these governments were involved in national scandals—such as the infamous Stavisky affair. Stavisky was a financier who, in 1933, had sold worthless bonds to the public. As a fugitive from justice, he had committed suicide in January 1934 but as the swindle had involved millions of francs, questions were asked in the French National Assembly. Here it was revealed that several members of the government together with at least one member of the Sûreté police were implicated. So serious did the scandal grow that the French Premier, Chautemps, had to resign.

The Popular Front

Such revelations hardly confirmed French confidence in democratic forms of government and several anti-democratic groups gained in numbers. Fascist organizations such as the Solidarité Française (founded by François Coty, the make-up millionaire) had been in existence for some years; now the most prominent were the Croix de Feu and their extremist members, the Cagoulards (the Hooded Ones). To cope with this Fascist threat, the Socialists and Communists linked up to form a new coalition government (Front Populaire) in 1936. It banned the Croix de Feu, promised a whole series of social and economic reforms and a general 'cleansing of public life'. But little was achieved; the Popular Front quickly split over foreign policy and the attitudes that France should adopt towards the Spanish Civil War and Nazi Germany.

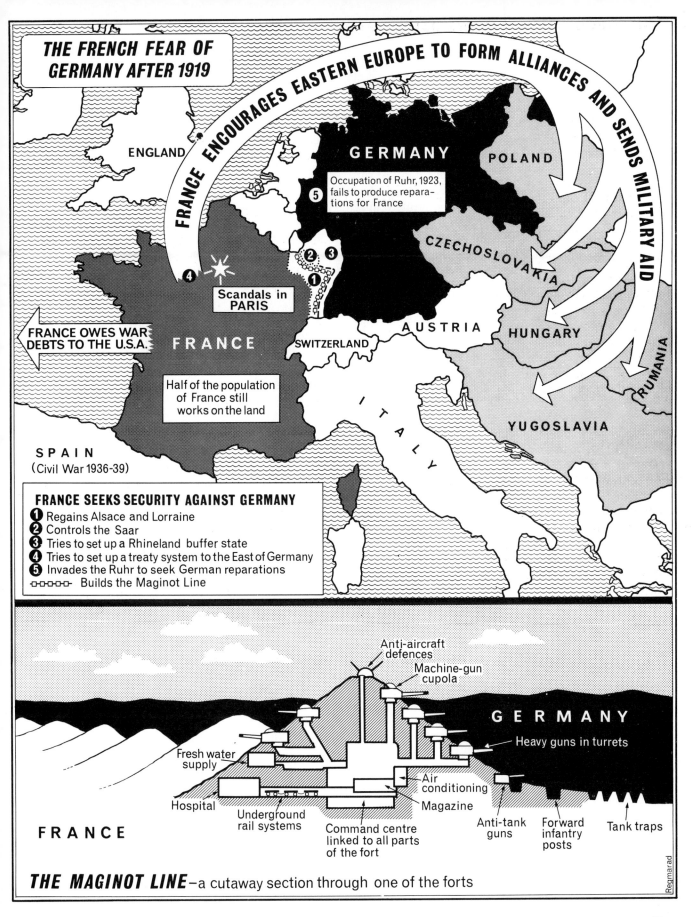

THE FRENCH FEAR OF GERMANY AFTER 1919

FRANCE ENCOURAGES EASTERN EUROPE TO FORM ALLIANCES AND SENDS MILITARY AID

ENGLAND

GERMANY

POLAND

⑤ Occupation of Ruhr, 1923, fails to produce repara-tions for France

CZECHOSLOVAKIA

② **③**

④ **①**

Scandals in PARIS

AUSTRIA

HUNGARY

FRANCE OWES WAR DEBTS TO THE U.S.A.

FRANCE

SWITZERLAND

RUMANIA

Half of the population of France still works on the land

ITALY

YUGOSLAVIA

SPAIN
(Civil War 1936-39)

FRANCE SEEKS SECURITY AGAINST GERMANY

① Regains Alsace and Lorraine
② Controls the Saar
③ Tries to set up a Rhineland buffer state
④ Tries to set up a treaty system to the East of Germany
⑤ Invades the Ruhr to seek German reparations
-ᴑ-ᴑ-ᴑ-ᴑ- Builds the Maginot Line

Anti-aircraft defences

Machine-gun cupola

GERMANY

Heavy guns in turrets

Fresh water supply

Air conditioning

Hospital

Magazine

Underground rail systems

Command centre linked to all parts of the fort

Anti-tank guns

Forward infantry posts

Tank traps

FRANCE

Regmarad

THE MAGINOT LINE – a cutaway section through one of the forts

21: The condition of the democracies: Britain

The price of victory

Before 1914 Britain had enjoyed the status of a major world power, immensely wealthy and trusting in the supremacy of the Royal Navy. But because of the manner in which the war was fought, she had lost this naval supremacy and emerged as a second-class land power, deeply in debt. She had conscripted huge armies—there were $4\frac{3}{4}$ million British and Imperial troops under arms in 1918—and had suffered heavy casualties—higher in 1918 than they were to be in the whole of World War II. The price of victory, it seemed, was not much different from the price of defeat. One thing was certain; there must never be another war—and this conviction explains the rise of pacifism in post-war Britain and a willingness to tolerate the actions of European dictators.

Deflation

After 1918 the country endured a long period of deflation. Simply, this meant that there was a national shortage of money. The government tried to repay its American loans; industry economized by cutting wages and dismissing workers. Deflation had two main effects. The cost of living fell as both retailers and consumers adjusted to the low wages and unemployment benefits (the 'dole') on which thousands of families existed. Secondly, as people had less money to spend on manufactured goods, industry was forced to lay off more workers and make further wage cuts. Miners were especially hard hit. During the war the government had nationalized the mines and had paid high wages; now in 1921 the government decided to restore the mines to the private owners who, on average, cut the pay per shift from £1.0.3d to 9/3d.

General Strike

Many people blamed the war for these dismal conditions. In fact, the coal mines and railways were suffering from old-age and obsolescence before 1914, when there had been several wage disputes and strikes. The war had camouflaged the defects, but after 1918 Britain paid the price of having been the first of the modern industrialized states. Her industry and system of communications were inefficient. Crisis came in 1926 when the big unions declared a General Strike in sympathy with the miners who were facing yet another pay cut. The General Strike lasted nine days, after which the Trade Unions abandoned the miners, who were left to struggle alone until their surrender six months later.

The Slump

Baldwin, the Conservative Prime Minister, was praised as the 'man who kept his head', who 'had saved the nation' during the General Strike. But Ramsay MacDonald, the Labour leader, defeated him in the 1929 elections. This was the year of the Wall Street Crash in America, which soon led to a slump in world trade. British unemployment figures climbed to nearly 3 million. In 1931, Ramsay MacDonald formed a new 'National Government' with the support of Baldwin's Conservatives. This tried to protect British industry by resorting to 'tariffs' or customs duties on foreign goods and by cutting government expenditure—including the dole. There were some ineffectual demonstrations and even a brief mutiny in the Royal Navy at Invergordon, but most people made the best of things. They voted for the National Government in 1931 and again in 1935. For many people, especially in the southern part of the country, the worst effects of the depression soon passed. Everyday life was improved by all sorts of new luxuries; cars, carpet sweepers and other household appliances could be bought on hire purchase, the cinema enjoyed a growing popularity especially after the first 'talkies' in 1929, football pools were introduced, and more and more people were able to enjoy a holiday (with pay) by the seaside. Very few joined extremist groups such as Mosley's Fascist Party or the British Communist Party.

The late Thirties

After 1935 unemployment decreased considerably with the general improvement in world trade. In 1936 King George V died and for the next eighteen months the British people were absorbed by the dramatic story of King Edward VIII's abdication and George VI's coronation. Most people were only dimly aware of the growing menace of the European dictators. Above all the British people wanted peace.

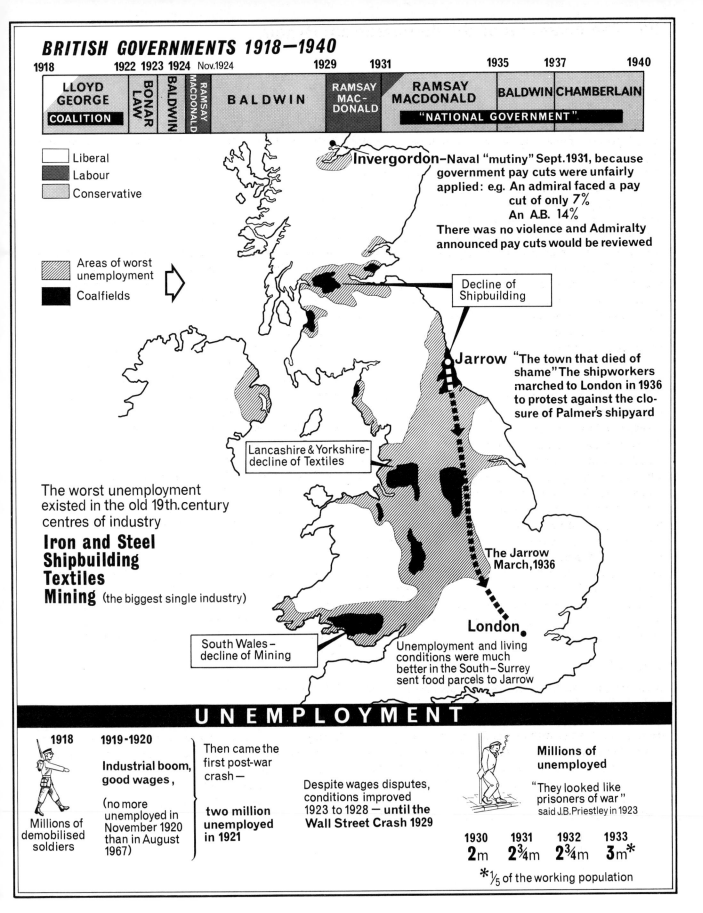

BRITISH GOVERNMENTS 1918—1940

1918	1922	1923	1924	Nov.1924		1929	1931		1935	1937	1940

LLOYD GEORGE — COALITION
BONAR LAW
BALDWIN
RAMSAY MACDONALD
BALDWIN
RAMSAY MAC-DONALD
RAMSAY MACDONALD — "NATIONAL GOVERNMENT"
BALDWIN
CHAMBERLAIN

Liberal
Labour
Conservative

Areas of worst unemployment
Coalfields

Invergordon – Naval "mutiny" Sept. 1931, because government pay cuts were unfairly applied: e.g. An admiral faced a pay cut of only 7%
An A.B. 14%
There was no violence and Admiralty announced pay cuts would be reviewed

Decline of Shipbuilding

Jarrow "The town that died of shame" The shipworkers marched to London in 1936 to protest against the closure of Palmer's shipyard

Lancashire & Yorkshire-decline of Textiles

The worst unemployment existed in the old 19th. century centres of industry

Iron and Steel
Shipbuilding
Textiles
Mining (the biggest single industry)

The Jarrow March, 1936

London
Unemployment and living conditions were much better in the South – Surrey sent food parcels to Jarrow

South Wales – decline of Mining

UNEMPLOYMENT

1918
Millions of demobilised soldiers

1919-1920
Industrial boom, good wages,
(no more unemployed in November 1920 than in August 1967)

Then came the first post-war crash —
two million unemployed in 1921

Despite wages disputes, conditions improved 1923 to 1928 — **until the Wall Street Crash 1929**

Millions of unemployed
"They looked like prisoners of war" said J.B. Priestley in 1923

1930	1931	1932	1933
2m	2¾m	2¾m	3m*

*⅕ of the working population

49

22: More troubles for Britain: Ireland and India

IRELAND: Rebellion

In 1800 the British Parliament had passed the Act of Union which made Ireland an integral part of the United Kingdom; and from that moment onwards many Irishmen dedicated themselves to winning their national independence, to secure 'Home Rule' for Ireland. A century's bitterness flared into rebellion during the Easter Rising of 1916, when a few members of the Sinn Fein ('Ourselves Alone') movement tried to set up a free Irish Republic. British troops soon crushed the rebellion. But in the 1918 General Election, the Sinn Feiners won nearly all the Southern Irish seats. The people were obviously behind them. Now the Sinn Feiners established an illegal republican government and formed the I.R.A.—Irish Republican Army. Lloyd George's government tried a compromise solution: it partitioned Ireland into the 26 Southern Counties (mainly Roman Catholic) and the 6 Northern Counties (mainly Protestant) and offered each its own Parliament if it would stay within the United Kingdom. This failed to satisfy the Sinn Feiners who resorted to terrorism. Britain replied by forming counter-terrorist units—the Black and Tans—so that 1920 degenerated into a year of murder. The I.R.A. made terrorist attacks in Manchester and Liverpool—and as it was thought they would try to assassinate Lloyd George the entrance to Downing Street was barricaded for safety.

Dominion status

Eventually the rebel leaders came to London to discuss an Anglo-Irish Treaty and thus the British began what was to be a long history of negotiation with rebels prior to granting most of their demands. In 1921 Southern Ireland became a self-governing member of the British Empire with full dominion status, but this brought no peace to the Irish who fought among themselves in a bitter civil war which lasted until April 1923. Led by Eamon de Valera, one of the survivors of the Easter Rebellion, the 'Irish Free State' took the name of Eire in 1937. Two years later, when Britain was at war with Germany, Eire was the one member of the Commonwealth to remain neutral.

INDIA: Amritsar

In 1919 'the brightest jewel on the British crown' was a sub-continent of 400 million people, mostly governed by British officials. During the First World War Indian divisions had fought for the British who, in 1917, promised that India would be granted 'gradual development of self-governing institutions with a view to the progressive realization of responsible government'. But many Indians did not want to wait and clamoured for independence. British rifles dispersed one such demonstration at Amritsar in 1919. There were some 1600 casualties.

Mahatma Gandhi

Amritsar brought an Indian leader to the forefront; he was Mahatma Gandhi. Gandhi offered India a programme of 'Satyagraha', civil disobedience on a national scale designed to paralyse British government in India but without resort to violence. Gandhi's views in his day seemed extraordinary; he said that the answer to famine and unemployment was self-help and issued two million spinning wheels to the peasantry. He was backed by the Indian Congress Party but he resigned from its leadership in 1925 in order to tour the country and to preach 'economy' and the 'pure life'. 'Independence', he said, 'is an attitude of mind'. He fasted for days on end, dressed in the simplest clothes and organized his civil disobedience. Best known was his protest against the salt-tax in which he walked from Ahmedabad to Dandi, where he solemnly gathered salt from the sea-shore. When he visited Britain in 1931 for the 'Round Table Conference' on India, Churchill called him a half-naked fakir and refused to see him. But King George V did—and was impressed. Gandhi toured parts of Britain, telling the workers: 'Your average unemployment dole is £3.10.0 a month; our average income is 7/6 a month!' But he aroused very little support. He was frequently jailed and, as a pacifist, he bitterly complained that on 3 September 1939 the British Viceroy in India had declared war on Germany on behalf of 400 million Indians. But Gandhi's demands had to wait; his views would not prevail until *after* Adolf Hitler had been defeated.

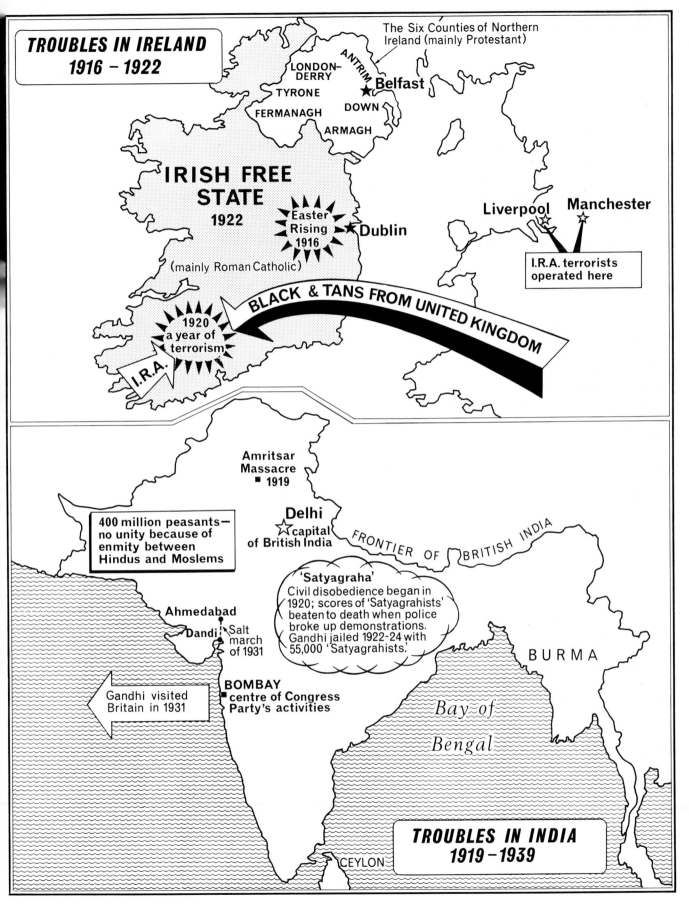

TROUBLES IN IRELAND 1916 – 1922

The Six Counties of Northern Ireland (mainly Protestant)

LONDON-DERRY
TYRONE
FERMANAGH
ARMAGH
ANTRIM
DOWN
★ Belfast

IRISH FREE STATE 1922

Easter Rising 1916

★ Dublin

(mainly Roman Catholic)

1920 a year of terrorism

I.R.A.

BLACK & TANS FROM UNITED KINGDOM

Liverpool   Manchester

I.R.A. terrorists operated here

Amritsar Massacre ■ 1919

400 million peasants— no unity because of enmity between Hindus and Moslems

Delhi
☆ capital of British India

FRONTIER OF BRITISH INDIA

'Satyagraha'
Civil disobedience began in 1920; scores of 'Satyagrahists' beaten to death when police broke up demonstrations. Gandhi jailed 1922-24 with 55,000 'Satyagrahists.'

BURMA

Ahmedabad
Dandi   Salt march of 1931

Gandhi visited Britain in 1931

BOMBAY ■ centre of Congress Party's activities

Bay of Bengal

CEYLON

TROUBLES IN INDIA 1919 – 1939

23: Trouble in the Far East: the first threat to world peace

Growth of Japanese power

Ever since the Japanese had beaten the Russians in the war of 1904–5, their ambitions seemed boundless. They had a firm grip on Korea and the Liao-tung Peninsula; they had stationed a large army in Southern Manchuria to guard their railway interests. Now they cast greedy eyes towards the new Chinese Republic, created after the anti-Manchu revolution in 1912. Their power had increased enormously during World War I, in which they captured Germany's Far Eastern possessions and worked their industries at full blast to produce ships and war munitions for the Allies. After the war, the Japanese fleet was the strongest in the Pacific. Of all the countries involved in the war, Japan seemed to have made the biggest profits.

Japanese problems

But in fact Japan had developed rather too quickly. More and more Japanese left the land and fishing industry to seek work in the factories. Food prices—rice was the staple diet—doubled during the war, while the population was increasing at the rate of nearly a million a year. All of these factors caused hardship to the Japanese people. There were rice riots in 1918; in 1923 matters were made worse by earthquake disasters which wrecked most of Tokyo and Yokohama. And throughout the Twenties the threat of unemployment hung over the heads of millions of wage-earners. Japan's problem was largely one of maintaining her industries at a high and profitable level of production. To do this she needed the precious raw materials which were lacking in Japan itself: iron ore, wool, aluminium, rubber—these all had to be imported. And to pay for these imports, Japan had to sell her manufactured goods and raw silk abroad. This became almost impossible when the world slump began in 1929 and the Japanese searched desperately for a way out of their troubles. Their army came up with one answer: if we need more land, more markets, more raw materials why not increase the size of the Imperial Army and take them? This was not the view of the Emperor and his government in Tokyo and they were almost as surprised as the rest of the world when in 1931 the news was announced that Japanese troops were occupying the whole of Chinese Manchuria.

The Manchurian Affair

This act of aggression was a deliberate breach of the Covenant of the League of Nations. Would the League act to stop the reckless Japanese Army? China appealed to the League for help; the Japanese retorted that China had started the war anyway by exploding a bomb on the South Manchurian Railway. Of course the League asked both sides to stop fighting, but the Japanese troops continued to fan out across Manchuria. Finally, the League sent out a Commission of Inquiry under Lord Lytton to sort out the whole affair, but before he was able to report back the Japanese had annexed the whole of Manchuria, renamed it 'Manchukuo' and recognized its 'independence' in September 1932. A month later Lord Lytton condemned Japanese aggression! In 1933 Japan resigned from the League, taking her prize with her.

The significance of the Manchurian Affair

The Manchurian Affair of 1931–33 had three very important results for world history. Firstly, it showed that the League of Nations was incapable of enforcing world peace and that, in the words of the *Spectator* 'a straight road back to 1914 lies open'. Secondly, it encouraged the European dictators to try the same tactics in Africa and Europe. And thirdly, the Japanese had no more qualms about extending their empire by armed force. They launched a full-scale attack on China in 1937 and this war continued, fiercely resisted by communist guerrillas under Mao Tse-tung and Nationalist armies led by Chiang K'ai-shek, until in the end it became merged with the story of the Second World War.

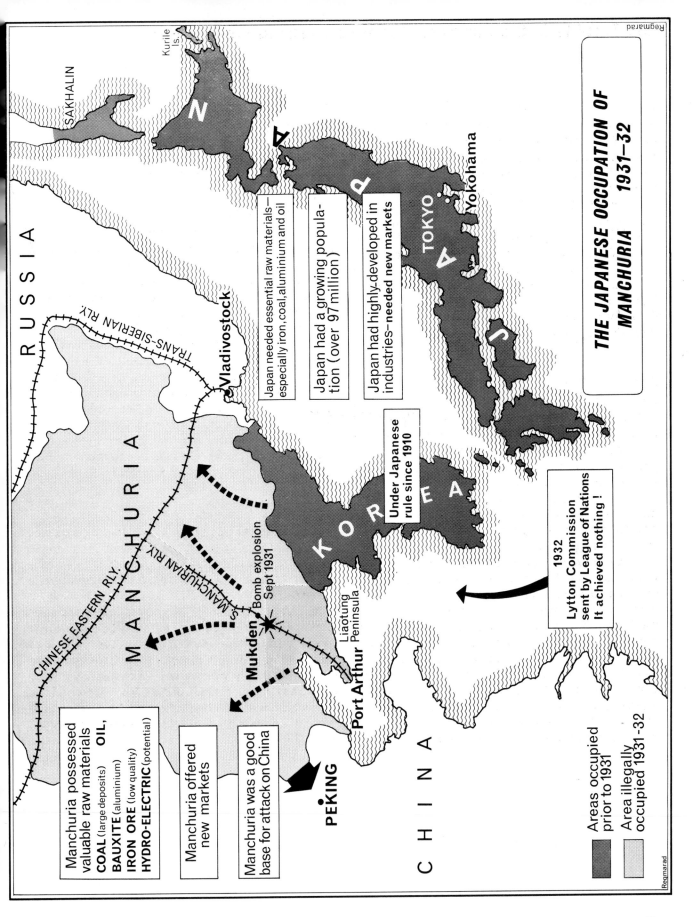

THE JAPANESE OCCUPATION OF MANCHURIA 1931–32

Japan needed essential raw materials— especially iron, coal, aluminium and oil

Japan had a growing population (over 97 million)

Japan had highly-developed industries— needed new markets

Under Japanese rule since 1910

1932 Lytton Commission sent by League of Nations It achieved nothing!

RUSSIA

SAKHALIN

Kurile Is.

N

A

P

A

J

TOKYO

Yokohama

KOREA

Vladivostock

TRANS-SIBERIAN RLY.

CHINESE EASTERN RLY.

MANCHURIA

MANCHURIAN RLY.

Mukden

Bomb explosion Sept 1931

Liaotung Peninsula

Port Arthur

CHINA

PEKING

Manchuria possessed valuable raw materials **COAL** (large deposits) **OIL,** **BAUXITE** (aluminium) **IRON ORE** (low quality) **HYDRO-ELECTRIC** (potential)

Manchuria offered new markets

Manchuria was a good base for attack on China

Areas occupied prior to 1931

Area illegally occupied 1931-32

Regmarad

Regmarad

24: Another war: the Italian invasion of Abyssinia and the 'failure of sanctions'

Since 1965 we have heard a great deal about the use of sanctions as a way of bringing back Mr. Smith's illegal government in Rhodesia to the 'rule of law'. Thirty years before, the League of Nations had tried to impose sanctions in order to prevent Mussolini's savage conquest of the Abyssinian people.

Mussolini attacks Ethiopia

Mussolini saw in his Italian Fascist state the rebirth of the ancient Roman Empire. He dreamt of vast colonial territories in Africa, such as Rome had once possessed. He called the Mediterranean Sea 'Mare Nostrum'—'Our Sea'—and occasionally he wore a toga. Already Italy had several colonies in Africa: Libya and Tripolitania, Eritrea and Italian Somaliland. But the Duce also wanted the ancient Empire of Ethiopia—Abyssinia. Once before, in 1896, the Italians had tried to conquer it but had suffered inglorious defeat at the Battle of Adowa. Now, in 1935, Mussolini made his bid against the badly armed soldiers of the Emperor Haile Selassie. On 3 October, he hurled his army, equipped with armour, artillery and automatic weapons, and his Air Force, fitted with mustard gas sprayers, into Abyssinia.

Reaction of League

This onslaught aroused far more world indignation than had the Manchurian affair four years earlier. The League was stirred to act and on 7 October 1935 it condemned Mussolini's aggression; and in less than a fortnight, with the approval of fifty-one nations, it decided to impose economic sanctions on Italy. Unfortunately, the sanctions excluded vital commodities such as steel, copper and oil whilst at the same time the League stopped all arms exports (except those actually in transit) to the combatants. Clearly, the Abyssinians weren't going to get any military aid! Nevertheless, there had been *some* positive action; perhaps the League would at last show some strength and stop the fighting. Yet it was soon obvious that the sanctions were having absolutely no effect on Mussolini—who was threatening a general war if anyone dare cut off his oil supplies. Finally Anthony Eden, then a minister with special interest in the affairs of the League, suggested that an oil embargo might begin during December.

Hoare-Laval Pact

Then came an extraordinary event. Samuel Hoare, the British Foreign Secretary, was off on holiday to Switzerland and on the way he visited Paris a few days before the oil sanctions were due to be imposed. He had some talks with his French opposite number, Pierre Laval, in which the pair agreed on an iniquitous plan, known as the Hoare-Laval Pact. Simply, if Mussolini would stop fighting immediately he could have most of Abyssinia. He had already captured more than half of it! When some reporters got wind of this arrangement and published the details in the British and French Press there was a tremendous public outcry—and Hoare had to resign. The Hoare-Laval Pact was never carried out—but the damage had been done. Obviously, neither Britain nor France, the most powerful members of the League, really intended to take any positive action and soon the other supporters of sanctions drifted away. Mussolini completed his conquest of Abyssinia during 1936 without interruption and forced Haile Selassie to flee abroad. The Duce's own words were significant:

> If the League had extended economic sanctions to oil, I would have had to withdraw from Abyssinia within a week.

Failure of the League

So the oil sanctions never *failed*, because they were never even applied. What had failed, and for the second time since 1931, was the League of Nations. The story of the Abyssinian war was the last nail in the coffin of the League, and after 1936 men sought other ways of maintaining world peace, eventually turning to the policy known as 'appeasement'.

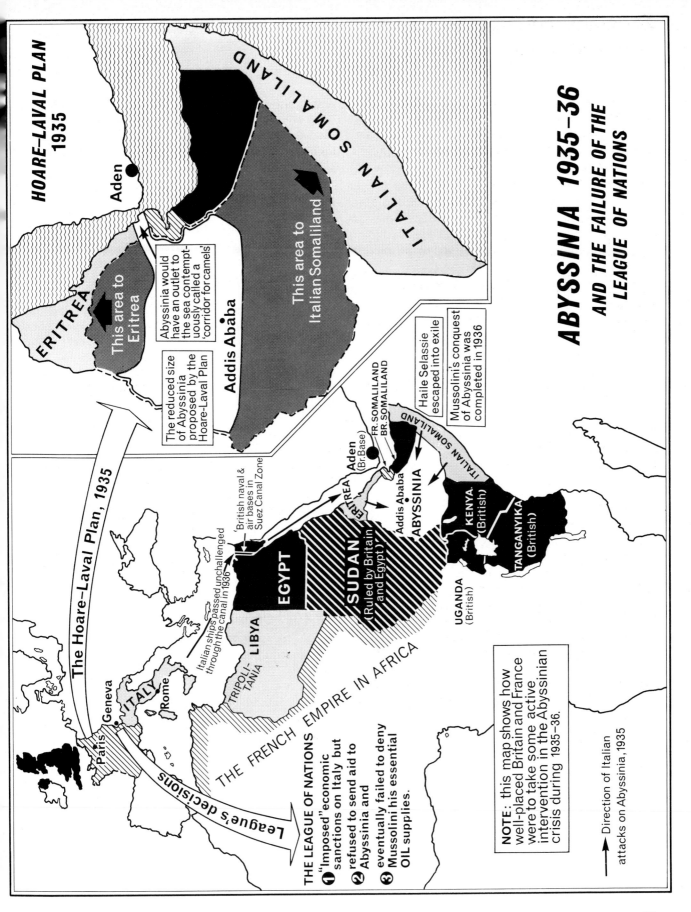

ABYSSINIA 1935–36
AND THE FAILURE OF THE LEAGUE OF NATIONS

HOARE–LAVAL PLAN 1935

ERITREA

This area to Eritrea

Abyssinia would have an outlet to the sea contemptuously called a 'corridor for camels'

The reduced size of Abyssinia proposed by the Hoare–Laval Plan

Addis Abãba

This area to Italian Somaliland

ITALIAN SOMALILAND

Aden

The Hoare–Laval Plan, 1935

League's decisions

Geneva
Paris
ITALY
Rome

LIBYA

TRIPOLITANIA

THE FRENCH EMPIRE IN AFRICA

Italian ships passed unchallenged through the canal in 1936

British naval & air bases in Suez Canal Zone

EGYPT

SUDAN (Ruled by Britain and Egypt)

Aden (Br.Base)

ERITREA

FR. SOMALILAND
BR. SOMALILAND

Addis Ababa
ABYSSINIA

ITALIAN SOMALILAND

Haile Selassie escaped into exile

Mussolini's conquest of Abyssinia was completed in 1936

KENYA (British)

UGANDA (British)

TANGANYIKA (British)

THE LEAGUE OF NATIONS
① "imposed" economic sanctions on Italy but
② refused to send aid to Abyssinia and
③ eventually failed to deny Mussolini his essential OIL supplies.

NOTE: this map shows how well-placed Britain and France were to take some active intervention in the Abyssinian crisis during 1935–36.

→ Direction of Italian attacks on Abyssinia, 1935

25: The Spanish Civil War 1936–1939

Spain's problems

Spain's problems were unique. They did not arise from the aftermath of World War, for Spain was neutral between 1914–18, but from her own history and institutions. Ever since the loss of Cuba and the Philippines in 1898, the Spanish industries based on Bilbao and Barcelona had been robbed of traditional overseas markets, so that industrial workers were either unemployed or underpaid. Though most Spaniards were peasants, $2\frac{1}{2}$ million of them were landless 'braceros' who worked for wages on the vast estates called 'latifundia'. Often the braceros were unemployed and close to starvation. These conditions helped to make Spain a hotbed of political unrest. There were communists who, after 1917, demanded a government along Russian lines; there were socialists who wanted a closer central control of Spanish economic conditions; and there were anarchists who wished for no government at all! They were all enemies of the king, Alfonso XIII, who looked for his support to the wealthy, landowning Catholic Church, to the Civil Guard (the police) and to the powerful army, constantly embroiled in colonial wars in Morocco.

The Spanish Republic

In 1917 Spain experienced a general strike. The army crushed it. During the next six years there were twelve different governments. Then in 1923 the Army provided a dictator—Primo de Rivera. He ruled Spain for seven years and then retired from politics after a quarrel with the king. This left Alfonso alone and unhappy—and in the midst of the 1931 general elections he abdicated. In this way Spain became a republic. However, the Republican governments met little success. They tried to give lands to the braceros, but this was a slow and frustrating process. Furious peasants would squat on farming lands—then clash with the Civil Guard and perhaps burn down local churches. As one miserable Spaniard said: 'We cannot live in anarchy'. So once more the Army acted. In July 1936 General Francisco Franco invaded Spain from Morocco, whilst elsewhere in Spain other officers took control of towns and villages. In Madrid the Republican government, supported by communists, socialists and anarchists alike, decided to fight the invader and so civil war began.

Civil War

At first the great powers decided not to take sides and solemnly signed a 'non-intervention' agreement. But almost immediately, the Fascist dictators broke their word and sent all sorts of military aid to Franco. Communist Russia, justifiably complaining that the agreement had been broken, sent help to the Republicans. But Britain and France steadfastly maintained an official policy of 'non-intervention'. Outside Spain, the Civil War appeared either as a struggle between a legal Republican government and the 'Fascist' invaders, or as a Nationalist bid to eradicate Communism in Spain. It depended on one's political point of view. Many young men chose to join International Brigades and fought side by side with Russian communists in defence of the Republic.

'Non-interventionism' certainly restricted the civil war to Spain and most people remained passive—even when stirred by atrocity reports and the news of the German bombing of Guernica in 1937. Germany used the civil war as a way of testing her new air force under battle conditions. Mussolini sent 60,000 troops to Spain. Communist Russia discovered that her tanks and aircraft had certain design weaknesses and soon withdrew her aid. By March 1939 the war was over and Spain surrendered to the dictatorship of General Franco.

After nearly three years of fighting, in which more than half a million people died, a nation lost all trace of democratic freedom. And in 1939, as men listened to Hitler's endless demands for more 'living space' the Spanish Civil War was seen as the shape of things to come.

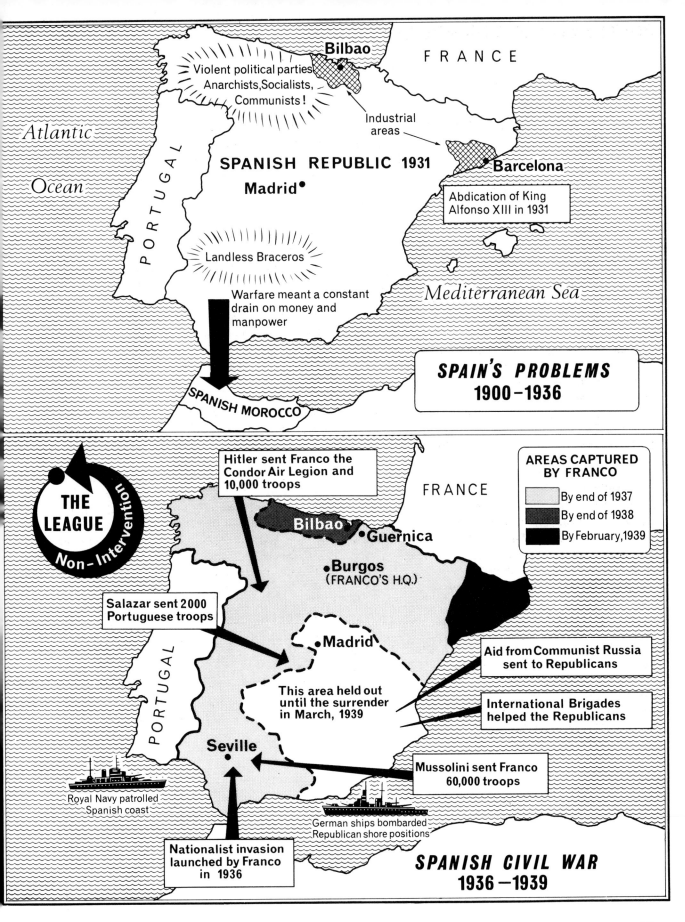

SPAIN'S PROBLEMS 1900–1936

Atlantic Ocean

FRANCE

Bilbao

Violent political parties
Anarchists, Socialists,
Communists!

Industrial areas

SPANISH REPUBLIC 1931

Madrid

Barcelona

Abdication of King
Alfonso XIII in 1931

PORTUGAL

Landless Braceros

Mediterranean Sea

Warfare meant a constant
drain on money and
manpower

SPANISH MOROCCO

SPANISH CIVIL WAR 1936–1939

Hitler sent Franco the
Condor Air Legion and
10,000 troops

THE LEAGUE
Non-Intervention

FRANCE

AREAS CAPTURED BY FRANCO

By end of 1937
By end of 1938
By February, 1939

Bilbao
Guernica

Burgos
(FRANCO'S H.Q.)

Salazar sent 2000
Portuguese troops

PORTUGAL

Madrid

Aid from Communist Russia
sent to Republicans

This area held out
until the surrender
in March, 1939

International Brigades
helped the Republicans

Seville

Mussolini sent Franco
60,000 troops

Royal Navy patrolled
Spanish coast

German ships bombarded
Republican shore positions

Nationalist invasion
launched by Franco
in 1936

57

26: Hitler's Germany 1933–1938

The Führer

Once in power Hitler destroyed all who opposed his rule. The Gestapo, commanded by Heinrich Himmler, herded leading Communists and Social Democrats into concentration camps. All political parties, other than the Nazi Party, were banned. Hitler even distrusted his own friends; in 1934 Ernst Roehm, the Stormtrooper Leader, was arrested and shot. And when President Hindenburg died a few weeks later, Hitler combined the offices of President and Chancellor into one, proclaimed himself Führer (Leader) and ordered all German soldiers to take an oath of allegiance to him.

Germany's reaction

Did the German people agree with what Hitler had done? He asked them to vote in a plebiscite during 1934 and of the 42 million voters, 38 million echoed a resounding *Yes*! Hitler, who carried out his revolution *after* coming to power, had the approval of the vast majority of the German people. They allowed their children to be fed with Nazi propaganda about the evil communists and Jews both in school and in organizations such as the Hitler Youth. They turned a blind eye to the concentration camps and the persecution of German Jews, for Hitler was promising all 'pure Germans' a glorious new future and was actually ending unemployment.

Rearmament

Just before he came to power Hitler had told the German industrialists that he would create, with their help, a great new German 'Reich'—armed to strike. So when he became Führer he began setting up, in complete defiance of the terms of the Treaty of Versailles, a German state that was geared to war. He left the League of Nations and authorized the production of U-boats, tanks and planes for the new Luftwaffe (Air Force). He virtually ended unemployment by conscripting half a million soldiers into the Wehrmacht (Army) and by finding work for thousands in the Labour Corps which, incidentally, helped to build the famous German autobahnen (motorways).

Testing his strength

By 1936 Hitler was ready to strike. First he marched a few of his troops into the Rhineland—demilitarized since 1919. Not a finger was raised against them. Next he looked for allies, coming to an understanding with Fascist Italy (which Mussolini called the Axis agreement) and then signing an anti-communist pact with Japan. So far everything that Hitler had done seemed acceptable to the western democracies: he had simply taken over parts of Germany that were legally his—the people of the Saar, for example, had willingly voted to rejoin the Reich in the 1935 plebiscite. But after 1936 Hitler began to demand territories that were not legally his. He argued that Germany was in dire need of Lebensraum (living-space) and that outside Germany's frontiers lived millions of Germans who needed the Führer's protection. And there is little doubt that, during 1937, Hitler had decided to back up his demands for Lebensraum with force, if necessary.

Anschluss

In 1938 Hitler demanded an Anschluss (union) with Austria. Herr Schuschnigg, the Austrian Chancellor, yielded to Hitler's threats and Austria joined the Reich. Hitler's policy of Lebensraum seemed to be enjoying boundless success. But when the Führer showed an interest in the Czechoslovakian Sudeten territories later that year he found that the Czechs, confident of French and Russian support, would rather fight than surrender. Once more the threat of war hung over Europe—and at this point Britain intervened in a desperate play for peace. The story of this intervention is the story of the 1938 Munich Crisis.

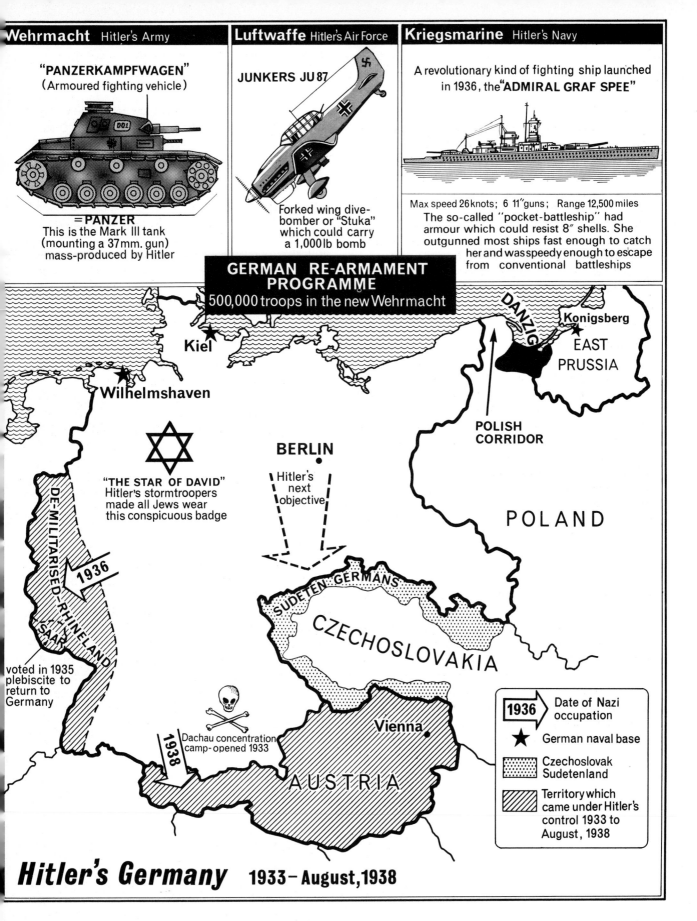

Wehrmacht Hitler's Army

"PANZERKAMPFWAGEN"
(Armoured fighting vehicle)

= PANZER
This is the Mark III tank
(mounting a 37mm. gun)
mass-produced by Hitler

Luftwaffe Hitler's Air Force

JUNKERS JU 87

Forked wing dive-
bomber or "Stuka"
which could carry
a 1,000 lb bomb

Kriegsmarine Hitler's Navy

A revolutionary kind of fighting ship launched
in 1936, the **"ADMIRAL GRAF SPEE"**

Max speed 26 knots; 6 11" guns; Range 12,500 miles
The so-called "pocket-battleship" had
armour which could resist 8" shells. She
outgunned most ships fast enough to catch
her and was speedy enough to escape
from conventional battleships

GERMAN RE-ARMAMENT PROGRAMME
500,000 troops in the new Wehrmacht

Kiel

DANZIG

Konigsberg

EAST PRUSSIA

Wilhelmshaven

"THE STAR OF DAVID"
Hitler's stormtroopers
made all Jews wear
this conspicuous badge

POLISH CORRIDOR

BERLIN
Hitler's next objective

POLAND

DE-MILITARISED-RHINELAND

1936

SAAR

voted in 1935
plebiscite to
return to
Germany

SUDETEN GERMANS

CZECHOSLOVAKIA

1938

Dachau concentration
camp-opened 1933

Vienna

AUSTRIA

1936 → Date of Nazi
occupation

★ German naval base

Czechoslovak
Sudetenland

Territory which
came under Hitler's
control 1933 to
August, 1938

Hitler's Germany 1933 – August, 1938

27: The 1938 Munich Crisis and its results

Appeasement

The thought of another European war with the new attendant horrors of air attack was abhorrent to the British people in the Thirties—and particularly so to Neville Chamberlain, the man who became Prime Minister in 1937. Realizing that the peace of the world depended on the actions of the half-mad German Führer, he nevertheless sympathized with Hitler's demands. Chamberlain wanted to see Germany regain her rightful place in Europe. But this would not happen until the question of the three million Germans living in Czechoslovakia had been settled. Hitler wanted, he said, 'self-determination' for these Sudeten Germans; might it be possible to placate or appease the Führer by arranging a meeting with him to discuss a settlement?

Munich

Whilst Hitler threatened the Czechs, Chamberlain flew to meet the Führer in Berchtesgaden (15 September 1938). Here Hitler promised to delay an attack on Czechoslovakia and gave Chamberlain until 1 October to arrange the withdrawal of Czech troops from the Sudetenland. Chamberlain managed to persuade Dr. Benes, the Czech Premier, to agree to transfer to Germany *those parts of the Sudetenland where the majority of the population was German.* On 22 September, Chamberlain flew back to Germany and at Godesberg he offered Hitler the deal. The Führer replied: 'I'm very sorry, but I regret that this is of no use now.' He wanted the *whole* of the Sudetenland—and renewed his threat of war. Chamberlain was now disconsolate; he could see no way of preventing war. On the evening of 27 September he broadcast on the BBC: 'How horrible, fantastic, incredible it is that we should be digging trenches and trying on gasmasks here because of a quarrel in a far away country between people of whom we know nothing... I would not hesitate to pay a third visit to Germany if I thought it would do any good.' Next day he had his chance. He flew to Munich for talks with Hitler, Mussolini and Daladier, the French Premier. The Czechs were excluded from the conference room; the Russians were not even invited. On 30 September—the day before Hitler's threatened attack upon Czechoslovakia—the decision was announced. Hitler was to have the whole of the Sudetenland; he promised he had no more territorial demands to make in Europe. The Czechs, betrayed and isolated, had to agree. So the crisis was solved. Hitler was appeased—because he had had his own way; and the price of appeasement was the sacrifice of the frontiers of Czechoslovakia.

More demands

Everything was peaceful for the next six months. Then, to Chamberlain's horror, Hitler showed how untrustworthy he was. On 15 March 1939 German troops occupied Bohemia and Moravia. A week later they marched into the Lithuanian city of Memel. Where next would Hitler strike? The British rightly judged that it would be in the Polish Corridor and on 21 March they promised to protect the Poles against German aggression. Exactly how this would be done, no-one explained at the time. But surely the threat was enough. Hemmed in by the democracies in the west and by Communist Russia in the east, Hitler would never dare to resort to war now.

The pact with Russia

Then came the bombshell: on 23 August 1939 Communist Russia and Nazi Germany signed a non-aggression pact. They promised not to make war on one another. Whilst the rest of the world tried to fathom out this development, Hitler attacked Poland on 1 September. Now Britain was forced to honour her promise to the Poles. She gave Hitler a deadline: unless he withdrew his troops from Poland by Sunday 3 September Britain would declare war on Germany.

Munich—AND ITS RESULTS, 1938–1939

RUSSO-GERMAN NON-AGGRESSION PACT, Aug 1939

Memel

Germany gains Memel, 1939

Danzig

Germany attacks Poland, 1 Sept.1939

POLAND

GERMANY GAINS SUDETENLAND 1938

•Godesberg

BOHEMIA
•Prague

Skoda arms works

MORAVIA

TESCHEN—taken by Poland 1938

SLOVAKIA

②

③

①

•Munich

Hungary takes this territory, March, 1939

•Berchtesgaden

Germany gives this territory to Hungary, Oct. 1938 "The Vienna Award"

German frontier March, 1939
Sudetenland
Bohemia and Moravia
Chamberlain's flights, 1938

THE DESTRUCTION OF CZECHOSLOVAKIA

1. **Sudetenland**—to Germany
2. **Teschen**—to Poland
3. To Hungary
4. **Bohemia Moravia**—to Germany
5. **Ruthenia**—to Hungary

1

4

2

SLOVAKIA

3

5

Slovakia survived, officially as an independent state in March, 1939, but in reality as a German satellite.

28: America and her problems 1919–1939

Isolation

Three thousand miles across the Atlantic, the U.S.A. remained virtually untouched by the rapid changes taking place in Europe. From 1919 onwards the Americans had isolated themselves from that war-scarred continent, retaining only an interest in financial matters. After all, Europe owed them $12,500,000,000. America was interested in maintaining prosperity in Europe: that was why she helped Germany over her inflationary troubles during 1923–4; why Americans invested their dollars in Europe's industries; why America supported gestures of peace and goodwill, such as the 1928 Kellogg Pact. But she never committed herself, never signed the Versailles Treaty, never joined the League. Americans had rejected Woodrow Wilson's ideas in 1920 and for the next 12 years 'isolationist' Republican Presidents led the American people.

The Crash

During the Twenties the Americans concentrated on their internal development. They had vast reserves of food and mineral resources. Their industries, which had made huge profits during the war, now mass-produced consumer goods such as radios, cars and washing-machines. For many Americans it *was* an age of prosperity, though marred by gangsters such as Al Capone and by the persecution of the southern negro by organizations such as the Ku Klux Klan. But affluence did not last. America overproduced; millions of people ran up hire-purchase debts and soon money became scarce. Shareholders tried to exchange their investments for cash and in October 1929 share prices collapsed on their Wall Street Stock Exchange. This was the Great Crash, which led first to the American depression and then to a slump in world trade. By 1930 the Americans were beginning to understand the misery of unemployment—something which Europe had already experienced. By 1932 over 12 million Americans had lost their jobs and more than 30,000 firms had gone bankrupt. America tried to call in her overseas loans and clamped down on the import of foreign goods. As a result Brazilian coffee growers destroyed their crops rather than flood a market already suffering from falling prices and in Germany unemployment returned overnight to give the Nazis their chance.

Franklin D. Roosevelt

President Hoover had no answer to this breakdown in the American economy—and so the American electors were encouraged to vote for his Democrat rival, Franklin D. Roosevelt in the 1932 elections. Roosevelt was offering the American people a 'New Deal'—his answer to unemployment. Once elected, he gave vast sums of Federal aid to the 48 states so that they could put money back into the pockets of the wage earners. He introduced 'social security'—unemployment and sickness pay; he began great 'work-finding' schemes such as irrigation projects, bridge building and dam construction. Most famous was his Tennessee Valley Authority (TVA), a remarkable scheme which boosted agriculture and industry in a number of states. He had to face plenty of opposition from his political opponents. The Republicans disliked his interference in the affairs of individual states and the charge of 'Fascist dictator!' was often bandied about. But the American people were behind 'F.D.R.', who was destined to win the next *three* presidential elections.

America and the world

Slowly the Americans began to emerge from their depression at approximately the same time as war was once more threatening Europe. They were still determined to keep out of trouble, although Roosevelt was well aware of the dangers that existed in Germany and Japan. In 1935 and 1937 Congress passed 'Neutrality Acts'—the nation wanted peace. No American, of course, could foresee that in the not too distant future his country would be at war with both Japan and Germany—and allied with a most unlikely partner, the Communist state of Russia.

The New Deal !

C.C.C. **Civilian Conservation Corps.** Gave jobs to young unemployed Americans in U.S. forestlands; 2½ million found a job with the C.C.C.

P.W.A. **Public Works Association.** Spent over $3000m on national construction to find work for the unemployed.

H.O.L.C. **Home Owners' Loan Corporation.** Lent cash to those who could not keep up mortgage repayments.

T.V.A. **Tennessee Valley Authority.** Covered 41,000 sq. miles. Provided cheap hydro-electric power, irrigation, fertilisers, new industries and retraining programmes. Stopped flooding and soil erosion. Transformed valley from poverty into a new age of prosperity.

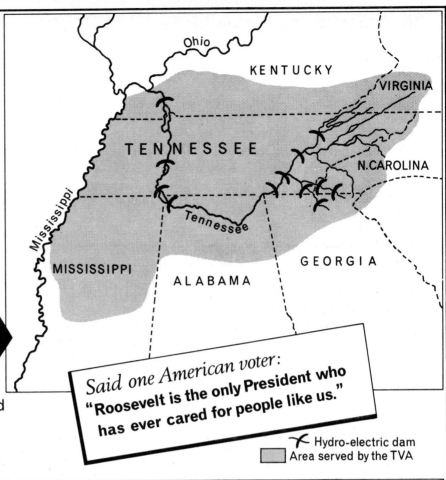

Said one American voter:
"Roosevelt is the only President who has ever cared for people like us."

Hydro-electric dam
Area served by the TVA

12,000,000 unemployed in America

America withdraws short term loans from Germany. $ investment ends.

The whole of Latin America depended on export (mainly to the U.S.A.) of a few commodities. e.g. Brazil depended on the sale of her coffee. The depression in the U.S.A. therefore led to suffering in Latin America.

No sale for Brazilian coffee

GERMAN INDUSTRY COLLAPSES

Trade with rest of Europe is cut

Leads to mass unemployment

Rise of violent political parties
Nazis
Communists

THE EFFECTS OF THE WALL STREET CRASH, 1929

Regmarad

29: The Communist achievement in Russia 1924–1939

Stalin and the Five Year Plans

Between 1924 and 1928 Josef Stalin schemed to become dictator of Russia. In 1927 he expelled his leading rivals—including Trotsky—from the Communist Party, so that by 1928 Stalin was the most powerful man in the Soviet Union. He then began one of the most ambitious projects in the history of the world: the rapid industrialization and collectivization of Russia. First he designed a series of 'Five Year Plans' to modernize the vast and backward land over which he ruled. In the First Plan, which began in 1928, he demanded that Russia must concentrate on factory building and the expansion of her natural power resources. He called for steel-mills and coal-mines, brick factories and cement plants, power stations and oil refineries. An enormous tractor plant opened in Stalingrad: a brand new iron and steel industry began in the Urals-Kuzbass region. But the Russians had a long way to go and in 1931 Stalin made an uncanny prophecy: 'We are fifty to a hundred years behind the advanced countries. We must make good this distance in ten years—either we do this or they will crush us'. The next year saw the start of the Second Plan, when even more demands were made on the Russian people, who were still inadequately clothed, underpaid and undernourished. Not until 1937 did the Third Plan begin to concentrate on the production of essential consumer goods. Even twenty years later, when Russia had launched the world's first space satellite, the people of Moscow would still make a wry joke:

Good, now we're in space perhaps we can have some shoes. There is no doubt that the Russian people were little more than slaves during this period of reconstruction. But the changes they brought about *were* rapid and quite startling. Whilst the rest of the world suffered mass unemployment Stalin managed to end unemployment—admittedly, by using the methods of the labour camps—and increased Russian industrial production to a figure seven times above the 1914 level.

Collectivization

Stalin adopted an equally ruthless approach to the collectivization of agriculture. This meant that all Russian farmland would be nationalized and that the 'kulaks'—wealthy peasant farmers who tended to hoard food supplies to keep prices up—would be replaced by giant farms on which workers would labour collectively. The farm produce would then be sold to the state. There would be no more private trading in foodstuffs. Stalin warned that he would 'liquidate the kulaks as a class' and after 1929 tens of thousands were forced into the labour camps or resettled in other parts of Russia. Unknown numbers were killed, sometimes by the secret police, sometimes by the Red Army and Air Force. By 1937 there was hardly a single private farm left in Russia.

The price

From the Communist point of view, collectivization was both a success and a necessity. From the ordinary Russian's point of view it meant appalling hardship. Misuse of the new agricultural machinery, poor harvests and eventual food shortages became a commonplace. More than 12 million people died of hunger and disease during the dreadful famines of 1932–34; in the midst of these Stalin actually exported Ukrainian wheat to pay for his imports of engineering equipment. The climax to Stalin's ruthless policies came between 1935 and 1938 when thousands of untrustworthy men—in the dictator's judgment—military and civilian alike, were liquidated during the infamous 'purges'. No nation has ever paid such a price in the name of progress as did Russia during that first decade of Stalin's dictatorship. Yet even this was to pale when compared with the sacrifice that 20 million Russians were destined to make in the 'Great Patriotic War' against Hitler.

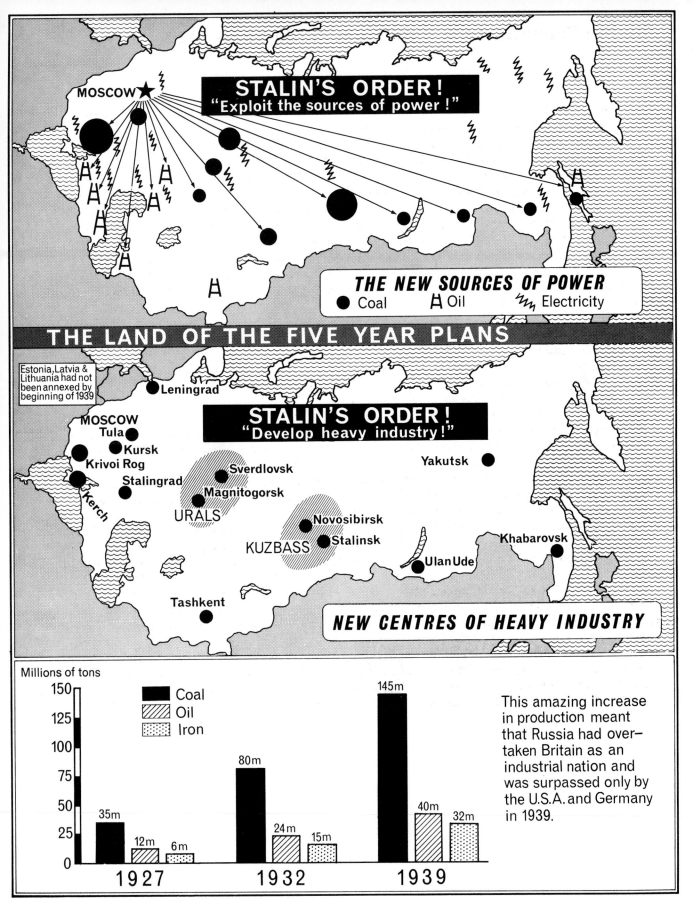

STALIN'S ORDER!
"Exploit the sources of power!"

MOSCOW

THE NEW SOURCES OF POWER
● Coal   Ħ Oil   ⌇ Electricity

THE LAND OF THE FIVE YEAR PLANS

Estonia, Latvia & Lithuania had not been annexed by beginning of 1939

Leningrad

MOSCOW
Tula
Kursk
Krivoi Rog
Stalingrad
Kerch

STALIN'S ORDER!
"Develop heavy industry!"

Sverdlovsk
Magnitogorsk
URALS

Yakutsk

Novosibirsk
Stalinsk
KUZBASS

Ulan Ude

Khabarovsk

Tashkent

NEW CENTRES OF HEAVY INDUSTRY

Millions of tons

■ Coal
▨ Oil
▦ Iron

150
125
100
75
50
25
0

1927   35m   12m   6m
1932   80m   24m   15m
1939   145m   40m   32m

This amazing increase in production meant that Russia had over-taken Britain as an industrial nation and was surpassed only by the U.S.A. and Germany in 1939.

Part 3 – Book List

19. See individual references in Encyclopedia Brittanica
20. *Twentieth Century France*   P. Holland   OUP
21. *A Picture of the Twenties*   R. Bennett   Vista Books
22. *Britain between the Wars*   C. L. Mowat   pp 110–112, 337–378, 426–428, all on India
pp 57–78, 79–108, all on Ireland
23. *Britain between the Wars*   C. L. Mowat   pp 419–422
24. *Britain between the Wars*   C. L. Mowat   pp 542–563
25. *Franco and the Spanish Civil War*   L. E. Snellgrove   Longmans
26. *Twentieth Century Germany*   B. Catchpole   OUP
27. *Britain and Germany between the Wars*   M. Gilbert   Longmans
28. *Franklin Roosevelt*   C. P. Hill   OUP
29. *Twentieth Century Russia*   S. Pickering   OUP

Both Stalin and Hitler contrived to present an image of geniality by frequently posing for photographs with children. (*S.C.R. Photo Library* and *Heinrich Hoffman*)

PART 4

The Second World War
1939–1945

The war that Hitler unleashed on 1 September 1939 brought far more misery and killing than did the mass battles of World War I.

At first, Hitler's intuition, the skill of his generals and the undoubted bravery and efficiency of his armies brought victory after victory. Soon Europe was his, a Europe which at once fell victim to the maniacal racial beliefs of the Nazi leadership. Millions of European Jews and tens of thousands of resistance fighters were to die in the German death camps.

That Hitler did not invade and conquer Britain in 1940 was due to a series of blunders for which the British people had good cause to be grateful. Firstly, Hitler failed to capture the British armies stranded on the Dunkirk beaches; secondly he failed to press home his advantages in the Battle of Britain; and thirdly he decided, against the advice of most of his General Staff, to invade the Soviet Union where, in 1941, he committed two-thirds of the German armed forces in a fruitless struggle against the Russian people. Then, after the sudden Japanese attack on Pearl Harbor at the end of 1941, he declared war on the United States of America. Very wisely, President Roosevelt agreed to concentrate on the defeat of Nazi Germany before destroying the enemy in the Pacific.

In a sense, therefore, two separate wars were being fought out between 1939 and 1945. No real spirit of comradeship and co-operation existed between the Germans and the Japanese and the course of fighting in one theatre had few significant results upon the other. Nevertheless, victory in both these theatres of war required the total defeat of the enemy. Before the Nazis would agree to unconditional surrender, the Allies had to devastate the German countryside; Japan suffered frightful fire raids prior to the ultimate atomic holocaust of 1945.

It has been often said that wars achieve nothing. But World War II did remove the evil cancers of German Nazism and Japanese militarism, with the result that both countries were required to adopt new forms of government after their defeat. More significantly the war led to a direct confrontation between the two superpowers, Russia and the USA, an event which has shaped all our lives.

30: Blitzkrieg!

Britain declares war

In the early hours of the morning of 1 September 1939 the scream of divebombers and the roar of lowflying fighters filled the air above Poland. On the ground Hitler's panzers were smashing in all directions through the Polish defences as they cut a path for the rapidly advancing infantry. This was Europe's first taste of the Führer's *Blitzkrieg* or lightning war. In Britain, Chamberlain's reaction was to send an ultimatum to Hitler: he required Hitler to withdraw his troops from Poland or face war with Britain. Chamberlain waited until Sunday 3 September for Hitler's reply; then he spoke to the British people: 'I have to tell you now that no such undertaking has been received and consequently this country is at war with Germany'.

The phoney war

Once more a British Expeditionary Force sailed to France—which had also declared war on Germany. Once more they marched towards the Belgian frontier while the French manned their impregnable Maginot Line. Everywhere there was an air of expectancy, but nothing happened. The Germans completed their conquest of Poland—after 17 September they were actually assisted by the Russian armies. But the western democracies did nothing. They simply watched a great part of Eastern Europe fall into the hands of the Nazi and Communist dictators; and after this they seemed far more interested in the spirited fight put up by the Finns in their 'Winter War' against the Russian aggressors than in their own commitments against Hitler. This period was known as the 'phoney war'—a war in which no British soldier died in combat on the Western Front before December 1939. Yet Chamberlain was sure that this inactivity would bring Hitler to his knees; on 5 April 1940 he went so far as to say that Hitler had 'missed the bus'.

Attack in the West

He had to eat his words within a few days. On 9 April Hitler's soldiers invaded Denmark and Norway. A month later they launched the Blitzkrieg against Holland and Belgium and then, after skirting round the tip of the Maginot Line, invaded France on 12 May. Within six days the panzers had reached the English Channel—they had sliced the Allied armies in France into two. In the north the B.E.F. and the French were compressed into a shrinking perimeter around Dunkirk, from which 338,000 troops eventually escaped by evacuation to England. But in the south the Germans wheeled to attack the bewildered French forces, who capitulated on 22 June 1940.

The Battle of Britain

After this spectacular achievement by Hitler's fighting men, Britain and the Commonwealth countries stood alone in the struggle against Nazi aggression. Winston Churchill, the new Prime Minister, could promise the British people only blood, sweat, toil and tears. On the one hand the British faced slow starvation under a U-boat blockade; on the other there was the prospect of a German invasion. Only a few miles across the Channel the Germans were preparing for Operation Sealion—the codeword for the invasion. Its first phase involved the destruction of the R.A.F. and the British aircraft factories and on 13 August 1940 the Luftwaffe began the Battle of Britain. For weeks the German fliers tried to smash British resistance in the air—and they very nearly succeeded. However, Hitler called off the daylight attacks on 12 October. He mistakenly believed that the British could be finished off by a series of night attacks. So throughout the winter of 1940–41 London, Liverpool, Hull, Coventry, Plymouth and scores of other towns burned under the Luftwaffe's incendiary and high explosive raids—while in Germany the Führer's twisted mind concocted his most grandiose scheme of all: Operation Barbarossa—invasion of the Soviet Union.

Radar and Ultra

Credit for victory in the Battle of Britain is deservedly given to the men and women of Britain's armed services in general and the pilots of Fighter Command in particular. But the British also possessed two devices which gave their defences advanced warning of German plans. *Radar* picked up the enemy aircraft as they left their bases on the other side of the Channel. *Ultra* gave advanced information about their destinations! Ultra was in fact an "Enigma" mechanical cypher machine capable of intercepting and decoding German signals.*

*See F. W. Winterbotham, *The Ultra Secret* (Weidenfeld and Nicolson, 1974).

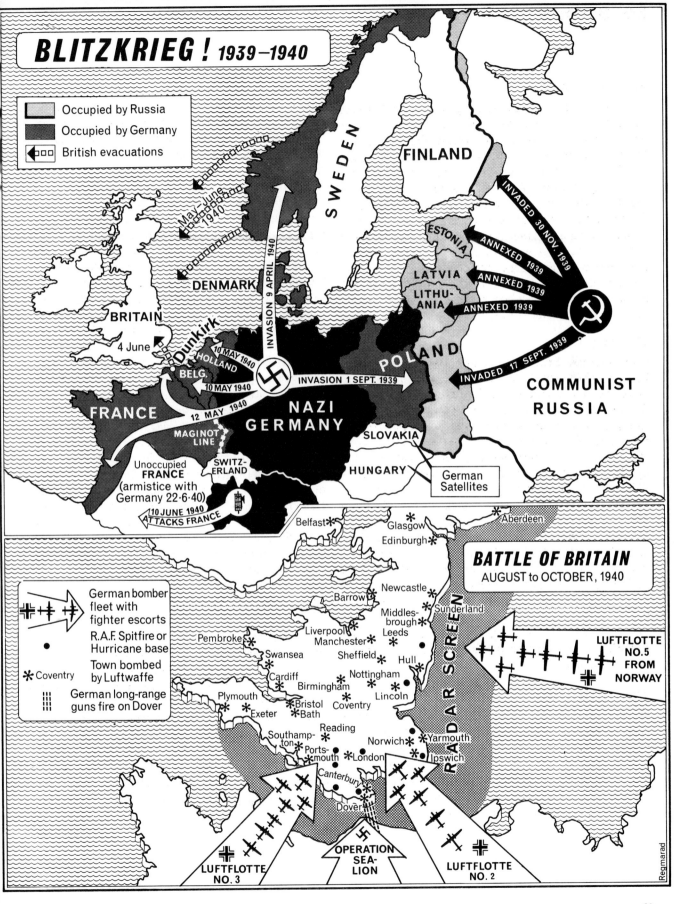

BLITZKRIEG ! *1939–1940*

Occupied by Russia
Occupied by Germany
◄□□ British evacuations

SWEDEN
FINLAND
May–June 1940
DENMARK
BRITAIN
Dunkirk
4 June
ESTONIA
LATVIA
LITH-
ANIA
INVADED 30 NOV. 1939
ANNEXED 1939
ANNEXED 1939
ANNEXED 1939
INVASION 9 APRIL 1940
HOLLAND
10 MAY 1940
BELG
10 MAY 1940
POLAND
INVASION 1 SEPT. 1939
INVADED 17 SEPT. 1939
COMMUNIST
RUSSIA
FRANCE
12 MAY 1940
NAZI
GERMANY
MAGINOT
LINE
SWITZ-
ERLAND
SLOVAKIA
HUNGARY
German
Satellites
Unoccupied
FRANCE
(armistice with
Germany 22·6·40)
10 JUNE 1940
ATTACKS FRANCE

Belfast ✳
Glasgow ✳
Edinburgh ✳
Aberdeen ✳

BATTLE OF BRITAIN
AUGUST to OCTOBER, 1940

German bomber
fleet with
fighter escorts
• R.A.F. Spitfire or
Hurricane base
✳ Coventry Town bombed
by Luftwaffe
⫴ German long-range
guns fire on Dover

Newcastle ✳
Barrow ✳
Middles-
brough ✳
Sunderland ✳
Liverpool ✳
Manchester ✳
Leeds ✳
Pembroke ✳
Sheffield ✳
Hull ✳
Swansea ✳
Cardiff ✳
Nottingham ✳
Lincoln ✳
Birmingham ✳
Plymouth ✳
Bristol ✳
Coventry ✳
Exeter ✳ Bath ✳
Reading ✳
Southamp-
ton ✳
Ports- ✳
mouth
✳ London
Norwich ✳
✳ Yarmouth
Ipswich ✳
Canterbury
Dover

RADAR SCREEN

LUFTFLOTTE
NO. 5
FROM
NORWAY

LUFTFLOTTE
NO. 3
OPERATION
SEA-
LION
LUFTFLOTTE
NO. 2

Regmarad

69

31: Barbarossa

Preliminary operations in the Balkans

Before Hitler attacked Russia, he brought the Balkan countries under his control. To some extent he was forced to do this as a result of the inept activities of his ally, Mussolini. The Italian dictator had envied Hitler's successes and this has led him to declare war on the Allies just before the Battle of France ended in June 1940. Seeking an easy military victory, he sent his troops into Greece during October but, to his horror, the Greeks repulsed the Italians and Il Duce faced a military disaster. When he asked Hitler for help, the Führer realized that Mussolini's plight gave him a chance to consolidate Germany's power in the rest of Europe. He forced Bulgaria, Hungary and Rumania to become his allies; then in April 1941 his troops overran Yugoslavia and Greece—thus relieving Mussolini of a very embarrasing situation. Within three weeks the Greeks had surrendered and in May Hitler rounded off his Balkan campaigns with a completely successful airborne assault on the island of Crete.

Hitler's hopes

By the summer of 1941, Germany was supreme in Europe. Under his command the Führer had nearly three million troops ready to carry out his dearest wish—the conquest of the U.S.S.R. Why did he want to do this? Ever since he had published 'Mein Kampf' he had made no secret of his desire to carve out more 'living space' in Russia; to him the Russian Slavs were 'sub-humans' fit only to be slaves of German colonists. Moreover, the expanding German Reich needed the wheatlands of the Ukraine and the oilfields of the Caucasus. All of this could be his, he imagined, by the end of 1941. He would capture Moscow, Leningrad, Kiev and the Ukraine—then the Russians would capitulate.

The attack

'Operation Barbarossa' began on 22 June 1941 and as usual the Bitzkrieg tactics were completely successful. The panzers swarmed all over Western Russia and by September they had captured Kiev and were besieging Leningrad. Moscow itself was now not many miles to the East. A million Russians were prisoners: countless thousands were dead. 'The enemy in the East has been struck down,' crowed an exultant Führer. But this mastermind who believed in the invincibility of his Wehrmacht had omitted to provide it with adequate winter equipment. And November saw the onset of a bitter Russian winter. Many a German tank stalled for lack of anti-freeze; many a German soldier died not from a Russian bullet but from frostbite. Nevertheless, the Wehrmacht pushed doggedly towards Moscow and in December its advance patrols claimed to have spotted the Kremlin's spires. Then, unbelievably the Russians forced the Germans back—leaving Hitler to revise his plans for the conquest of Russia, plans that were to involve the German armies in the greatest 'pincer-movement' in history.

Global warfare

But before 1941 had ended the entire character of the war had changed. On 7 December 1941 aircraft of the Japanese Navy attacked the American Pacific base at Pearl Harbor. A few days later Hitler declared war on the United States so that when the year ended a trio of unlikely allies—Great Britain, America and Russia—were united in a common cause: the destruction of Hitler's Germany.

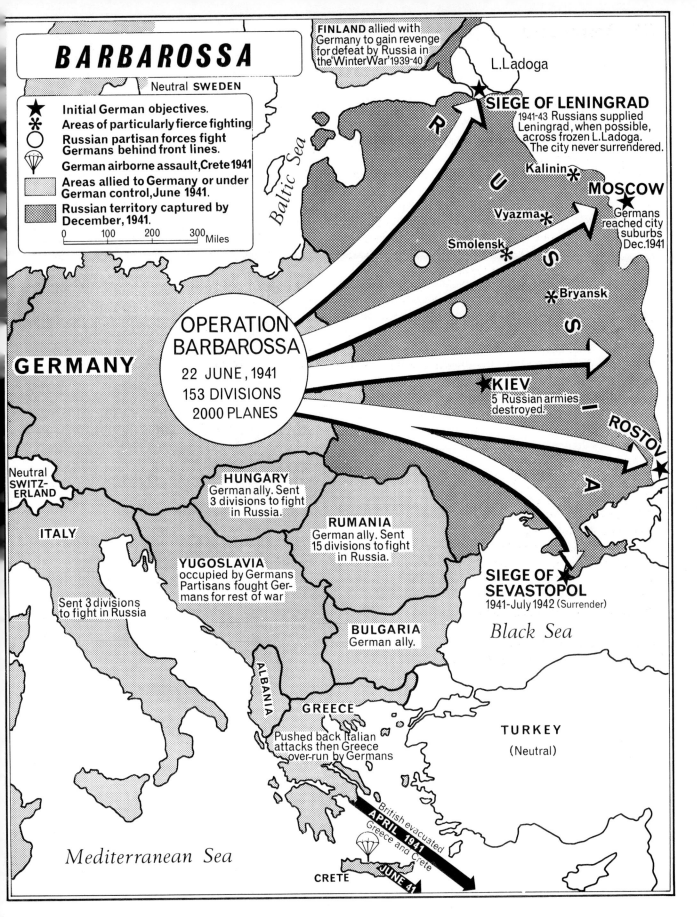

BARBAROSSA

Neutral SWEDEN

★ Initial German objectives.
✳ Areas of particularly fierce fighting
◯ Russian partisan forces fight Germans behind front lines.
⛑ German airborne assault, Crete 1941
▨ Areas allied to Germany or under German control, June 1941.
▨ Russian territory captured by December, 1941.

0   100   200   300 Miles

FINLAND allied with Germany to gain revenge for defeat by Russia in the 'WinterWar' 1939-40

L.Ladoga

SIEGE OF LENINGRAD
1941-43 Russians supplied Leningrad, when possible, across frozen L.Ladoga. The city never surrendered.

Baltic Sea

Kalinin ✳

MOSCOW
Germans reached city suburbs Dec.1941

Vyazma ✳

Smolensk ✳

✳ Bryansk

OPERATION BARBAROSSA

22 JUNE, 1941
153 DIVISIONS
2000 PLANES

R U S S I A

ROSTOV

GERMANY

★ **KIEV**
5 Russian armies destroyed.

Neutral SWITZ-ERLAND

HUNGARY
German ally. Sent 3 divisions to fight in Russia.

ITALY

RUMANIA
German ally. Sent 15 divisions to fight in Russia.

Sent 3 divisions to fight in Russia

YUGOSLAVIA
occupied by Germans Partisans fought Germans for rest of war

SIEGE OF SEVASTOPOL
1941-July 1942 (Surrender)

Black Sea

BULGARIA
German ally.

ALBANIA

GREECE
Pushed back Italian attacks then Greece over-run by Germans

TURKEY
(Neutral)

British evacuated Greece and Crete
APRIL 1941
JUNE 41

Mediterranean Sea

CRETE

32: Japan's Pacific Blitzkrieg 1941–42

Pearl Harbor

Dawn was breaking on 7 December 1941 as 183 Japanese aircraft sped from six carriers steaming across the Pacific Ocean. Many of the pilots and crews were veterans of air battles fought out over China and Outer Mongolia, but none had ever flown such a dangerous and important mission as this. Their target was the American air and naval base of Pearl Harbor. As the squadrons swept over the islands, the first pilots radioed back to the carriers 'Tora! Tora!' ('Tiger! Tiger!')—the code sign to indicate they had caught the Americans napping. Bombs screamed down, torpedoes rammed home—and almost immediately parked aircraft exploded and battleships began to sink at their moorings. Thirty minutes later a second wave of Japanese planes completed the work of destruction. By half-past nine that Sunday morning 18 ships had been rendered useless; 2,400 Americans lay dead.

The reason why

Later President Roosevelt was to speak to a horrified American nation of this 'unprovoked and dastardly attack by Japan'. Why did it happen? There is little doubt that the Japanese were impressed by Hitler's victories during 1940–41. He had conquered Europe; they would conquer the Pacific. They needed the resources of the Far East—especially the oil fields of the East Indies—and they envied the wealthy Dutch, British and American empires. Between 1938 and 1940 the Japanese had drawn up a plan to take over the whole area—to set up a 'New Order in Asia' and a 'Co-Prosperity Sphere'. These fine words meant that Japan would have to fight not only the British and Dutch colonial forces but the great industrial nation of America as well. Yet the Japanese, led by their bellicose General Tojo, were prepared to take this risk. Tojo argued that all he needed was a foolproof plan to neutralize U.S. naval power in the Pacific. His brilliant admiral, Yamamoto, was com-missioned to prepare such a plan—and the attack on Pearl Harbor was the result.

Isolation ends for America

Another result was the rapid awakening of 130 million Americans from their dreams of isolationism. Now they were ready to heed Roosevelt's warnings about the evil dictators—doubly so after Hitler unwisely declared war on the U.S.A. (11 December 1941). But in reality, America was quite unprepared for a Pacific War. Certainly her factories had been producing tanks, planes and guns for the British since Congress had passed the Lend-Lease Act of March 1941; moreover America had been conscripting troops for more than a year. But full-scale mobilization and training of her armed forces would take months—and time seemed short.

Japanese conquests

Meanwhile the Japanese raced through the Pacific and Far East. Displaying astounding skill and military superiority they defeated the Allies on land and sea. For example, three days after Pearl Harbor Japanese divebombers sank two British capital ships, the *Repulse* and *Prince of Wales*, off Malaya. And as empire after empire crashed, the Japanese claimed to come as liberators, releasing native populations from the tyranny of western imperialism. 'This is a war of emancipation for the Far East,' they said. By the middle of 1942 the Japanese had cut the Burma Road to China and threatened to invade India and Ceylon. They bombed North Australia and occupied the Aleutians. But victory brought its own problems—the Japanese had to defend the vast areas they had conquered; they had to be ready to frustrate General MacArthur's famous promise uttered when he was forced to leave the Philippines in 1942:

'We will return'.

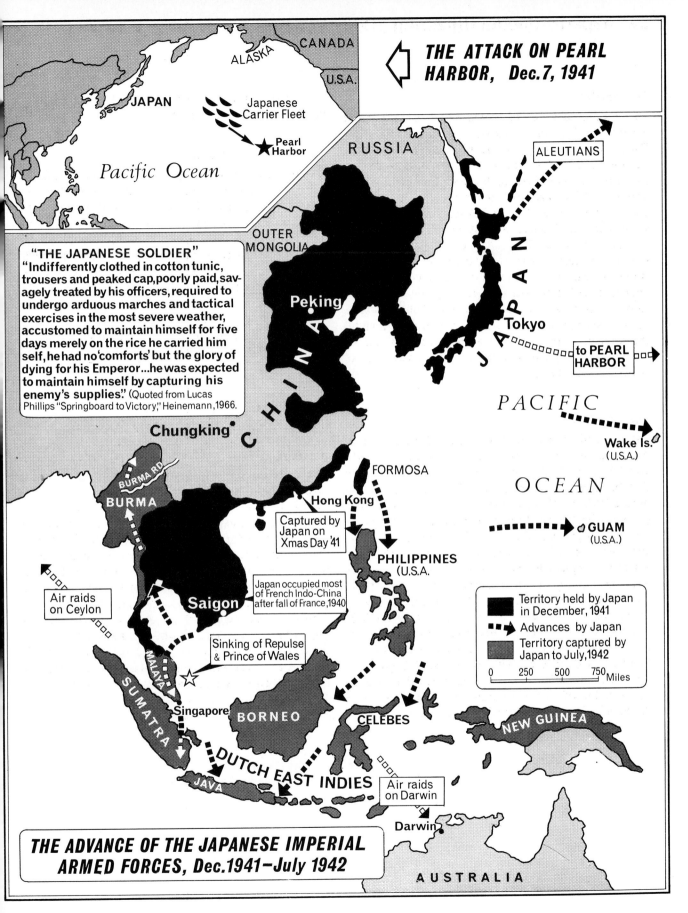

THE ATTACK ON PEARL HARBOR, Dec.7, 1941

ALASKA
CANADA
U.S.A.
JAPAN
Japanese Carrier Fleet
Pearl Harbor
Pacific Ocean

RUSSIA

ALEUTIANS

OUTER MONGOLIA

"THE JAPANESE SOLDIER"
"Indifferently clothed in cotton tunic, trousers and peaked cap, poorly paid, savagely treated by his officers, required to undergo arduous marches and tactical exercises in the most severe weather, accustomed to maintain himself for five days merely on the rice he carried himself, he had no 'comforts' but the glory of dying for his Emperor...he was expected to maintain himself by capturing his enemy's supplies." (Quoted from Lucas Phillips "Springboard to Victory," Heinemann, 1966.

Peking

JAPAN
Tokyo
to PEARL HARBOR

PACIFIC

Chungking

Wake Is. (U.S.A.)

OCEAN

BURMA RD.
BURMA

FORMOSA

Hong Kong

Captured by Japan on Xmas Day '41

GUAM (U.S.A.)

PHILIPPINES (U.S.A.)

Air raids on Ceylon

Japan occupied most of French Indo-China after fall of France, 1940

Saigon

Sinking of Repulse & Prince of Wales

MALAYA

Singapore
BORNEO
CELEBES
NEW GUINEA

Territory held by Japan in December, 1941
Advances by Japan
Territory captured by Japan to July, 1942
0   250   500   750 Miles

SUMATRA

DUTCH EAST INDIES

Air raids on Darwin

JAVA

Darwin

THE ADVANCE OF THE JAPANESE IMPERIAL ARMED FORCES, Dec.1941–July 1942

AUSTRALIA

33: 'The turn of the tide': Hitler tastes defeat 1942–43

Defeat in Africa

Before 1942 the Axis had suffered two reverses only: British Commonwealth forces had liberated Abyssinia from Italy and defeated Mussolini's troops in Libya. During 1942 Hitler sent Rommel's Afrika Korps to Libya to stiffen the Italian resistance. Rommel's job was to act as the southern jaw of Hitler's pincer movement—to capture the Suez Canal and the Middle East oil fields. Rommel advanced until he met the British defences drawn across that narrow neck of land between the Mediterranean and the Qattara Depression—the spot called El Alamein. Here Rommel tried to smash through the defences—at the First Battle of Alamein (July) and at the Battle of Alam Halfa (August–September)—without success. Then on 23 October General Montgomery fought and won his great Battle of El Alamein. Rommel retreated westwards, hotly pursued by the 8th Army. The Germans sought refuge in Tunisia but when in November 1942 an Anglo-American force commanded by General Eisenhower landed in Morocco and Algeria they found themselves hemmed in. They fought bravely—Hitler sent them the latest 'Tiger' tanks and monster six-engined transports flew in reinforcements. 'Fight to the last cartridge!' demanded the Führer. But there was little point, for the war in Africa was over. In May 1943 the Afrika Korps surrendered. This meant that an invasion of Southern Europe was possible and in July 1943 the Allies landed in Sicily.

The Italian campaigns

In September 1943 the Allies invaded Italy where Mussolini toppled from power—and the Italian people changed sides in the war. But these developments brought little gain. Hitler rushed troops into Italy and soon the war there became another bitter, slow-moving conflict, made all the more difficult by the mountainous terrain and fast-flowing rivers of the Italian peninsula.

Defeat in Russia—Stalingrad

In Russia the changes in fortune were equally dramatic. During the Spring of 1942 the Germans resumed their advance, planning now to capture the Crimea, the Caucasus oil fields and Stalingrad. Then perhaps they would attack Moscow again—possibly from the east. By the summer they were within sight of the Caucasus Mountains and actually fighting in the streets of Stalingrad. But they had overtaxed their strength. Russian partisans harried the supply lines; there were too few troops to man the battle line—now 3000 miles long—as well as fight pitched battles inside cities. Yet the madman Hitler chose to do this and committed the entire VIth Army to this venture. Before long 240,000 Germans were surrounded by the Russians at Stalingrad, now in the grip of a Russian winter. Hitler tried to rescue them—but failed. 'Fight to the last man!' he ordered—140,000 Germans did but the rest surrendered in January 1943.

Defeat in Russia—Kursk

Stalingrad was the limit of Hitler's advance but not the last of his offensives. He wanted revenge for his humiliation at Stalingrad and in July 1943 he ordered the latest German tanks—the Panthers and Tigers—plus the newest guns and every available reserve to be thrown against the Russian defences at Kursk. He would win a great battle at Kursk, he said. But the Russian armour and the 'Sturmovik' ground attack planes pulverized the panzers at Kursk. Never again would Hitler launch a great offensive in the east; from now on he was on the defensive. He had been stopped at El Alamein, Stalingrad and Kursk, three major disasters each of which cost him an entire army and the cream of his military equipment. This was the 'turn of the tide', but not the end of the war. Before this could happen Hitler would have to be beaten on his own ground.

Dieppe 1942

To prevent a major allied assault on the Continent, Hitler had decided to transform the occupied countries in the west into a European fortress—*Festung Europa*! Along the most vulnerable French and Belgian coastlines, forced labour gangs began to build the Westwall—a series of heavily defended positions. To test the strength of the enemy defences, the allies launched Operation Jubilee against Dieppe in 1942. Six thousand men—Royal Marine Commandos and Candian infantry regiments—made the assault against intense German resistance. One after the other, the Canadian units tried to capture 'Jubilee', the code-name for Dieppe: the Royal Regiment of Canada, the Essex Scottish Regiment, the Hamilton Light Infantry, the South Saskatchewans and the Queen's Own Cameron Highlanders. The Germans broke up every attack. In desperation the last reserves—the Fusiliers Mont-Royal—went in, only to be pinned down in the shallow sand of the beaches. Operation Jubilee was a disaster; 3,379 Canadians were lost. But these heavy Canadian losses were not entirely in vain; the allied planners had learned their lesson. The full-scale invasion of Europe must NOT be launched at a heavily defended port where the attacking forces could be outgunned by the German defenders and exterminated on the beaches.

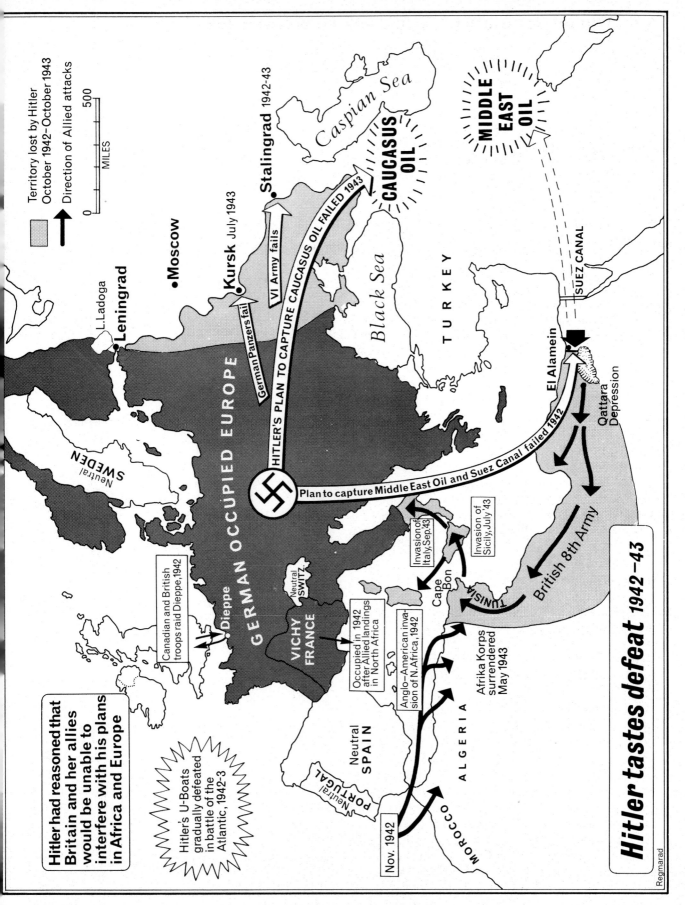

Territory lost by Hitler
October 1942–October 1943

Direction of Allied attacks

MILES

500

0

Caspian Sea

MIDDLE EAST OIL

CAUCASUS OIL

Stalingrad 1942-43

Moscow

Kursk July 1943

HITLER'S PLAN TO CAPTURE CAUCASUS OIL FAILED 1943

VI Army fails

German Panzers fail

L. Ladoga

Leningrad

SUEZ CANAL

Black Sea

TURKEY

El Alamein

Qattara Depression

Neutral SWEDEN

GERMAN OCCUPIED EUROPE

Plan to capture Middle East Oil and Suez Canal failed 1942

Plan to capture Middle East Oil

British 8th Army

Canadian and British troops raid Dieppe, 1942

Dieppe

Neutral SWITZ.

VICHY FRANCE

Occupied in 1942 after Allied landings in North Africa

Invasion of Italy, Sep. 43

Invasion of Sicily, July 43

Cape Bon

TUNISIA

Anglo–American invasion of N. Africa, 1942

Afrika Korps surrendered May 1943

Neutral SPAIN

Neutral PORTUGAL

ALGERIA

MOROCCO

Nov. 1942

Hitler had reasoned that Britain and her allies would be unable to interfere with his plans in Africa and Europe

Hitler's U-Boats gradually defeated in battle of the Atlantic, 1942-3

Hitler tastes defeat 1942–43

Regmarad

75

34: The defeat of Hitler's Germany 1944–1945

The bombing of Germany

From 1942 onwards Stalin urged Churchill to open a Second Front in Europe. He had justification; the Red Army was fighting two-thirds of the German Wehrmacht and desperately needed some relief. However, the main allied effort—apart from the incessant war against the U-boats in the Battle of the Atlantic—was in the air. R.A.F. Bomber Command, now being equipped with four engined 'Halifaxes' and 'Lancasters,' pounded German cities with incendiaries and high explosive. Yet these night attacks met with only moderate success. Speer, that wizard of German industrial organization, dispersed his most important factories so that arms production actually increased under the R.A.F. attacks. U.S. B.17 'Fortress' and B.24 'Liberator' bombers, stationed mainly in East Anglia, flew exceptionally dangerous daylight missions against specific targets, such as the Ploesti oil refineries and the Schweinfurt ball-bearing plant in 1943. But these slow-moving aircraft flying in their giant 'box-formations' suffered very heavy losses until long-range escort fighters such as the P.51 'Mustang' were developed to protect them.

The Normandy Landings

Bomber raids alone would never defeat a resilient enemy and the allies gradually built up their strength for a full-scale attack on Hitler's 'European Fortress'. On D-Day, 6 June 1944, the invasion forces landed on the Normandy beaches, where the Germans least expected an attack. Soon a strong beach-head existed—due largely to remarkably slow reactions on the part of the Germans who were sure that the Normandy attacks were in fact a feint, to the work of the French Resistance workers who dislocated German communications in the rear, and to allied command of the air. Tactical Air Force fighter-bombers ruled the skies and shot up any moving target; a lumbering convoy, a troop-train or even a solitary staff-car would attract the cannon-fire and rockets of a ferocious fighter-bomber. This was the sort of air power which would win wars. Coupled with the determination of allied troops, the quality and quantity of their armour (there were bridge-carrying tanks, flame-thrower tanks, flail-tanks to destroy mine-fields) it spelt success.

Advance in the west

Once the allies had broken German resistance in France at the Battle of the Falaise Gap in August, the way was open for the 'great swan'—the rapid, mobile advance through Western Europe. But the Germans were far from finished: their V.1 'doodlebug' flying bombs and V.2 rockets still fell upon England; their panzer forces annihilated the British paratroopers dropped on Arnhem in September; while in December Hitler launched 'Operation Christrose', his counter-attack in the Ardennes. This was the famous Battle of the Bulge, a short-lived German advance which the allies rolled back by the beginning of January 1945. By 24 March 1945 the allies were able to cross the Rhine and, a month later, to link up with the spearhead of the Red Army advancing from the east.

Russian success

The speed of the Russian advance had been spectacular. All the territory originally conquered by Hitler was recaptured and by the beginning of 1945 the Russians had entered Poland, Hungary and Rumania. By April they were in Berlin where, on 30 April 1945, Adolf Hitler shot himself. By now most of Germany was occupied and between 2–8 May 1945 the Wehrmacht surrendered. Hitler's Germany had been totally defeated; though the joy of victory was marred by the discovery of the death-camps in which the Nazis had carried out their 'Final Solution'—the extermination of six million Jews.

DOODLE-BUG! The Germans fired 9,200 V1s at Britain during 1944–5. (*Imperial War Museum*)

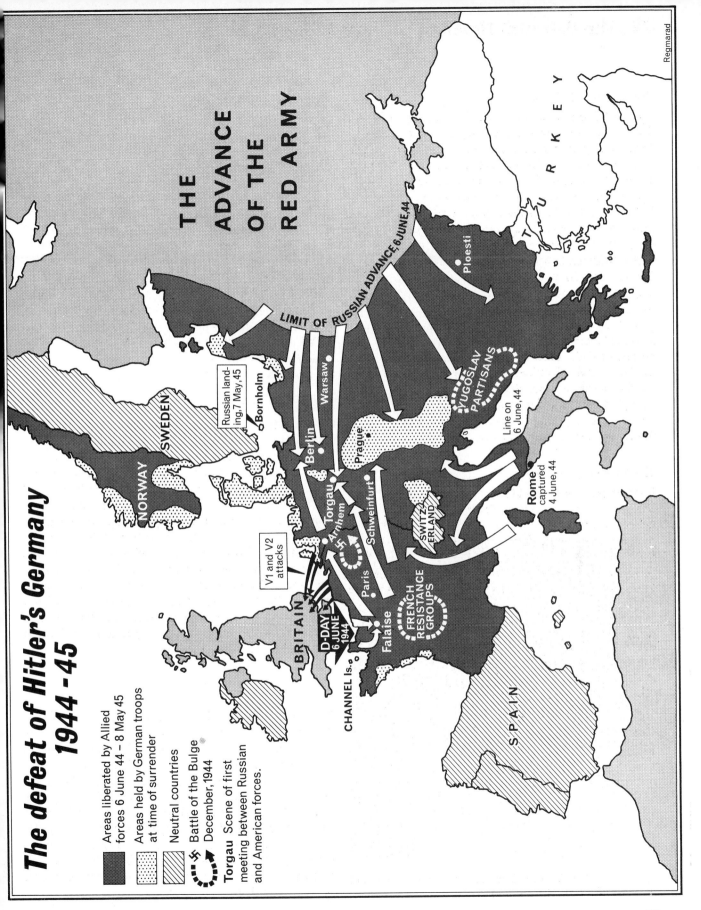

The defeat of Hitler's Germany 1944 - 45

Areas liberated by Allied forces 6 June 44 – 8 May 45

Areas held by German troops at time of surrender

Neutral countries

✠ Battle of the Bulge December, 1944

Torgau Scene of first meeting between Russian and American forces.

THE ADVANCE OF THE RED ARMY

TURKEY

LIMIT OF RUSSIAN ADVANCE, 6 JUNE, 44

Ploesti

Russian land-ing, 7 May, 45

Bornholm

Warsaw

SWEDEN

NORWAY

Berlin

Prague

Torgau

Arnhem

Schweinfurt

YUGOSLAV PARTISANS

Line on 6 June, 44

SWITZ-ERLAND

Rome captured 4 June, 44

V1 and V2 attacks

BRITAIN

Paris

Falaise

FRENCH RESISTANCE GROUPS

D-DAY 6 JUNE 1944

CHANNEL Is.

SPAIN

Regmarad

77

35: Japanese defeat in the Far East 1942–45

Back to the Philippines

After the initial Japanese successes in the Pacific, the United States managed to win two very important naval actions: the Battle of the Coral Sea (May 1942) and the Battle of Midway (June 1942). Now that the Americans had partial control of the Pacific, they began their 'atoll-hopping' tactics. This meant leaping from one atoll to another—perhaps hundreds of miles away—and bypassing Japanese forces on the less important islands. Relentlessly, the Americans advanced towards Japan in a costly process which involved the U.S. Marines in scores of frontal assaults on enemy beaches. For example, at Tarawa in 1943 the Americans suffered 3000 casualties as they wiped out 5000 defenders. The fighting got worse during 1944. In Burma British Commonwealth forces repelled heavy Japanese attacks and finally won a great victory at Kohima. In New Guinea the Australians advanced under the most difficult conditions, while in the Pacific the Americans entered the Marianas and captured Saipan Island, only 1300 miles from Toyko. From this base the new B.29 Superfortress bombers began their fire raids against enemy cities, thus bringing the war home to the Japanese people. One result was the downfall of General Tojo, but he was soon replaced by leaders who were determined to go on fighting. When next the Americans landed in the Philippines during 1944 and managed to sink most of the Japanese Navy at the Battle of Leyte Gulf, they still had to contend with fanatical Japanese soldiers fighting in the Philippine jungles for another year. There seemed no end to the bitter contest.

Iwo Jima and Okinawa

But during 1945 the Americans drew closer to Japan itself. Seeking islands suitable for fighter bases, the Marines attacked Iwo Jima in February. On this tiny island fighting lasted a month; there were 20,000 American casualties and 23,000 Japanese dead. In April the Marines attacked Okinawa. Here the fighting was even more ghastly and 40,000 American casualties resulted. These heavy losses were due partly to the suicidal power-dives made by Japanese Kamikaze pilots, who made no less than 1,900 attacks on the U.S. Fleet at Okinawa. But apart from these 'suicide attacks', the Japanese made little attempt to defend their own air space. American bombers, supported by British carrier planes, ranged freely over Japan, destroying most of her cities and her shipping. Yet they could not destroy the two million undefeated troops and the 5000 Kamikaze aircraft still stationed in Japan—and all of these would be used in a fight to the death when the American invaders came. For the Americans did intend to invade: the first assault against Southern Japan was planned for 1945; the second, against Honshu, for 1946. President Truman, who had succeeded Roosevelt after the latter's death in April 1945, knew that these operations would probably cost one million American lives.

Atomic warfare

The invasions never took place. On 6 August 1945 a single B.29 took off from Tinian Island. Over Hiroshima it released an atomic bomb. There was a great flash—and, in the words of Rutherford, the world entered 'No Man's Land'. Two days later the Soviet Union attacked Japanese Manchuria and Korea and on 9 August another atomic bomb destroyed Nagasaki. Understandably, the Japanese recoiled from the double threat of invasion and atomic warfare. On 14 August 1945 they surrendered unconditionally. World War II had ended.

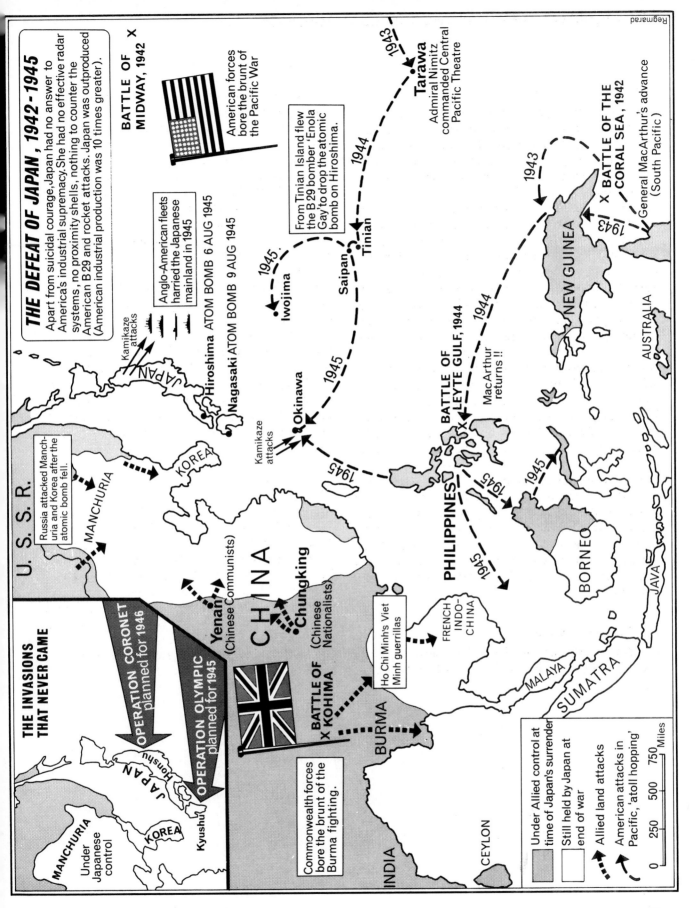

79

Part 4—Book List

General reference: Purnell's "History of the Second World War" in six volumes

30.	*The Narrow Margin*	Derek Wood	Arrow Books	
	History of the Second World War		Purnell	Vol. 1
31.	*Hitler's War on Russia*	P. Carell	Harrap	
32.	*History of the Second World War*		Purnell	Vol. 2&3
33.	*Rommel*	D. Young	Fontana	
	History of the Second World War		Purnell	Vol. 3&4
	African Nationalism	N. Sithole	Oxford	
34.	*History of the Second World War*		Purnell	Vol. 5&6
35.	*Hiroshima*	J. Hersey	Penguin	

HIROSHIMA 1945. (*Imperial War Museum*)

PART 5

The years of fantastic change 1945–1975

During these twenty-eight years the world's political, social and economic structure underwent a great deal of change. It became divided into communist and capitalist blocs; its old empires at last disappeared as a whole host of modern nation states emerged—not always without bloodshed and civil war. By 1975 the world map was dotted with their unfamiliar names—Mali and Malawi, Botswana and Lesotho, Zaire and Bangladesh. All of them joined a new form of world government which in 1945 had replaced the defunct League of Nations. It was called the United Nations Organization and its agencies at once began to attack the problems that had troubled mankind for centuries—disease, blight, flooding, erosion and ignorance—all magnified in the post-war years by the 'population explosion' which in 1966 U Thant, Secretary-General of the UN, had described as 'a world problem no less than the threat of nuclear destruction.

During these years many parts of the world such as Europe, America and the Soviet Union achieved great advances in living standards and increased their peoples' leisure and opportunities for personal prosperity. Less fortunate countries, among them India, adopted democratic forms of government but met with indifferent success. 800 million Chinese followed the teachings of Mao Tse-tung in the hope that communism would bring a solution to their troubles.

But few countries were able to survive the post-war years without aid from the 'superpowers', Russia and the USA. Only one or two underpopulated countries, such as Canada, Australia and New Zealand, were able to encourage immigration.

So it remained a world, for all the fantastic changes, where many people still went undernourished. Man's knowledge and scientific abilities had never been greater or more competent to improve life on this earth. Yet the oldest problem of all—human survival—was now complicated by the manufacture of nuclear weapons capable of eliminating the human race. In these years of fantastic change, 'keeping the peace' had a new urgency.

36: The beginning of the Cold War 1945—48

Confrontation in Europe

Perhaps the most dramatic result of World War II was the sudden confrontation in Europe between Russia and America. Previously, continental countries had always resisted Russia's attempts to break into Europe, while America had chosen to avoid entanglements there whenever possible. But as the U.S.S.R. was now occupying a great deal of the Continent—and bent on increasing her power there—only America would be strong enough to offer resistance. At first America was unwilling to adopt such a role. Roosevelt had already tried to settle Europe's affairs when he met Stalin and Churchill at the Yalta Conference in February 1945. Here the leaders had broadly agreed to restore Hitler's conquests to their rightful owners and to divide Germany up into four occupation zones. But Roosevelt had died shortly after this and his Vice-President, Harry Truman, succeeded him. In Britain, Churchill lost the 1945 General Election and Clement Attlee became Prime Minister.

Potsdam

In July these two new Western leaders met Stalin at the Potsdam Conference and they soon realized that Stalin was unwilling to keep his earlier promises. For now the Russian dictator suggested 'temporary' changes (they were still in force in 1968) in the frontiers of Eastern Europe. Reluctantly the west accepted his proposals—which enabled Stalin to work for the installation of communist governments in every country occupied by the Red Army. Stalin was also anxious that the French and Italian communist parties should take control of their own governments—but his hopes were dashed. Stalin even tried to break through to the Mediterranean, but here the British kept him at bay by supporting the Greek and Turkish governments who controlled the exit from the Black Sea. While British money flowed into Turkey, British troops fought communist guerrillas in Greece.

The Truman Doctrine

By 1947, the strain on the British economy was too great and Attlee told Truman that British troops would have to pull out of Greece. Truman saw the implications of such a move—the Russians would step in. Accordingly, he announced in March 1947 his famous 'Truman doctrine':

> I believe that it must be the policy of the United States to support free peoples who are resisting attempted subjection by armed minorities or by outside pressures.

In practical terms the Truman doctrine meant that America would tolerate Russian communism within its 1947 limits (*The Principle of Coexistence*) but would resist any extension of communist power (*The Principle of Containment*); and that America would help any nation with dollars and supplies if that country asked for help.

Cold war begins

Within a year the U.S.A. had to stand by these promises. Under the 1947 Marshall Plan—originally intended to give aid to communist as well as non-communist countries—millions of dollars poured into the needy areas. But the Russians would allow none of it to enter their satellite states. Then in 1948 communists seized control of Czechoslovakia with alarming ease and with the consent of the Czech government. America stood by helplessly. But when in 1948 there was a Russian threat to West Berlin, the Americans won a signal victory in the famous Berlin Airlift. Thus by 1948 the wartime alliance had disintegrated. Politically the atmosphere was distinctly chilly in this divided world, a world, people said, in the midst of a 'Cold War'. Did this mean another World War? Many people felt that the answer to this depended on how the superpowers made use of a new instrument of international control—the United Nations Organization.

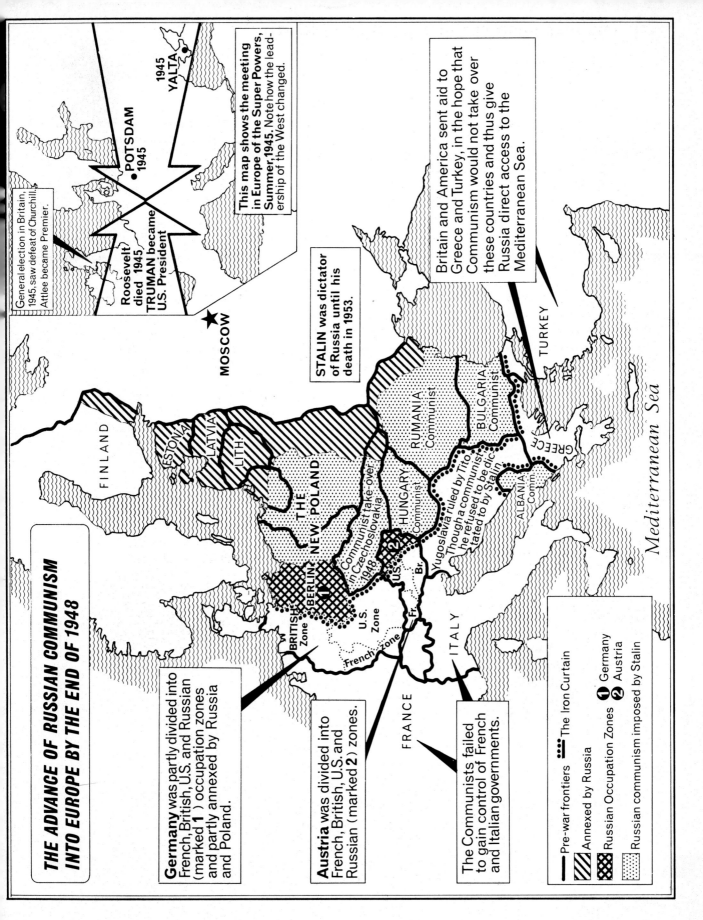

THE ADVANCE OF RUSSIAN COMMUNISM INTO EUROPE BY THE END OF 1948

Germany was partly divided into French, British, U.S. and Russian (marked **1**) occupation zones and partly annexed by Russia and Poland.

Austria was divided into French, British, U.S. and Russian (marked **2**) zones.

The Communists failed to gain control of French and Italian governments.

General election in Britain, 1945, saw defeat of Churchill. Attlee became Premier.

Roosevelt died 1945. TRUMAN became U.S. President

POTSDAM 1945

1945 YALTA

This map shows the meeting in **Europe of the Super Powers, Summer, 1945.** Note how the leadership of the West changed.

STALIN was dictator of Russia until his death in 1953.

Britain and America sent aid to Greece and Turkey, in the hope that Communism would not take over these countries and thus give Russia direct access to the Mediterranean Sea.

MOSCOW

FINLAND

ESTONIA

LATVIA

LITH.

THE NEW POLAND

BRITISH Zone

BERLIN

U.S. Zone

French Zone

Fr.

Communist take-over in Czechoslovakia 1948.

HUNGARY Communist

U.S.

Br.

RUMANIA Communist

BULGARIA Communist

Yugoslavia ruled by Tito. Though a communist he refused to be dictated to by Stalin.

ALBANIA Comm.

GREECE

TURKEY

ITALY

FRANCE

Mediterranean Sea

— Pre-war frontiers ∴∴∴ The Iron Curtain

▨ Annexed by Russia

❶ Germany ❷ Austria

▦ Russian Occupation Zones

⋰ Russian communism imposed by Stalin

83

37: The United Nations Organization (UNO)

The Atlantic Charter

The United Nations was born into a world that had already shown itself far from united either in friendship or political belief. The idea of a United Nations Organization stemmed from a meeting between Churchill and Roosevelt aboard a battleship off Newfoundland. There they produced a document called the Atlantic Charter in which they agreed that after the war mankind must have some guarantee of his basic rights—later defined as the 'Four Freedoms': the Freedom from Want; Freedom of Speech; Freedom of Religious Belief and Freedom from Fear.

The San Francisco Conference

On 26 June 1945, 51 states met in San Francisco to sign the Charter of U.N.O. which came into being on 24 October 1945. U.N.O.'s aims were: '. . . to save succeeding generations from the scourge of war, which twice in our lifetime has brought untold suffering to mankind, and to reaffirm faith in fundamental human rights, in the dignity and worth of the human person, in the equal rights of men and women and of nations large and small . . .' John D. Rockefeller, the American oil millionaire, donated a substantial sum so that U.N.O.'s impressive skyscraper headquarters could rise above Turtle Bay in New York—a site which the Russians would have preferred not to have chosen.

How U.N.O. works

Today this organization, now numbering well over 130 nation states, conducts its business in the *General Assembly*. Decisions on world affairs are reached here by a 2/3 majority of delegates present and voting. As each state sends up to five delegates, administration is a complicated affair, involving thousands of clerks, interpreters, translators and technical experts employed by the *Secretariat*. A Secretary-General, elected by the General Assembly for a five-year term, controls this work. The first was Trygvie Lie (1945–53); the second, Dag Hammarskjold, was killed in an air crash during the 1962 Congo crisis; the third was U Thant who agreed in 1966 to serve a second term. When he retired at the end of 1971, Kurt Waldheim became the new Secretary-General. After serving two terms of office, Kurt Waldheim gave way to a new Secretary-General at the end of 1981. He was the Peruvian diplomat, Pérez de Cuéllar. Another important branch of U.N.O. is the *Economic and Social Council*, elected for three years by the General Assembly. Eighteen nations serve on the Council, sorting out all the data collected by the Secretariat and recommending appropriate action to the General Assembly—one day it might be malaria control, another refugee aid. There also exists the *Trusteeship Council* whose tasks have almost disappeared (a few Trust Territories such as the Pacific Isles, South-West Africa and New Guinea are left*) and the *International Court of Justice* which has no means of enforcing its decisions. But the best known of U.N.O.'s bodies is the *Security Council*. In theory it is always ready to deal with a world crisis or an aggressor nation. There are five permanent members—Russia, America, France, Britain and the People's Republic of China**—each of whom may veto Security Council decisions. There are also ten other members of the Council.

Early Russian suspicion of U.N.O.

U.N.O.'s early history, from a political point of view, was discouraging. Members of the U.N. Relief and Rehabilitation Administration (U.N.R.R.A.) had worked behind the front line from 1943 onwards; many of them were Americans and they immediately aroused Russian suspicion: were they in fact U.S. agents? And was the 1947 Marshall Plan simply an American bid to bribe countries to support U.S. foreign policy? Was the U.N. simply a tool for American ambitions? Certainly the first five years of U.N.O.'s life were marred by mutual suspicion between the superpowers. Yet a great deal of good work was done in the world and the credit for much of it went to the *Specialized Agencies* of the United Nations.

*The New Guinea Trust Territory (Papua) became independent in September 1975.
**Between 1949 and 1971 Nationalist China (Taiwan) was the fifth member of the Security Council. Then came the historic General Assembly vote (25 October 1971) which recognized the government of the People's Republic as China's legal representative at the U.N. and expelled the representatives of Taiwan.

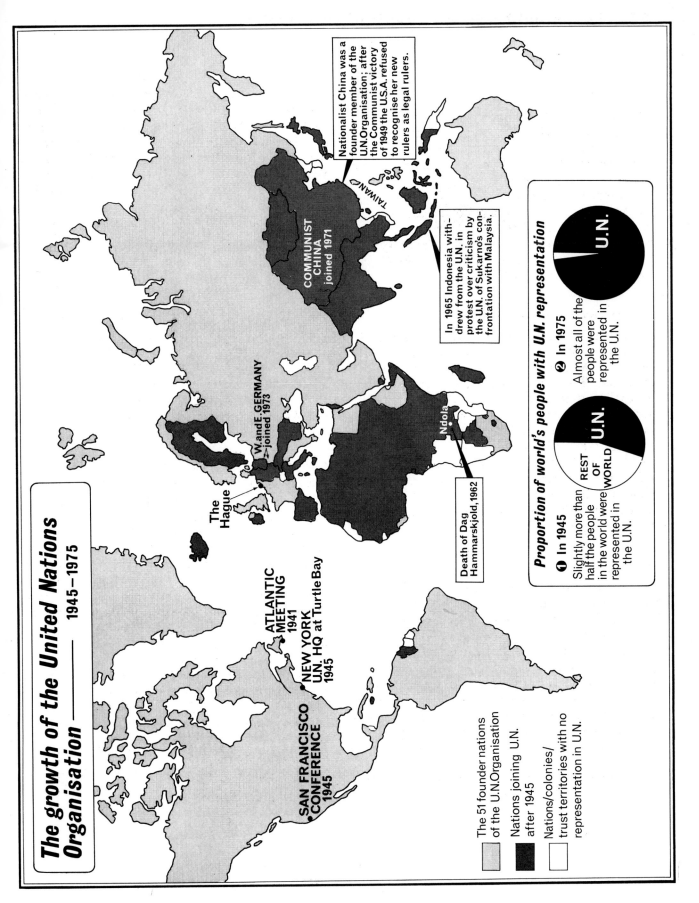

The growth of the United Nations Organisation —— 1945–1975

Nationalist China was a founder member of the U.N.Organisation; after the Communist victory of 1949 the U.S.A. refused to recognise her new rulers as legal rulers.

TAIWAN

COMMUNIST CHINA joined 1971

W.and E. GERMANY →joined 1973

In 1965 Indonesia withdrew from the U.N. in protest over criticism by the U.N. of Sukarno's confrontation with Malaysia.

The Hague

Ndola

Death of Dag Hammarskjold, 1962

ATLANTIC MEETING 1941

NEW YORK U.N. HQ at Turtle Bay 1945

SAN FRANCISCO CONFERENCE 1945

The 51 founder nations of the U.N.Organisation

Nations joining U.N. after 1945

Nations/colonies/ trust territories with no representation in U.N.

Proportion of world's people with U.N. representation

❶ In 1945
Slightly more than half the people in the world were represented in the U.N.

REST OF WORLD | U.N.

❷ In 1975
Almost all of the people were represented in the U.N.

U.N.

38: UNO—and the world food and population crisis

The size of the problem

Before 1939 the League of Nations had reported that half the world had not enough to eat. Today we know that many people in the world are suffering from malnutrition—they do not get enough of the right kind of food. Malnutrition leads to disease, deformity and death. Ironically, though, the population of the world has increased at an alarming rate and so the problem is: can this increase be fed? For although man has made progress in medical and sanitary arrangements and has reduced the killing power of many diseases, he has at the same time increased his expectation of life. And as millions of parents have no knowledge of birth-control they have very large families. It means that countries such as India have a *primitive birth-rate* allied with a *modern death-rate*. In 1973 the world's population exceeded 3,500,000. Though it seemed unlikely that it would reach 4000,000,000 by 1975 (U.N.O.'s original estimate), the projection of population growth over the last fifty years showed that there is a chance that world population will have doubled by the year 2000.

It is unlikely that all these people can be fed. Each day a man needs a diet which will yield him 2,200 calories. Since 1945 2/3 of the world's population may have existed on less, while many people who receive their daily 2,200 calories still lack essential proteins and vitamins. Look at these figures:

Surface area of the world	33,500 million acres
Area now under cultivation	3,200 million acres
Total area that COULD be cultivated	4,000 million acres

Obviously the area under cultivation may be increased—slightly. More crops may be grown with fertilizers, irrigation, drainage, improved seed and animal breeds, marine plankton harvesting and the mechanization of world agriculture. But some religious beliefs—such as the Hindu's reverence for the cow—stand in the way of improvements. Countries short of money cannot always afford to buy expensive equipment; populations in backward countries often resent change, trusting only the old ways. And a great deal of agricultural land grows crops that just cannot be eaten—rubber, timber and cotton.

Self-help

Of course, advanced nation states can pay for their own improvements. The U.S.S.R. has its vast collective farms and hopes to exploit the virgin lands of Siberia. British farmers are almost completely mechanized. North American farmers already produce 20% of the world's food. The Japanese have the highest rice yield in Asia—for they grow *japonica rice* which yields three times the crop of India's *indica rice*. But India cannot grow japonica because her climate is unsuitable.

F.A.O.

The less fortunate countries are helped by one of U.N.O.'s specialized agencies—F.A.O. (Food and Agricultural Organization). With its motto 'Fiat Panis' (Let there be bread) F.A.O. has worked tirelessly since October 1945. It has advised India on the use of tractors; fought rinderpest—a disease which killed two million cattle annually before 1946—with vaccinations; encouraged fish farming in Israel; improved citrus production in Libya; and fought locust plagues throughout the Middle East.

Controversy

F.A.O. has had its critics. Colin Clark* has accused it of staggering 'from one misstatement to another'; there is no evidence, he argues, to support F.A.O.'s claim (made in 1950) that $\frac{2}{3}$ of mankind were hungry or that half the people living in underdeveloped countries were undernourished. But a group of scientists writing in *The Limits to Growth*** disagreed: they say that $\frac{1}{3}$ of the world is undernourished. And though food production figures are up they are barely keeping pace with the population increase. However, there are some encouraging signs that the world population might stabilize at below 4000 million: the 1970 Decennial Census showed that in a number of countries—including Russia, America and China—the birth-rate was beginning to decline. At least some countries were at last recognizing that the population problem was the greatest world crisis of all. 'The clock is ticking,' warned the U.N. 'Every second there are two additional mouths to feed.' Birth control was therefore of the greatest urgency and 1974 was declared to be 'World Population Year'.

*See "The Myth of World Hunger" (Purnell's History of the Twentieth Century No. 124).
** Published by Universe Books 1972 and discussed in Dialogue Vol. 6, No. 1 (U.S.I.S.).

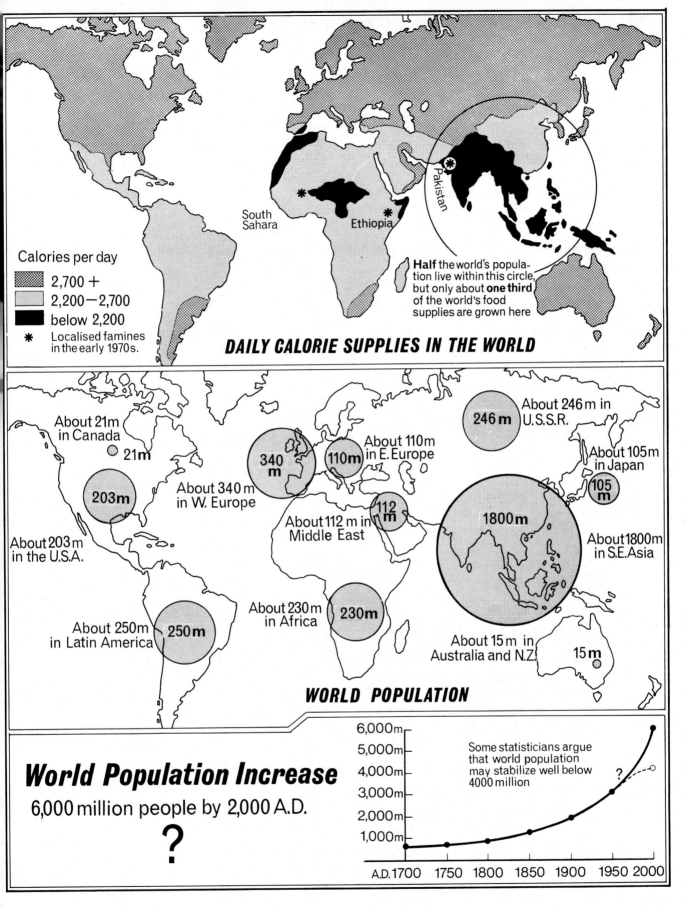

Calories per day

- 2,700 +
- 2,200 — 2,700
- below 2,200
- * Localised famines in the early 1970s.

South Sahara

Ethiopia

Pakistan

Half the world's population live within this circle, but only about **one third** of the world's food supplies are grown here

DAILY CALORIE SUPPLIES IN THE WORLD

About 21m in Canada 21m

About 203 m in the U.S.A. 203m

About 250 m in Latin America 250m

About 340 m in W. Europe 340 m

About 112 m in Middle East 112 m

About 230 m in Africa 230m

About 110 m in E. Europe 110m

About 246 m in U.S.S.R. 246 m

About 105 m in Japan 105 m

1800m

About 1800m in S.E. Asia

About 15 m in Australia and N.Z. 15 m

WORLD POPULATION

World Population Increase

6,000 million people by 2,000 A.D.

?

Some statisticians argue that world population may stabilize well below 4000 million

?

6,000m
5,000m
4,000m
3,000m
2,000m
1,000m

A.D. 1700 1750 1800 1850 1900 1950 2000

39: The importance of international aid

The sources of aid

There is hunger in the world—and hunger leads to disease. Some agencies try to cope with world food shortages; others try to improve the world's health. But this is a costly business simply because it is not just a matter of curing diseases. Any country, backward or otherwise, trying to raise its health standards is engaged at the same time in boosting its general standards of living—and this means finding money for airfields and roads, ports and factories, schools and teachers, farming implements and power stations, as well as cash for investments. Hospitals and clinics, doctors and nurses represent only one aspect of the needs of the state. Obviously, an under-developed country will be unable to afford even a few of these needs.

So a great deal of the money is provided by the member states of U.N.O.; America has sponsored many assistance schemes—most famous of which was the Marshall Plan of 1947. And she has also helped the British Commonwealth's Colombo Plan of 1951 in which member states finance one another in projects that will boost a nation's health and living standards. Roubles from Russia have aided many communist countries—as well as Cuba, Egypt and India. Private organisations help—the Ford Foundation has granted large sums for research purposes. Private individuals help by working in the V.S.O. (Voluntary Service Overseas) or in the American Peace Corps.

W.H.O. and U.N.I.C.E.F.

But there is one special agency which is expert in international medical aid. This is W.H.O. (World Health Organization) set up on 7 April 1948 with the backing of the U.N. Allied with U.N.I.C.E.F. (United Nations International Children's Emergency Fund), W.H.O. has campaigned against disease all over the world. *Yaws* is one of the frightful diseases it has almost beaten. Yaws covers the body with dreadful sores but twenty pence will buy enough penicillin to cure it. W.H.O. has almost eliminated the disease from Indonesia, one of the world's worst trouble-spots. Then between 1955 and 1959 W.H.O. and U.N.I.C.E.F. moved into action against the malarial mosquito. Armed with D.D.T. sprays their teams dealt with all the known mosquito haunts. Dramatically, world deaths from malaria began to decrease—especially in notorious areas such as Sicily, Italy, Mexico, Guyana and Ceylon. *Tuberculosis* kills millions of people every year; but W.H.O. can guarantee an 80% survival rate to children who are vaccinated with B.C.G.

Some diseases are difficult or impossible to cure. W.H.O. cannot eradicate the leper's crippling disease in the backward countries. It has not yet wiped out *trachoma* which blinds thousands annually. And the tsetse fly still carries the sleeping sickness *(trypanosomiasis)* to cattle and people in Tropical Africa. In the more sophisticated countries, lung cancer—caused probably by heavy cigarette smoking and a polluted atmosphere—and heart disease take an increasing toll.

This then is the size of the problem which is always with us and one which World Health may never hope to beat. But it can face a crisis or emergency. In 1960, for example, Agadir suffered two earthquakes, a tidal wave and a fire. W.H.O. called for international aid—and help came from all over the world.

Aid from the superpowers

One of the tragedies of the modern world is that it is not always compassion that impels the superpowers to distribute aid to the needy. Too often, the Soviet Union, the United States and the Chinese People's Republic have sent food and medical supplies side by side with arms shipments and squads of engineers whose task is to build roads, railways* and military bases. Too often, this has meant that the superpowers were fomenting or manipulating 'limited wars' in order to test their latest weapons or to extend their spheres of influence. Examples of this—where the Russians and Americans were accused of engaging in combat 'by proxy'—were the War in Viet Nam and the 1973 Arab-Israeli conflict.

* China's notable contribution is the building of the Tan-Zam Railway between Tanzania and Zambia.

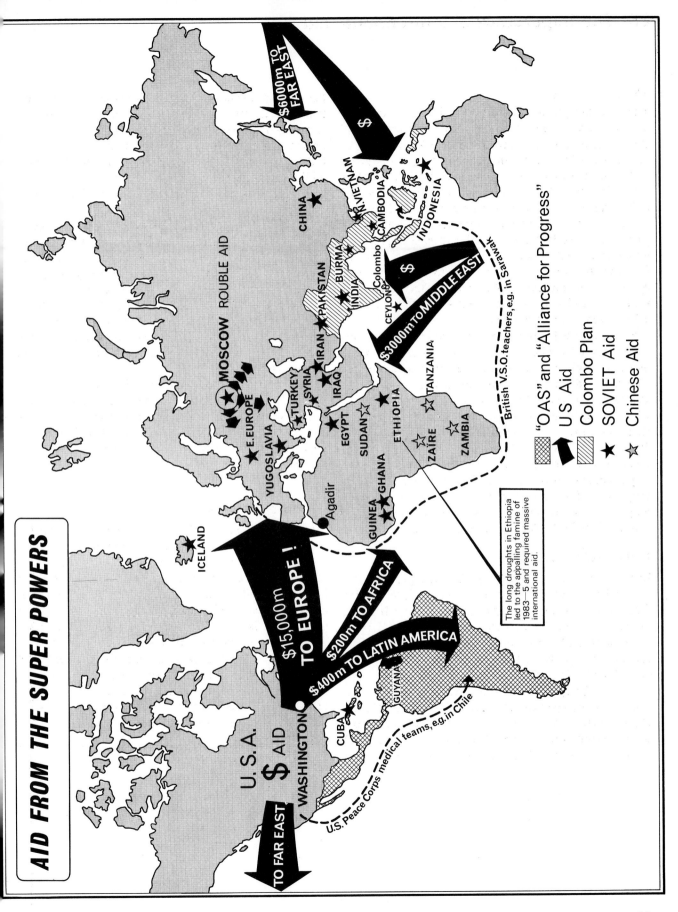

AID FROM THE SUPER POWERS

$6000m TO FAR EAST

MOSCOW ROUBLE AID

CHINA

$3000m TO MIDDLE EAST

British V.S.O. teachers, e.g. in Sarawak

PAKISTAN

BURMA

INDIA

Colombo

CEYLON

N.VIETNAM

CAMBODIA

INDONESIA

IRAN

SYRIA

TURKEY

IRAQ

E.EUROPE

YUGOSLAVIA

EGYPT

SUDAN

ETHIOPIA

TANZANIA

ZAIRE

ZAMBIA

GUINEA

GHANA

Agadir

ICELAND

$15,000m TO EUROPE !

$200m TO AFRICA

$400m TO LATIN AMERICA

The long droughts in Ethiopia led to the appalling famine of 1983—5 and required massive international aid.

U.S.A. $ AID

WASHINGTON

CUBA

GUYANA

U.S. Peace Corps medical teams, e.g. in Chile

TO FAR EAST

"OAS" and "Alliance for Progress"

US Aid

Colombo Plan

SOVIET Aid

Chinese Aid

40: The world's refugee problem

Origins in World War II

In almost every area where fighting took place in World War II, whole civilian populations were involved. Bombs and shells destroyed their towns, villages and farms; abandoning their possessions they fled in search of safety, becoming refugees. But few found a place of refuge because, in the wake of battle, came the Japanese and German occupation armies. The Japanese occupied vast tracts of the Far East and their treatment of native populations was relatively humane—they reserved their brutality for Allied troops who surrendered. But Hitler's Third Reich based its economy on the employment of slave labour in the factories, mines and on the land. Germany was dotted with forced labour camps, built side by side with the death camps designed to slaughter the Jews. Thus in World War II the Germans were responsible for shifting many nationalities all over Europe. When 1945 brought the Allied victory there was little happiness for 'refugees' and 'displaced persons'. Some fled westwards to escape the advancing Red Army; others, liberated by British and American troops, tried to find their way home. Most huddled where best they could, seeking shelter in bombed houses and bartering cigarettes in exchange for food and clothing on the many 'Black Markets'. Choked with refugees, and with industry at a standstill, post-war Europe was in a state of chaos.

U.N.O.'s work

As early as 1943 plans had been made to help the homeless. U.N.R.R.A. and the International Refugee Organization did sterling work, feeding and sheltering the homeless. In 1949 U.N.O. took over most of their responsibilities and in 1951 the Office of the U.N. High Commissioner for Refugees began its operations. More than a million refugees needed its help. Most of the money for this work came from voluntary sources and in 1959–60 U.N.O. held its 'World Refugee Year' to publicize both this fact and the plight of the refugee. Thousands of refugee families found homes, including—thanks to the Swiss and Canadians—the most difficult to resettle: disabled refugees.

The problem increases

But the refugee was not just a result of World War II. Wherever there have been hostilities since 1945, civilian populations have been the first to suffer. It is easy to explain how their plight arises; far less easy to solve the refugee problem that results. For example:

1945–46 The Russians—understandably—expelled thousands of Germans from Eastern Europe. Many sought refuge in the western Allied occupation zones.

1947 In the partition of India and Pakistan, millions of refugees were victims of a civil war.

1948 Israel was established as a national home for refugee Jews—who began fighting with Arabs who were then expelled from *their* homes in Palestine!

1949 Communist victory in China—and thousands of refugees sought shelter in Hong Kong.

1950–53 The Korean War rained death on thousands of civilians north and south of the 38th Parallel.

1956 The Hungarian Uprising saw the flight of thousands of people to Austria.

And . . . 1954–1962 Thousands of civilians, French settlers and Algerian Moslems alike, died as the French army tried desperately to destroy the F.L.N. guerrilla uprising.

1960–1964 For 4 years the Congo was the scene of confused fighting in and around Katanga as the United Nations forces tried to restore law and order in the civil war which followed on immediately after Belgium granted independence to the Congo.

1967–1970 When the Ibo people set up their Biafran State the Nigerian Federal forces surrounded them; thousands of women and children have suffered from starvation and disease. Attempts to send in food via 'mercy flights' did not always meet with cooperation from the Federal government

1968 About 20,000 Czechs fled when Soviet tanks invaded their country in 1968.

1946–1973 During these years the people of North and South Viet Nam, Laos and Cambodia endured constant warfare. Viet Cong and Pathet Lao guerrillas murdered thousands of unco-operative villagers. US helicopter gunships and high-level B.52 bombers rained death upon North Vietnamese troops and civilians while American troops killed unknown numbers of people suspected of being sympathetic towards communism.*

1978–1979 The people of Cambodia (Kampuchea) suffered terribly first under the Pol Pot regime and then under the subsequent (1978) invasion by Viet Nam. Simultaneously, thousands of 'boat-people' (mostly ethnic Chinese) left Viet Nam to take their chance on the open sea.

1979–1985 Afghan refugees escaped to Pakistan.

* For example, the massacre at My Lai in 1968.

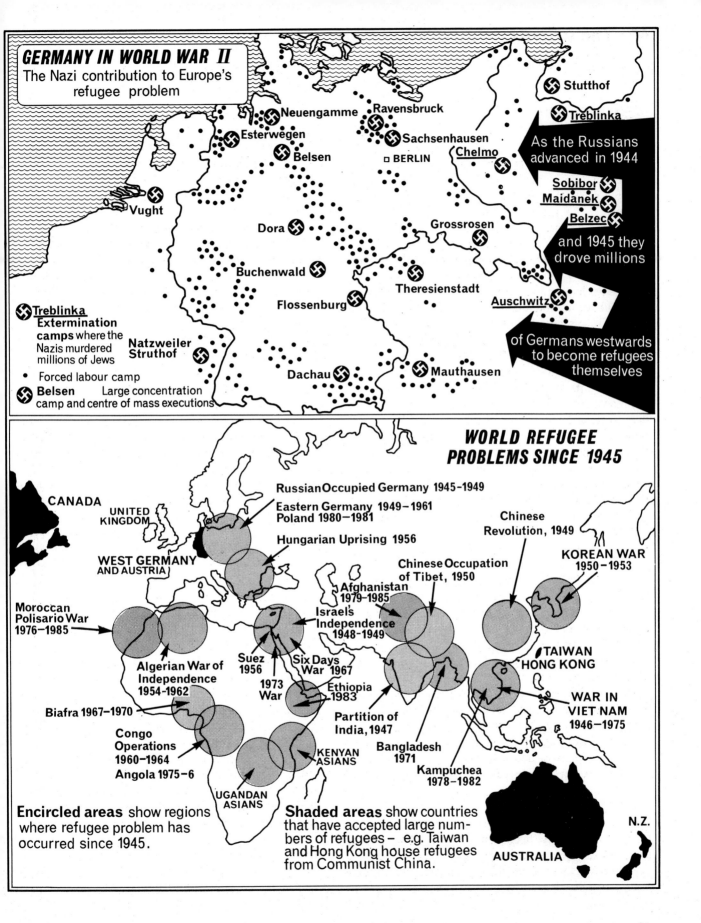

GERMANY IN WORLD WAR II
The Nazi contribution to Europe's refugee problem

Stutthof
Treblinka

Neuengamme Ravensbruck
Esterwegen Sachsenhausen
Belsen □ BERLIN Chelmo

As the Russians advanced in 1944

Sobibor
Maidanek
Belzec

and 1945 they drove millions

Vught

Dora

Grossrosen

Buchenwald

Theresienstadt

Flossenburg

Auschwitz

of Germans westwards to become refugees themselves

Treblinka
Extermination camps where the Nazis murdered millions of Jews

- Forced labour camp

Natzweiler Struthof

Dachau

Mauthausen

Belsen Large concentration camp and centre of mass executions

WORLD REFUGEE PROBLEMS SINCE 1945

CANADA

UNITED KINGDOM

Russian Occupied Germany 1945–1949
Eastern Germany 1949–1961
Poland 1980–1981

Hungarian Uprising 1956

Chinese Revolution, 1949

WEST GERMANY AND AUSTRIA

Chinese Occupation of Tibet, 1950

KOREAN WAR 1950–1953

Moroccan Polisario War 1976–1985

Afghanistan 1979–1985

Israel's Independence 1948–1949

Algerian War of Independence 1954–1962

Suez 1956

Six Days War 1967

TAIWAN
HONG KONG

1973 War

Ethiopia 1983

WAR IN VIET NAM 1946–1975

Biafra 1967–1970

Partition of India, 1947

Congo Operations 1960–1964
Angola 1975–6

KENYAN ASIANS

Bangladesh 1971

Kampuchea 1978–1982

UGANDAN ASIANS

N.Z.

Encircled areas show regions where refugee problem has occurred since 1945.

Shaded areas show countries that have accepted large numbers of refugees – e.g. Taiwan and Hong Kong house refugees from Communist China.

AUSTRALIA

41 : The growth of African nationalism to 1975

In 1945 only four independent states—Egypt, Liberia, Ethiopia and the Union of South Africa—existed in Africa; but by 1966 most of the continent had freed itself from colonial rule. One reason for this sudden growth of independence may be found in World War II, which saw the collapse of European empires both in Africa and Asia. In his book *African Nationalism* Ndabaningi Sithole tells the story of a British officer trying to recruit African soldiers to fight against the Axis armies:

> 'What's wrong with Hitler?' asked an African. 'He wants to rule the whole world,' said the British officer. 'What's wrong with that?' 'He is German, you see,' said the British officer, trying to explain in terms that would be conceivable to the African mind, 'it is not good for one tribe to rule another. Each tribe must rule itself. That's only fair. A German must rule Germans, an Italian, Italians, and a Frenchman, French people.'

And the Africans took the hint! After the war many agitated for the right of Africans to rule Africans, for the chance of creating in Africa their own modern nation states free from European domination.

Ghana

In 1874 Britain annexed a strip of West Africa and called it the Gold Coast Colony. During World War II it was especially important as a staging post for the movement of men and supplies en route for the African battlefields. Thousands of white men in the armed services passed through the ports of Takoradi and Accra—and so Gold Coast Africans were able to make new contacts with Europeans whose main concern was neither trade nor colonial government. Moreover, thousands of Gold Coast Africans joined the army and fought with distinction. By 1944, when the war in Africa was over many were demanding the right to govern themselves and enthusiastically supported their own leaders—one of whom was Kwame Nkrumah who, in 1949, founded the Convention People's Party (C.P.P.). In the towns and in the bush the C.P.P. rallied the Africans by using the same propaganda and tactics as do western politicians. But as well as the meetings, the speeches and the newspaper campaigns the C.P.P. also encouraged strikes and passive resistance—and this led Nkrumah into trouble with the British who, on two occasions, sent him to jail. But Britain was conscious of the genuine desire of the Africans for self-government and accordingly granted the Gold Coast a new constitution in 1951. After the 1953 elections Nkrumah became Prime Minister of the Gold Coast and three years later he again returned to office with tremendous African backing. Now Britain was certain that the Gold Coast was capable of self-rule and in 1957 the Gold Coast became independent Ghana—the first British colony in post-war Africa to win its independence. In 1960 Ghana became a Republic within the British-Commonwealth of Nations—and served as a model to other African colonies seeking independence.

Nigeria

More than 20% of Africa's population lives in Nigeria. It is a country of three distinct regions. In the north are 30 million Moslem Hausa; in the east 12 million Ibo; in the west 10 million Yoruba. There is no love lost between the three—and in particular between the Hausa and Ibo. The latter rebelled in 1967 and declared that their region was the independent state of Biafra, and thus the Federation of Nigeria, set up in 1960, was involved in civil war.

Kenya

Here the Kikuyu people form the largest tribe. During the 1940s and 1950s they became increasingly critical of the white settlers who farmed the rich agricultural areas known as the 'White Highlands'. Between 1952 and 1955 the Mau-Mau movement terrorized Kenya and murdered 20,000 people—most of them Kikuyus sympathetic to their white employers. The British accused Jomo Kenyatta, for years an advocate of Kenyan independence, of leading Mau-Mau. They threw him in jail but released him in 1961. Two years later Jomo Kenyatta became President of an independent Kenya.

Unrest after independence

Since the grant of independence many African states have seen a great deal of violence and political upheaval. This has been true of the former French and Belgian colonies as well as the British. In 1966 President Nkrumah fell from power in Ghana and fled to Guinea. In Nigeria the same year the Army took control after the assassination of the Federal Prime Minister, Abubakar Tafawa Balewa.

In other former colonial territories, such as Kenya, Uganda, and Tanzania the men who had led their countries to independence survived but they had to face sometimes violent opposition. In their struggle for independence most colonial peoples demanded 'One man, one vote!' but after independence they often found it impossible to cope with their countries' enormous problems through a European style democratic constitution. As a result many African states now operate on a one-party system or are ruled by military juntas.

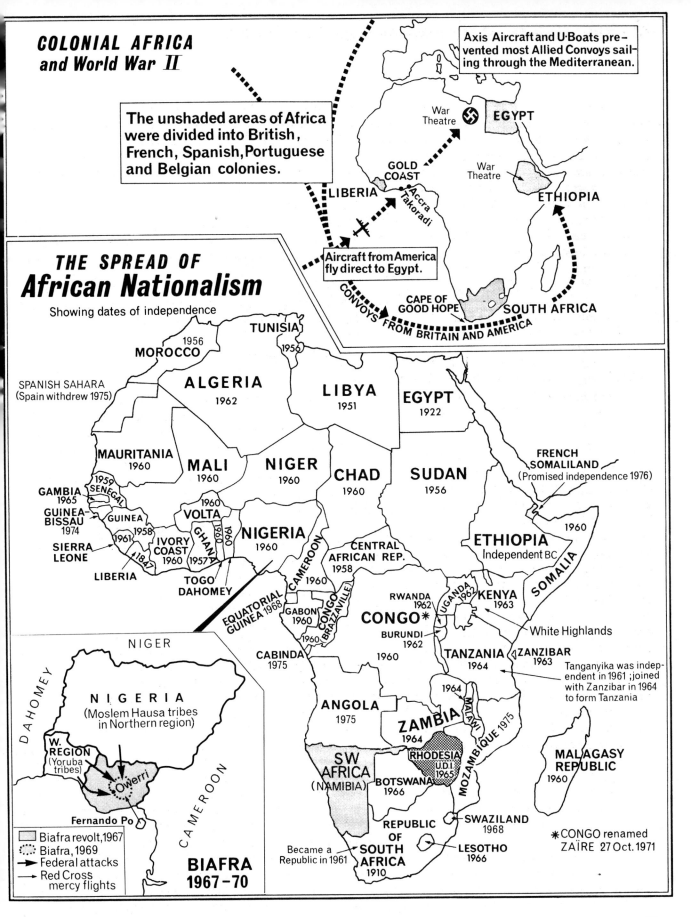

COLONIAL AFRICA and World War II

Axis Aircraft and U·Boats pre-vented most Allied Convoys sail-ing through the Mediterranean.

The unshaded areas of Africa were divided into British, French, Spanish, Portuguese and Belgian colonies.

War Theatre

EGYPT

GOLD COAST

LIBERIA

Accra
Takoradi

War Theatre

ETHIOPIA

Aircraft from America fly direct to Egypt.

CONVOYS FROM BRITAIN AND AMERICA

CAPE OF GOOD HOPE

SOUTH AFRICA

THE SPREAD OF African Nationalism

Showing dates of independence

MOROCCO 1956

TUNISIA 1956

SPANISH SAHARA (Spain withdrew 1975)

ALGERIA 1962

LIBYA 1951

EGYPT 1922

MAURITANIA 1960

MALI 1960

NIGER 1960

CHAD 1960

SUDAN 1956

FRENCH SOMALILAND (Promised independence 1976)

GAMBIA 1965

SENEGAL 1959

GUINEA-BISSAU 1974

GUINEA 1958

SIERRA LEONE 1961

VOLTA 1960

GHANA 1957

IVORY COAST 1960

TOGO 1960

DAHOMEY 1960

LIBERIA 1847

NIGERIA 1960

CAMEROON 1960

CENTRAL AFRICAN REP. 1958

ETHIOPIA Independent BC

1960

SOMALIA

EQUATORIAL GUINEA 1968

GABON 1960

CONGO (BRAZZAVILLE) 1960

RWANDA 1962

UGANDA 1962

KENYA 1963

CABINDA 1975

CONGO *

BURUNDI 1962

White Highlands

TANZANIA 1964

ZANZIBAR 1963

Tanganyika was indep-endent in 1961; joined with Zanzibar in 1964 to form Tanzania

ANGOLA 1975

1964

MALAWI

MOZAMBIQUE 1975

ZAMBIA 1964

RHODESIA U.D.I. 1965

MALAGASY REPUBLIC 1960

SW AFRICA (NAMIBIA)

BOTSWANA 1966

SWAZILAND 1968

* CONGO renamed ZAÏRE 27 Oct. 1971

Became a Republic in 1961

REPUBLIC OF SOUTH AFRICA 1910

LESOTHO 1966

BIAFRA 1967–70

NIGER

DAHOMEY

NIGERIA (Moslem Hausa tribes in Northern region)

W. REGION (Yoruba tribes)

Owerri

Fernando Po

CAMEROON

☐ Biafra revolt, 1967
⬚ Biafra, 1969
➜ Federal attacks
→ Red Cross mercy flights

93

42: New Nations in the Far East: Japan, Indonesia and Malaysia

Japan

Japan's resistance to the allies ended abruptly in 1945 with the atomic assaults on Hiroshima and Nagasaki. For the next seven years, when U.S. troops were in occupation, it may be said that Japan had lost her independence. However, despite the recent memories of the bitter Pacific War, America poured in aid to help the Japanese rebuild their shattered cities and restart their derelict industries. With determination, the Japanese threw themselves into the task of reconstruction and, by 1951, had reached their pre-war level of industrial production. In the same year they signed the Peace Treaty of San Francisco with the wartime allies; and though Japan lost her empire she did regain her independence. Before long the Japanese were competing with the rest of the world in the export of transistors, typewriters, television sets, cameras and cars. By 1973 they were the world's leading ship-builders and had even conducted their own space programme!

Indonesia

Meanwhile, in those areas which in 1945 had been freed from Japanese control, other voices demanded independence. The Japanese had already declared the people of the Dutch East Indies to be independent—in the hope of gaining their support. Now, on the return of peace, the Dutch tried to put the clock back—to re-establish colonial rule. At once the P.N.I.—Indonesian Nationalist Party—led by Sukarno resisted them and various clashes between the P.N.I. and Dutch troops went on between 1946–49. This conflict ended in 1949 with the defeat of the P.N.I. and the capture of Sukarno. But by now there was a good deal of world protest at the use of force by the Dutch; and in 1949 the U.N. arranged a Conference at the Hague. Here the Dutch agreed on a ceasefire and from this it was but a short step to the grant of independence to 'Indonesia' at the end of the year.

Malaysia

For Burma, invaded by the Japanese in 1942, independence came in 1948. Burma immediately left the British Commonwealth of Nations. But for Malaya, occupied by Japan from 1942 to 1945, Britain had different plans. Malaya was to be an independent union of states while Singapore would remain a British colony. These plans were almost wrecked by a serious communist uprising in 1948. For twelve years, in what was known as the 'Emergency', communist guerrillas threatened the peninsula. Nearly every guerrilla was Chinese and they tied down large numbers of British and Malay troops. The climax came between 1952 and 1954 when General Templer moved in not just against the guerrillas but also against their means of survival—the food stores kept by Chinese villagers in Malaya. Templer resettled thousands of Chinese suspected of aiding the communists and cleared the northern frontier of jungle to reduce Chinese infiltration across the border. The turning point of the 'Emergency' was not so much the military success as the open co-operation between the civilian Chinese and Malay leaders, T. H. Tan and Tunku Abdul Rahman. They formed the new Alliance Party and stood for the independence of Malaya. This undermined the communists' position—they claimed to be fighting for the very same thing! Slowly, the communist threat declined (though there were still a few communist bands in action during 1967). In 1955 the Alliance Party won the general elections in Malaya, formed a new government and demanded independence. This was granted on 31st August 1957 when the independent Federation of Malaya was born. And when it joined with Borneo (Sabah) and Sarawak in 1963 the name was changed to the Federation of Malaysia.

Confrontation

Indonesia noisily objected to these changes and claimed that Malaysia was now occupying lands rightfully belonging to Indonesia. Sukarno stopped all trade with Malaysia and then sent in guerrilla forces to harass the Malaysian defenders. And as Britain was committed to the defence of Malaysia, British troops once more found themselves in action. During 1964–65, Sukarno's 'confrontation with Malaysia' flared into a bitter war. The Indonesian President sent in seaborne commandos and airborne troops; the British retaliated with air strikes, artillery bombardments and Gurkha patrols. Then, when the Security Council deplored Sukarno's use of paratroopers, Indonesia withdrew from the U.N. in 1965. In 1966 Sukarno had to face a new and internal threat from the P.K.I.—the Indonesian Communist Party. Many communists died in bloodthirsty riots; while Sukarno himself lost support. By the end of the year the anti-communist General Suharto appeared to be in control. He ended the confrontation with Malaysia and, in 1967, his position was confirmed when President Sukarno retired from office.

NEW NATIONS IN THE FAR EAST—
JAPAN INDONESIA and MALAYSIA

1 Malaysia and Indonesia are of vital importance because they provide most of the world supply of **natural rubber** as well as large quantities of oil.

2 Effect of confrontation on Indonesia:
  (a) It cost Sukarno £300m. p.a.
  (b) It lost Indonesia nearly £100m. in trade with Malaysia.
  (c) It caused inflation.

SOVIET RUSSIA

CHINA

Resumed diplomatic relations in 1956

Joined 1956 → **U.N.**

Signed at San Francisco 1951 → **Peace Treaty**

Security Pact 1951 → **U.S.A.**

Large numbers of Chinese live in S.E. Asia and thus offer excellent chances of communist penetration e.g. Malaysia and Indonesia.

OKINAWA (restored to Japan 1972)

FORMOSA (TAIWAN)

BURMA independent 1948

Crew of Japanese fishing boat hit by radiation sickness. This led to panic in Japan and strong anti-American feeling in 1954.

FALL OUT

BIKINI Hydrogen bomb test in Mar. 1954 by U.S.A.

PHILIPPINES

Independent 1946. Ruled by Ferdinand Marcos 1985-86, when Mrs Corazon Aquino became president.

S. VIET NAM

MALAYA

MALAYSIA

BRUNEI

SARAWAK SABAH

CONFRONTATION 1963—1967

Indonesia wanted the Territory of New Guinea.

WEST IRIAN **NEW GUINEA**

Under Australian protection until it became independent Papua New Guinea in 1975.

1965

DJAKARTA

I N D O N E S I A

Singapore was ejected by the Malaysians from their independent Federation and it is now a separate state.

AUSTRALIA

95

43: Events in the Middle East: enmity between Jew and Arab 1945−56

Palestine 1917−47

For centuries the Jewish people have endured a history of persecution which reached its peak in Europe at the hands of Hitler and his henchmen. In their attempt to commit 'genocide'—the extermination of a race—the Nazis killed nearly six million Jews. Yet it is false to think of the Jews as a race. For most of their history they have been scattered among the peoples of the world and, before 1945, they had little hope of ever building a national home where they could follow their own religious and social customs without fear of interference. But after their hideous experiences under the Nazi regime, they renewed their determination to found their own national state. The place they sought was Palestine, the Biblical home of the Jews. The idea of a national home for the Jews had been supported by the British in the 1917 Balfour Declaration and, since then, under the powers of mandate granted by the League of Nations, the British had allowed a limited number of Jews to enter Palestine. This was not enough for the Jews—but it was far too much for the Arabs who were already living in Palestine. The result was that, both before and after World War II, the British had to face in Palestine sporadic attacks from discontented Jews and Arabs. The most notorious terrorists were the Jewish Irgun and Stern Gang. The Irgun, for example, blew up the King David Hotel in Jerusalem during 1946 and killed ninety-one people. So serious was the disorder that Britain told the U.N. that she would have to withdraw her troops; and as a solution to the problem the U.N. suggested in 1947 that Palestine should be partitioned between Jews and Arabs. This simply intensified the guerrilla war—in the midst of which the British withdrew. Gradually, the Jewish forces overcame the Arabs and on 14 May 1948 they proclaimed the creation of the Jewish state of Israel. This had two immediate results: the U.N. recognized Israel's independence; and the armies of the Arab League crossed the Palestine border to attack the Israelis.

The First Arab War

When the Arabs formed their league in 1945 one of their prime objects had been the elimination of the Jewish threat in Palestine. Now they welcomed the chance of a war against the Jews in 1948. The Egyptians moved north to destroy the main Israeli forces just below Tel Aviv while Jordan's crack Arab Legion (trained and equipped by the British) advanced on Jerusalem. But to the Arabs' alarm the Israelis not only repelled these attacks but actually advanced to occupy Arab territory. And when the U.N. sent out Count Bernadotte to restrain Israeli expansion, Jewish terrorists killed him.

The uneasy truce

Eventually the Jews and Arabs signed a truce in 1949. For Israel it meant victory and the chance to attract thousands of immigrant Jews to their new nation. For the Arabs it was an inglorious defeat, underlined by the fact that nearly a million of them were now refugees from their former homes in Palestine. This defeat had a profound effect on the Egyptian army, which in 1952 overthrew King Farouk of Egypt and set up a new military government led first by General Neguib but really controlled by Colonel Nasser.

Aswan and Suez

After he came to power in 1954 Nasser showed himself to be an energetic and incorruptible reformer. He promised the Egyptian people a wonderful new life—once the Aswan Dam project was complete. It would harness the Nile and bring irrigation and hydro-electricity to the land; it would guarantee the industrial and agricultural future of Egypt. But in its infancy the project depended on American dollars—until 1955–56. It was then that Nasser became increasingly friendly with the U.S.S.R.; and the U.S. government withdrew its aid on the assumption that, if Nasser were a communist, he would now be forced to show his true colours. Instead Nasser nationalized the Suez Canal.

The Suez War

His action enraged Britain and France for both had special interests in the Canal. Possibly Nasser reminded Sir Anthony Eden (British Prime Minister) of pre-war days when the Führer did what he liked. Nasser would enjoy no such privilege; Britain and France would teach him a short, sharp military lesson. The moment came— no doubt it was planned—when Israel suddenly attacked Egypt on 29 October 1956; Britain ordered the Egyptians and Israelis to withdraw from both sides of the Suez Canal. When Nasser refused, British and French planes attacked Port Said. Five days later Anglo-French forces blasted their way into the Canal Zone. This act of aggression provoked world-wide condemnation of Britain and stirred the U.N. to appoint an Emergency Force to take over from the British commandos and paratroopers. The Suez affair was a failure for Britain's policy in the Middle East: the Suez Canal was blocked by sunken ships: Israeli-Arab antagonism increased, whilst the prestige of President Nasser was higher than ever throughout the Arab world.

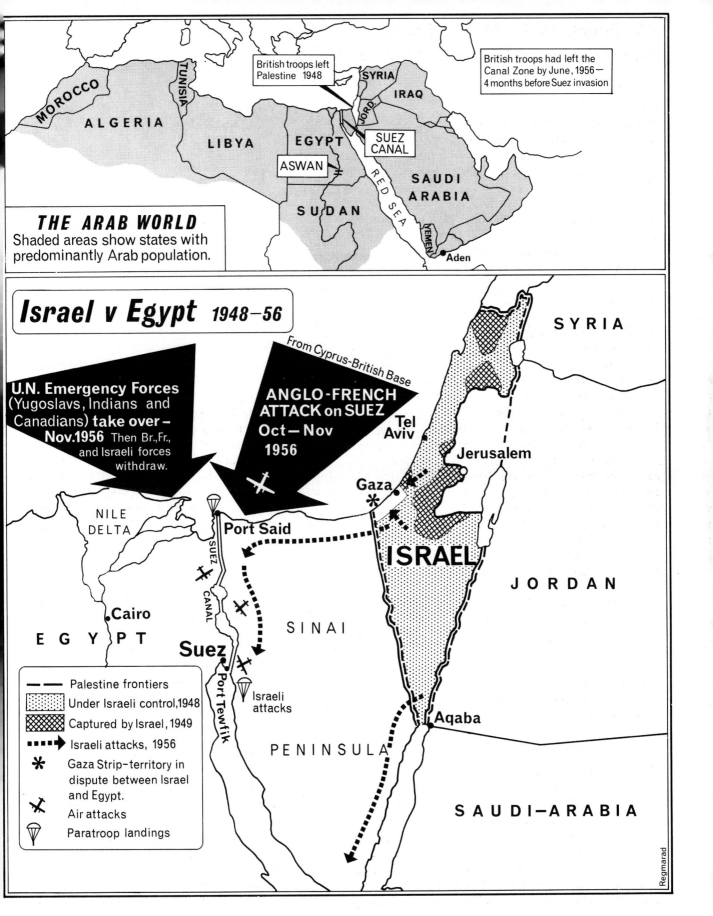

THE ARAB WORLD
Shaded areas show states with predominantly Arab population.

British troops left Palestine 1948

British troops had left the Canal Zone by June, 1956 — 4 months before Suez invasion

MOROCCO

TUNISIA

ALGERIA

LIBYA

EGYPT

ASWAN

SUDAN

SYRIA

IRAQ

JORD.

SUEZ CANAL

RED SEA

SAUDI ARABIA

YEMEN

Aden

Israel v Egypt 1948–56

From Cyprus–British Base

U.N. Emergency Forces (Yugoslavs, Indians and Canadians) take over – Nov. 1956 Then Br., Fr., and Israeli forces withdraw.

ANGLO-FRENCH ATTACK on SUEZ Oct – Nov 1956

Tel Aviv

Jerusalem

Gaza

NILE DELTA

Port Said

SUEZ CANAL

Cairo

EGYPT

Suez

Port Tewfik

SINAI

ISRAEL

JORDAN

Aqaba

PENINSULA

SAUDI–ARABIA

Israeli attacks

- - - Palestine frontiers
- Under Israeli control, 1948
- Captured by Israel, 1949
- ▪▪▪▶ Israeli attacks, 1956
- ∗ Gaza Strip–territory in dispute between Israel and Egypt.
- ✈ Air attacks
- ⛄ Paratroop landings

Regmarad

97

44: India and Pakistan: the problems of independence

The end of British India

'At the stroke of the midnight hour, when the world sleeps, India will awake to life and freedom.' And for India this came on August 15th 1947. But it was to be neither a united nor a peaceful India. *Two* independent republics, India and Pakistan, had been carved from this vast sub-continent, a division stemming from the days when Moslem invaders had lorded over the lands and holy rivers of the Hindu peoples, breeding a jealousy and hatred that flared into civil war at the time of partition. Partition meant that millions of Moslems had to trek into their new national home of Pakistan; similarly millions of Hindus had to find their way to India. An estimated 500,000 people lost their lives in this last mass migration of peoples in history. Of the atrocities committed, one group of army officers reported that they were 'more horrible than anything we saw in the war'. Appalled by these events the revered Mahatma Gandhi began yet another religious fast, but a fanatical Hindu assassinated him in 1948.

The special problems

This religious and racial enmity bedevilled the two republics for the next eighteen years. And yet during this time far more serious problems awaited their attention. India was the second most populous nation in the world; 100 million people lived in Pakistan's two 'wings'. Both countries faced a population explosion and desperately needed to reduce their birth-rate; both needed more food and money and, perhaps most urgently, both needed an educated leadership that would persuade more than 500 million people to adopt a more modern form of life. Many said that this in time would mean communism; to this Nehru, India's first Prime Minister, answered a most vehement 'No!' He was confident that India would choose the path of freedom. 'Freedom to starve?' both Communists and non-Communists wondered.

The Kashmir dispute

A peaceful, united approach to these problems has been made especially difficult by the quarrel over the ownership of Kashmir. Nehru (his family came from Kashmir) claimed it for India; Pakistan objected on the grounds that 75% of Kashmir's population were Moslems. After some skirmishes there in 1948–49, the United Nations managed to arrange a truce and a demarcation line across Kashmir. But for years the dispute remained unsettled. Meanwhile the leadership of the two republics changed: Ayub Khan took control in Pakistan in 1957; and when Nehru died in 1964, Shastri became Prime Minister. Within a year, the Pakistanis had attacked in Kashmir. 'We are fighting to retain our homeland' was their well-worn reason. As both sides had in the past received plenty of foreign aid the fighting soon became intense: Pakistanis flew American Sabrejets against Indians piloting British Hunters and Russian Mig 21s.

The Tashkent Conference

Though the 1965 war was fought over the disputed ownership of Kashmir, it was fundamentally about the great division which existed in the sub-continent. Pakistan could never become a truly united country with its 'wings' separated by 1,200 miles of Indian territory. And religious disputes might easily be provoked by the fact that some 50 million Moslems still live in India. So there was a constant risk of conflict between the two countries. However, in 1966 there was a dramatic intervention in their affairs. The Russian leaders invited both sides to settle their differences at the Tashkent Conference, where the U.S.S.R. played the role of Asian peacemaker with great success. Unfortunately Prime Minister Shastri died during the Conference. Mrs. Indira Gandhi then took over India's leadership and India's problems. An outstanding Prime Minister, she was assassinated in 1984.

The 1971 Indo-Pakistan War

Civil war flared in East Pakistan when Bangla Desh (Free Bengal) guerrillas clashed with government troops during March 1971. Thousands of civilians died in the slaughter and literally millions of terrified people stampeded across the border into India. Mrs. Gandhi resented having to shoulder her neighbour's problems and before long a serious crisis developed between her and Pakistan's new President, Yahya Khan. Then, on 3 December 1971, Pakistan's jets raided Srinigar while her armour rumbled across the Kashmir frontier to begin a full-scale war against India. Indian troops retaliated by invading East Pakistan where bitter fighting on land, sea and in the air forced Yahya Khan to surrender (16 December 1971). East Pakistan declared its independence and became the People's Republic of Bangladesh; Yahya Khan resigned; while his successor, President Bhutto, withdrew his mutilated state from membership of the British Commonwealth of Nations (30 January 1972).

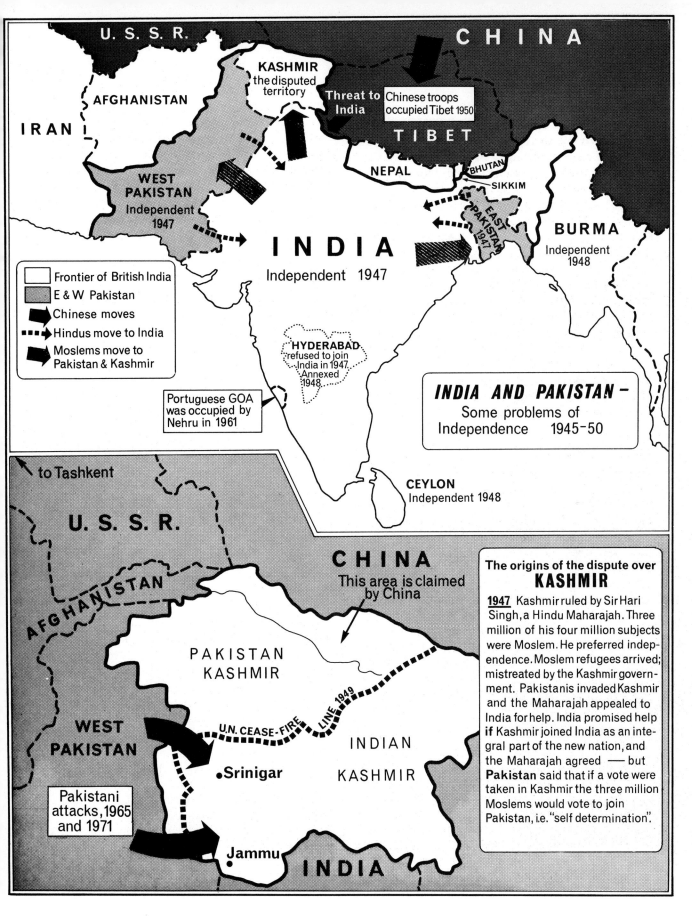

U.S.S.R.

CHINA

AFGHANISTAN

IRAN

KASHMIR the disputed territory

Threat to India

Chinese troops occupied Tibet 1950

TIBET

WEST PAKISTAN Independent 1947

NEPAL

BHUTAN

SIKKIM

EAST PAKISTAN 1947

BURMA Independent 1948

INDIA

Independent 1947

	Frontier of British India
	E & W Pakistan
	Chinese moves
	Hindus move to India
	Moslems move to Pakistan & Kashmir

HYDERABAD refused to join India in 1947. Annexed 1948

Portuguese GOA was occupied by Nehru in 1961

INDIA AND PAKISTAN –
Some problems of Independence 1945-50

CEYLON Independent 1948

U.S.S.R.

to Tashkent

CHINA

This area is claimed by China

AFGHANISTAN

PAKISTAN KASHMIR

U.N. CEASE-FIRE LINE 1949

INDIAN KASHMIR

WEST PAKISTAN

• Srinigar

Pakistani attacks, 1965 and 1971

• Jammu

INDIA

The origins of the dispute over
KASHMIR

1947 Kashmir ruled by Sir Hari Singh, a Hindu Maharajah. Three million of his four million subjects were Moslem. He preferred independence. Moslem refugees arrived; mistreated by the Kashmir government. Pakistanis invaded Kashmir and the Maharajah appealed to India for help. India promised help **if** Kashmir joined India as an integral part of the new nation, and the Maharajah agreed —— but **Pakistan** said that if a vote were taken in Kashmir the three million Moslems would vote to join Pakistan, i.e. "self determination".

45: The Communist victory in China

Sun Yat-sen

In 1911 the remarkable revolutionary, Sun Yat-sen, helped to topple the Manchu Empire. His dream was the liberation of the Chinese people and their advance towards a new way of life based upon his 'Three Principles':

'DEMOCRACY' 'NATIONALISM',
'THE PEOPLE'S LIVELIHOOD'.

He founded a political party called the Kuomintang (K.M.T.) to carry out his social revolution, but he lacked the basic tools for the task. He never gained control of the Chinese Army; many army commanders chose to become brigands or 'war-lords' and ravaged many parts of China.

Chiang Kai-shek

When Sun Yat-sen died in 1925 the leadership of the K.M.T. passed to one of his lieutenants. Chiang Kai-shek. Chiang had to contend with a new political force inside the K.M.T.—the Chinese Communist Party (C.C.P.), founded by men such as Mao Tse-tung and Chou En-lai. Chiang realised that the communists wanted to take over the K.M.T. and so in 1927 he purged the party of its communist element and forced many C.C.P. members to take refuge in the hills. Now Chiang had become the real ruler of China; now he had the chance of putting Sun Yat-sen's Three Principles into practice. But he failed to do this, instead he tried to modernize China along western lines by attracting British and American capital into the country.

The Japanese attacks

Unfortunately for Chiang's plans, Japanese troops also arrived and between 1931 and 1932 they occupied the whole of Chinese Manchuria. Yet Chiang did not unduly concern himself with the Japanese menace; he was more concerned with the threat from within—the Communists. He began full-scale military operations against Mao Tse-tung's Red Army and in 1934 forced it to make its famous 'Long March' into remote Shensi Province. There, free from K.M.T. attack, Mao set up a miniature Communist state and bided his time. Within three years the Japanese had attacked again, occupying a great deal of China's coastline in 1937. For the time being Mao and Chiang made an uneasy truce as they faced the common foe and eventually this Sino-Japanese conflict merged into World War II after 1941. Not until 1945 were the Japanese evicted from China. During these years the K.M.T. allowed, wherever possible, the communist troops to bear the brunt of the fighting. Chiang seemed more intent on stockpiling American weapons ready for the day when he would fight the communists again.

Defeat of the K.M.T.

The day came in 1946, after the Americans had failed to reconcile the two sides. For three years the K.M.T. resisted the communist attacks but they lost control of more and more of the Chinese countryside. Chiang's administrators were often corrupt; taxation was high; inflation was rife. To many peasants, the Communists came as liberators from oppression. A C.C.P. jeep would roar into a village: out would jump a propaganda team: 'We have liberated you from the Kuomintang! No more taxes! No more debts! Kill the landlord and the tax-collector! The fields and the rice-paddies are yours!' Control of the countryside; brilliant guerrilla tactics; sound propaganda: these were the methods which spelt out success for Mao Tse-tung. In 1949 the last of the K.M.T. fled to Taiwan (Formosa); on the mainland the Communist Chinese People's Republic was born.

Taiwan—Nationalist China

By the end of the Sixties mainland China was the most populous nation in the world; it possessed nuclear weapons; its armies were even bigger than those of the Soviet Union. But it was still not a member of the United Nations. America continued to recognize Chiang Kai-shek, now confined to Taiwan, as the legitimate ruler of China. U.S. aid enabled the two million K.M.T. troops based on Taiwan to defy the Communists and to retain control of the offshore islands of Quemoy and Matsu. Then, on 25 October 1971, the U.N. General Assembly made its dramatic decision: it recognized the government of the People's Republic as the *legitimate* representative of China at the United Nations. Taiwan, a nation of 14 million people, not only lost its place on the Security Council but also suffered expulsion from the U.N. General Assembly.

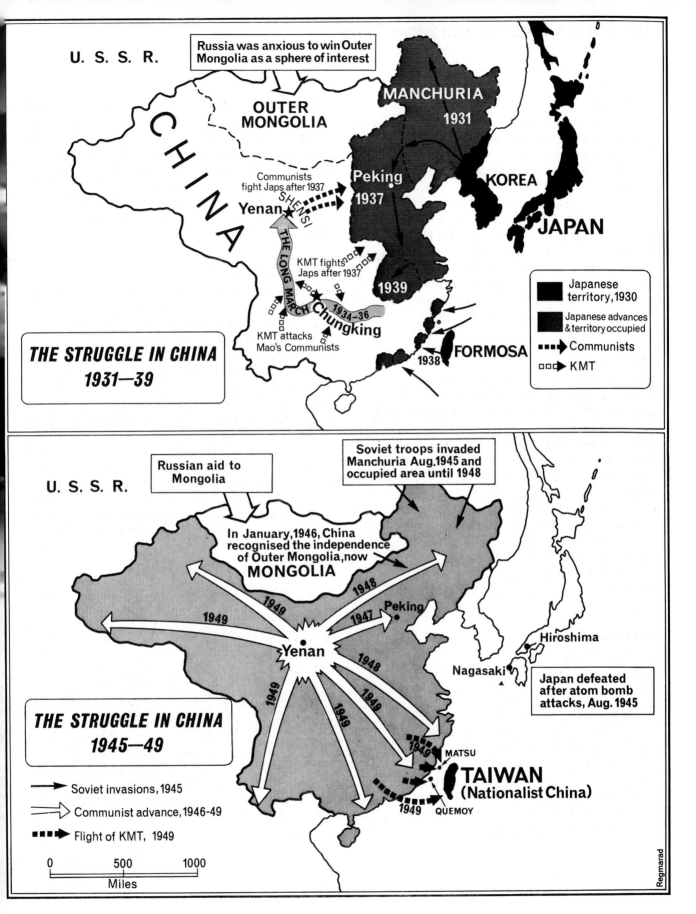

THE STRUGGLE IN CHINA 1931–39

U. S. S. R.

Russia was anxious to win Outer Mongolia as a sphere of interest

OUTER MONGOLIA

MANCHURIA 1931

CHINA

Communists fight Japs after 1937

SHENSI

Yenan

Peking 1937

KOREA

JAPAN

KMT fights Japs after 1937

1939

THE LONG MARCH

1934–36

Chungking

KMT attacks Mao's Communists

1938

FORMOSA

■ Japanese territory, 1930
▨ Japanese advances & territory occupied
▪▪▪► Communists
□□□► KMT

THE STRUGGLE IN CHINA 1945–49

U. S. S. R.

Russian aid to Mongolia

Soviet troops invaded Manchuria Aug. 1945 and occupied area until 1948

In January, 1946, China recognised the independence of Outer Mongolia, now
MONGOLIA

1948

1949

1949

1947

Peking

Yenan

1948

Hiroshima

Nagasaki

Japan defeated after atom bomb attacks, Aug. 1945

1949

1949

1949

1949

1949

MATSU

TAIWAN (Nationalist China)

1949

QUEMOY

→ Soviet invasions, 1945
⇒ Communist advance, 1946-49
■■■► Flight of KMT, 1949

0   500   1000
Miles

Regmarad

46: France tries to keep her empire: colonial wars 1946–1962

Indo-China: The Viet Minh

After 1945 France fought and lost two major colonial wars, the results of which have shaped a great deal of later world history. The first arose out of the French attempt to regain Indo-China. During World War II the French there had tamely accepted Japanese occupation while communist guerrilla forces, led by Ho Chi Minh*, had fought back. In 1945 Ho, a former London pastry-cook, set up his independent Democratic Republic of North Viet Nam which the French refused to recognize. By 1946 Ho's Viet Minh guerrillas began to attack the newly arrived French armies in Indo-China. From their hideouts in the Mekong Delta and Red River regions the Viet Minh would raid the well-equipped French forces which included crack units of 'les paras' (paratroopers) and the French Foreign Legion in their ranks. But the guerrilla commander, General Giap— once a history teacher—always tried to avoid pitched battles with the French. Then in 1954 Giap changed his tactics; the Viet Minh surrounded the French fortress at Dien Bien Phu and for two months pounded 15,000 trapped French soldiers with artillery. On 8 May 1954 the French surrendered.

Geneva Conference

Giap's dramatic victory stirred the interest of the great powers in this corner of Asia and at the Geneva Conference in 1954 they decided to divide Indo-China into four separate states. Ho Chi Minh would rule communist North Viet Nam; a non-communist government would administer South Viet Nam; to the west two *neutral* states. Laos and Cambodia, would form, in Anthony Eden's words, a 'protective pad' around the divided Vietnamese people. All foreign troops would then vacate Indo-China and within two years the Vietnamese were to hold free elections so that they would be re-united under a government of their own choice. Before these two years had passed, war returned to Viet Nam—war that was to be a major threat to world peace.

* President of North Viet Nam, died 1969.

Algeria: the F.L.N.

Having passed the Vietnamese problem into the hands of others, the French pulled out only to face yet another rebellion—this time in Algeria. Here lived nine million Algerian Muslims together with about a million Europeans, many of whom were third or fourth generation settlers. France regarded Algeria as an integral part of the French Fourth Republic; the Algerian people were French people who sent deputies to the National Assembly in Paris. Therefore rebellion was unlawful. However, the Algerian F.L.N. (National Liberation Front) thought otherwise and began terrorist attacks against French civilians. The French Army responded with bitter reprisals and so intensified the war. By 13 May 1958 the French settlers had tired of the government's dismal failure to protect their families and property. A mob stormed the Algiers Headquarters and, with the help of the soldiers, set up a 'Committee of Public Safety'. Now there were three rival powers in Algeria: the government, the Committee and the F.L.N. In France—where rumour had it that 'les paras' from Algeria might attempt an airborne assault on Paris—this led to chaos and the tottering French government collapsed. Now who would govern France?

General de Gaulle

From retirement General de Gaulle came forward to take control. First he became Premier and then, calling himself 'le garant' ('leader'), President of the French Fifth Republic. But to the horror of the settlers, the General began to negotiate with F.L.N. leaders during 1961. In 1962 he recognized Algeria's independence. This was how the General freed France from her disastrous policy of trying to revive the glories of a defunct colonial empire. In its place he was to try to offer France an alternative to military glory—the diplomatic leadership of Europe. So the French war in Indo-China led directly to the more dangerous war in Viet Nam; and the Algerian rebellion brought General de Gaulle to power in France.

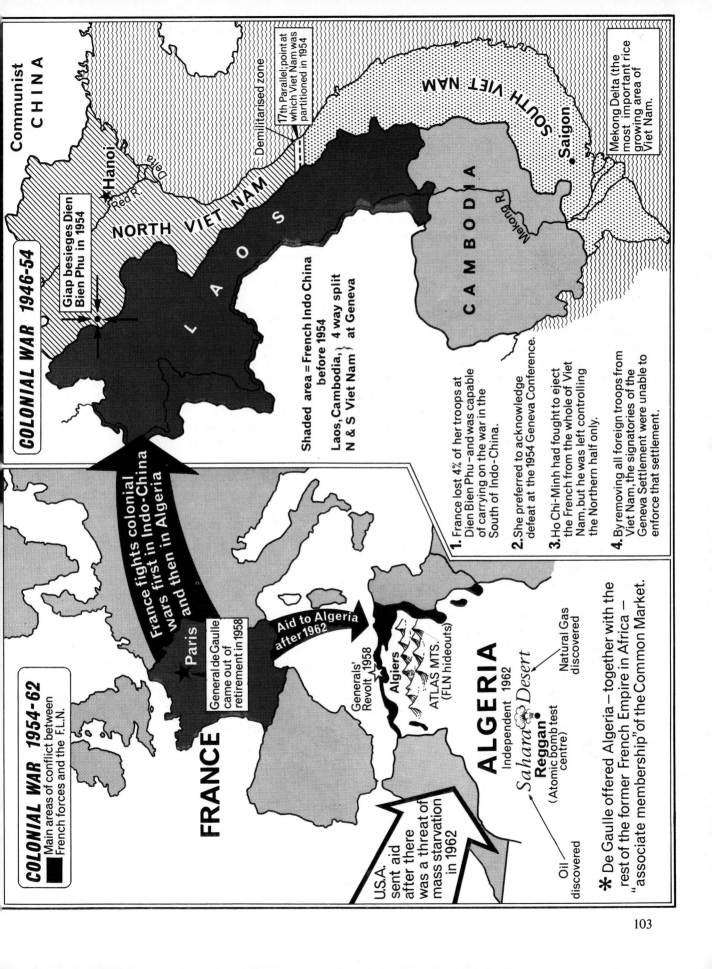

COLONIAL WAR 1946-54

Communist **CHINA**

Demilitarised zone

17th Parallel; point at which Viet Nam was partitioned in 1954

NORTH VIET NAM

Giap besieges Dien Bien Phu in 1954

★Hanoi

Red R.

Delta

SOUTH VIET NAM

Saigon ●

Mekong Delta (the most important rice growing area of Viet Nam.

LAOS

CAMBODIA

Mekong R.

Shaded area = French Indo China before 1954

Laos, Cambodia, } 4 way split
N & S Viet Nam } at Geneva

1. France lost 4% of her troops at Dien Bien Phu – and was capable of carrying on the war in the South of Indo-China.

2. She preferred to acknowledge defeat at the 1954 Geneva Conference.

3. Ho-Chi-Minh had fought to eject the French from the whole of Viet Nam, but he was left controlling the Northern half only.

4. By removing all foreign troops from Viet Nam, the signatories of the Geneva Settlement were unable to enforce that settlement.

COLONIAL WAR 1954-62

■ Main areas of conflict between French forces and the F.L.N.

France fights colonial wars first in Indo-China and then in Algeria

FRANCE

★Paris

General de Gaulle came out of retirement in 1958

Aid to Algeria after 1962

Generals' Revolt 1958

Algiers

ATLAS MTS. (FLN hideouts)

Sahara Desert

Reggan ●
(Atomic bomb test centre)

Natural Gas discovered

ALGERIA
Independent 1962

Oil discovered

U.S.A. sent aid after there was a threat of mass starvation in 1962

★ De Gaulle offered Algeria – together with the rest of the former French Empire in Africa – "associate membership" of the Common Market.

103

47 : South Africa and the policy of apartheid to 1973

The South African case

The Republic of South Africa is carrying out a policy of apartheid, the most extreme racial programme in the world. 'Apartheid' means 'separateness'; but it stands for racial segregation and the dominion of white over the black. Ignoring the evidence, South Africans claim that apartheid is just and that history is on their side. They point out that when the first Dutchman landed in 1652 the coastal region was populated by scattered San hunters and Khoi herdsmen; but when Dutch farmers trekked north they met Bantu settlers from tropical Africa. The two migratory peoples clashed and, after two centuries, the white man emerged victorious. When diamonds were discovered at Kimberley (1869) and gold on the Witwatersrand (1886) the Africans were tempted to desert their tribes and go to work for the white man. But the nation which grew up was a white nation—the blacks had simply come to *work* as unskilled labourers; they did not bring with them any right to *live* in South Africa. Thus, when the Union of South Africa was formed in 1910, the Afrikaners claimed that it was a white man's country and the very first modern national state in Africa. They completely ignored archaeological and linguistic evidence proving that Bantu settlers had been opening up southern Africa since about A.D. 1000. Today, almost the entire world condemns apartheid.

The African's misery

In 1948 the all-white Afrikaner government led by Dr. Malan began to enforce apartheid. Separate 'Bantustans', in which the Africans could live freely, were planned by Dr. Verwoerd, Minister of Native Affairs from 1950 to 1958. The first of these was the Transkei. At the same time a series of 'apartheid laws' removed the social and political rights of the vast majority of Africans living in or near the major towns and cities:

1952 The police were authorized to arrest any township African if he were 'idle'.

1953 Not more than ten Africans could assemble—unless they had police permission.

1957 All Africans had to carry the Reference Book—an identity card which the Africans called the dompass or 'accursed pass' because it made them feel like slaves.

1958 Dr. Verwoerd became Prime Minister. The African political party called the 'African National Congress' was banned.

1959 The representation of Africans in the South African Parliament was abolished.

Any opposition to the apartheid laws was punishable by a fine, five years in jail and a whipping.

Sharpeville

There was one unexpected reaction of this policy. To the south of Johannesburg was a fairly new African township called Sharpeville. About 16,000 Africans lived there and commuted daily to the mines and factories in and around Vereeniging. One day, frustrated by poor wages and living conditions, many went on strike, threw away their reference books and marched down to the police station. Here they all demanded to be arrested—they thought that this would give the police some difficulties. Crowds now assembled; government Sabre jets whistled overhead; Saracen armoured cars nuzzled the people. There was a scuffle, the police opened fire and 69 Africans died. It was 21 March 1960—the day of the Sharpeville Massacre. It stunned South Africa; it shocked the world deeply.

South Africa leaves the Commonwealth

In 1961 South Africa declared herself a Republic and threw off all allegiance to the Commonwealth. In this new republic, the blacks and coloured people outnumbered the whites by roughly 4:1. But the whites were well-armed with automatic weapons, 'Buccaneer' strike aircraft and 'Canberra' bombers. In 1962 they passed the 'Sabotage Act' which punished political opposition with the death penalty. In 1963 they passed the 'No Trial' Act. South Africa had become a police state. In the words of Ronald Segal: 'There is no longer in South Africa any legal protection against the Minister of Justice; he may imprison whom he pleases for as long as he likes.' On 6 September 1966 Dr. Verwoerd was assassinated. His successor was Dr. Vorster, an equally enthusiastic supporter of apartheid. He tightened up state security with B.O.S.S.* and the 1967 Terrorism Act, but found it progressively difficult to deny the blacks their long-overdue wage increases. Serious strikes in Natal and S.W. Africa (Namibia) during 1972–3 culminated in the riot at Western Deep where 12 black miners died in clashes with the police. But something was achieved; by the end of 1973 the mine owners had given their workers wage increases of 25%.

* Bureau of State Security, created 1969; now replaced by Department of National Security.

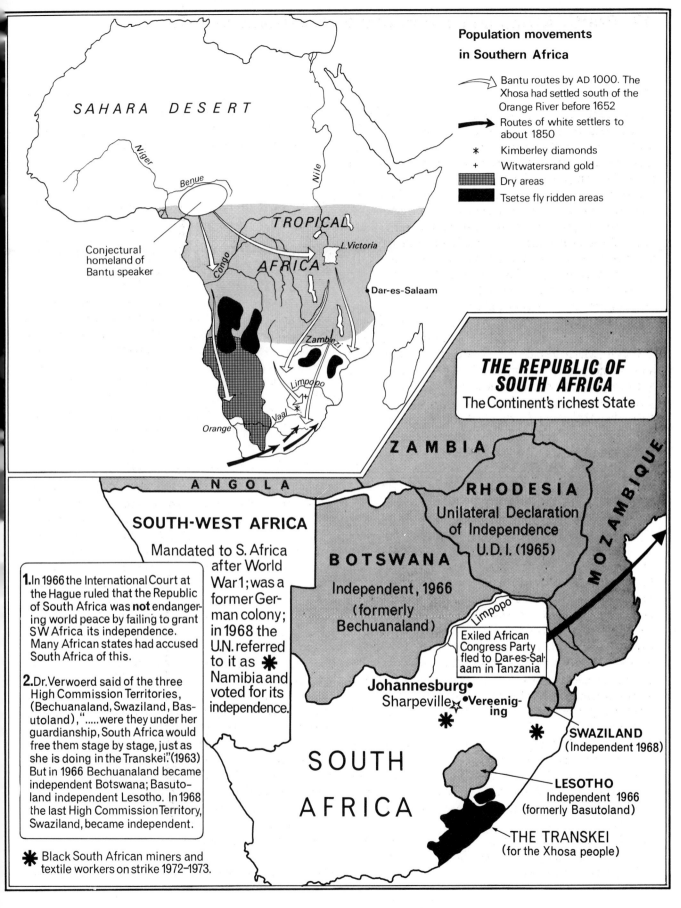

Population movements in Southern Africa

↪ Bantu routes by AD 1000. The Xhosa had settled south of the Orange River before 1652

→ Routes of white settlers to about 1850

∗ Kimberley diamonds

+ Witwatersrand gold

▦ Dry areas

■ Tsetse fly ridden areas

SAHARA DESERT

Niger

Benue

Conjectural homeland of Bantu speaker

Congo

TROPICAL

L.Victoria

AFRICA

• Dar-es-Salaam

Zambiezi

Limpopo

Vaal

Orange

∗

+

THE REPUBLIC OF SOUTH AFRICA
The Continent's richest State

ANGOLA

ZAMBIA

MOZAMBIQUE

RHODESIA
Unilateral Declaration of Independence
U.D.I. (1965)

SOUTH-WEST AFRICA

BOTSWANA
Independent, 1966
(formerly Bechuanaland)

Mandated to S. Africa after World War 1; was a former German colony; in 1968 the U.N. referred to it as ∗ Namibia and voted for its independence.

Limpopo

Exiled African Congress Party fled to Dar-es-Salaam in Tanzania

1. In 1966 the International Court at the Hague ruled that the Republic of South Africa was **not** endangering world peace by failing to grant SW Africa its independence. Many African states had accused South Africa of this.

2. Dr. Verwoerd said of the three High Commission Territories, (Bechuanaland, Swaziland, Basutoland), "..... were they under her guardianship, South Africa would free them stage by stage, just as she is doing in the Transkei". (1963) But in 1966 Bechuanaland became independent Botswana; Basutoland independent Lesotho. In 1968 the last High Commission Territory, Swaziland, became independent.

Johannesburg•
Sharpeville ☆ •Vereeniging
∗

∗ **SWAZILAND**
(Independent 1968)

SOUTH

AFRICA

LESOTHO
Independent 1966
(formerly Basutoland)

THE TRANSKEI
(for the Xhosa people)

✳ Black South African miners and textile workers on strike 1972–1973.

105

48: Latin America: economic problems

The people

South of the U.S.A. are the twenty-two nations which form Latin America. Most of the republics have a great deal in common. All were once the colonies of European powers such as Spain and Portugal. Most Latin Americans speak either Spanish or Portuguese and nearly all are Roman Catholics. Because of these common factors, there has been in the West a tendency to regard the different peoples and countries of Latin America as alike and to emphasize their similarities.

The problems

Certainly the republics share common problems, most of which arise out of their unique history. Firstly, their wealth has always hinged on the export of a few raw materials. Chile has depended on nitrates and copper; Venezuela on oil; Argentina (after the invention of the refrigerator ship) has relied on meat exports. And because the republics spent their profits from these exports on the purchase of *imported manufactured goods*, industrialization was slow to take root in Latin America. Secondly, the U.S.A. has traditionally been both the main customer and supplier of Latin America. Thirdly, large urban areas which have *not* depended on the growth of industries have developed; this is in complete contrast with the growth of large towns in most other parts of the world. Today Latin America is dotted with large cities such as Caracas, Santiago, Buenos Aires and Rio de Janeiro—all of which have a population of a million or more. And it is not just the upper and middle classes who direct Latin America's trade who live in these large cities; tens of thousands of very poor people are condemned to live in the 'shanty town' areas. This has caused one of the biggest problems facing Latin America: the tremendous gap between the incomes of the rich and the wages of the poor who since 1968 have suffered from a rise in the cost of living far more serious than that experienced in Western Europe. And as it is usually the poor families which have the most children they in turn cause Latin America's other great problem: a population explosion.

Examples

(i) Venezuela

More than 90% of Venezuela's wealth comes from her oil exports to the U.S.A.—yet only about 2% of her people work in the oilfields. 35% still scratch a living on the soil. They can only afford wooden or adobe houses. The floors are made of earth and few of the windows have any glass in them. These people are 'living on an unsatisfactory diet of maize, beans or roots and tubers'. In 1920 Venezuela's population was $2\frac{1}{2}$ million; in 1966 it topped $8\frac{1}{4}$ million—and half of these were young people under 18. Yet the oil profits have built motorways that would put British roads to shame.

(ii) Argentina

Argentina has different problems. During his dictatorship (1946–55), President Peron and his attractive and highly popular wife Eva tried to raise the standard of living of the poor city dwellers. Peron increased their wages and gave them holidays with pay; in return they formed trade unions and gave the President their enthusiastic support. But Peron failed to improve the lot of the peasants and, after the droughts and bad harvests of 1952, their discontent grew. Eva Peron died in the same year and soon the dictator's power began to wane and he finally gave up office in 1955.* Nevertheless, Argentina had become the world's biggest meat exporter and an important grain producer. Her population explosion is less marked than in the other republics and her educational standards are higher.

Solutions

Most of the other republics have even more difficult problems and many hope to find a solution in rapid industrialization and by increasing trade with one another. In this way they might reduce their dependence on the U.S.A. So they have formed a *Central American Market* and a *Latin American Free Trade Association*. Brazil led the way in new methods of industrial and agricultural production—but at no small cost to humanity. For example, in a determined attempt to reclaim land for arable crops and for growing sugar to make alcohol (Brazil's replacement fuel for petrol), she destroyed millions of acres of Amazonian rain forests. Thousands of Amerindians died in the process; and the rest of the world is in danger of losing its most important rain forest—a major source of oxygen.

*He returned to Argentine in 1973.

U. S. A.

THE U.S.A.
SELLS TO LATIN AMERICA:
⅓ OF HER CHEMICAL EXPORTS
⅓ OF HER CAR EXPORTS
¼ OF HER MACHINERY EXPORTS
¼ OF HER TEXTILE EXPORTS

MEXICO

BR. HONDURAS
Mexico City ★

CUBA
COFFEE 70%
DOMINICAN
REPUBLIC
HAITI
JAMAICA
BANANAS 60%
HONDURAS
NICARAGUA
GUATEMALA
EL SALVADOR
COSTA RICA
PANAMA
COFFEE 70%

OIL 92%

SURINAM (DUTCH)
FRENCH GUIANA
Caracas ★
VENEZUELA
GUYANA

Panama Canal

★ Bogota
COFFEE 80%
COLOMBIA
Quito ★
ECUADOR

COFFEE 60%

B R A Z I L
Suffers from
constant inflation

P E R U
★ Lima

BOLIVIA
★ La Paz

Brasilia
★

A new capital has
been built here at
fantastic expense

LATIN AMERICA
SELLS TO U.S.A.
ALMOST ALL OF HER COFFEE EXPTS.
½ OF HER OIL AND BANANA EXPORTS
¾ OF HER COPPER AND SUGAR EXPTS

TIN 90%
C H I L E
PARAGUAY
Asuncion ★

★ Rio de Janeiro

ARGENTINE
Buenos
Aires ★
WOOL 55%
★ Montevideo

Santiago ★
COPPER 70%

The richest &
most advanced
of any of the
Latin American
Republics

CUBA — Sugar not sold to
U.S.A. after 1961

★ — Important cities

OIL 92% — The dominant export—
note how most republics
depend on the export
of one commodity.

Trade in The Americas

Regmarad

49: Latin America: some political problems

Revolutions

Since 1945 most of the dictators and landowning classes have tended to lose power in Latin America. The governments which have replaced them are more concerned with improving the general standard of living—with varying degrees of success. For example, in Brazil, where the dictator Vargas ruled from 1930 to 1945, governments are now elected by the people 'with the exception of beggars, illiterates, soldiers and those whose political rights have been suspended'. Now Brazil claims to be the most highly industrialized republic in Latin America—although 60% of her people still work on the land and she still depends on her coffee exports.

Bolivia's recent history has been more violent. Life is very hard in this republic. Most of the Bolivian people are indigenous Indians living at great altitudes on the Andes Mountains. 5% of the population work in the tin mines and produce 90% of the exports; 85% work on the land and fail to produce adequate quantities of food! In 1952 a university professor called Paz Estenssoro led a revolution (the 179th revolt in Bolivia's history) and redistributed the landed estates to the peasants. But this meant that Bolivia degenerated into a land of inefficient smallholdings and that the food shortage worsened. Meanwhile the tin miners were even worse off when the world demand for tin slackened at the close of the Korean War (1953).

Since the mid-Fifties many Latin Americans have turned to the Communist Party for an answer to their economic and political problems. In Chile they scored their first democratic success by electing Salvador Allende's Marxist government in 1970; in Uruguay, Venezuela, Guatemala and Bolivia* they have joined guerilla bands operating from the security of the mountain and forest hide-outs. Best known are the Tupamaros who achieved international publicity by kidnapping Geoffrey Jackson, the British ambassador to Uruguay.

U.S. interest in Latin America

However, the United States is reluctant to see any expansion of communist power in Latin America. In

*It was in Bolivia that the famous communist guerrilla fighter, Ché Guevara, was killed (October 1967).

fact since 1823, when President Monroe formulated his famous doctrine, the U.S.A. has opposed any foreign power who has wished to meddle in Latin American affairs. But the U.S.A. rarely interferes herself in the affairs of the republics—unless it is Cuba or Panama where she claims special interests for historical reasons or in the case of governments whose actions 'endanger the security of the region'. The recent history of the Dominican Republic illustrates this. Here the Dominican dictator, Rafael Trujillo, was assassinated in 1961. None of the governments which followed him was efficient and civil war broke out in 1965. U.S. marines promptly landed in the island in an effort to restore order, but many Latin American countries—as well as the whole of the communist world—labelled this intervention an American act of aggression.

West Indies

Off the Latin American mainland are many islands which belong to the British Commonwealth. In 1958 most of these islands sought their independence by forming a 'Federation of the West Indies'. But this experiment in independence failed during the next four years, largely due to the unwillingness of Jamaica and Trinidad to help the smaller, less prosperous islands. Both Jamaica and Trinidad demanded and secured their independence within the Commonwealth in 1962. But the idea of federation did not die. Some of the islands—Barbados, Grenada, St. Vincent, St. Lucia, Dominica (not to be confused with the Dominican Republic), St. Kitts-Nevis, Antigua and Montserrat—planned to form a 'West Indies Federation'. Then Grenada withdrew from the scheme while the politicians in Barbados demanded complete independence for their island. They achieved this at midnight 29–30 November 1966 when Barbados became the 26th independent member of the British Commonwealth of Nations. Grenada (independent 1974) became the scene of another US intervention in 1983. Maurice Bishop, leader of the New Jewel Party, was murdered and a military council, aided by Cuban advisers, ran the island. Four thousand US troops landed on Grenada, overthrew the council, captured the Cubans and left a Caribbean security force in charge of the island.

Defence Aid from United States

Dictator Batista overthrown 1959 in Cuba (now pro-communist)

Dominican Republic, dictator Trujillo assassinated 1961

MEXICO

Pro-communist Arbenz régime fell in Guatemala in 1954

VENEZUELA

West Indies (Commonwealth)

Independent Guyana (Commonwealth)

Independent Surinam

Guiana (French)

COLOMBIA

Venezuela, dictator Jimenez overthrown 1958

ECUADOR

Peru, dictator Odria resigned 1956

PERU

BRAZIL

■ These Latin American states joined in a defence pact with the U.S.A. called the O.A.S., 1948 (Organisation of American States)

POLITICAL EVENTS IN LATIN AMERICA SINCE 1945

BOLIVIA

Brazil, dictator Vargas overthrown 1945

Allende's government overthrown in 1973

PARAGUAY

Paraguay, dictator Stroessner in power since 1954

CHILE

ARGENTINA

Uruguay, paralyzed by bank raids and bomb attacks since 1964

Argentina, dictator Peron fell from power, 1955, but returned in 1973 only to die the following year.

U.S.A.

U.S. intervention in Dominican Republic 1965

RAF Harrier jump-jets stationed here since 1975 to deter invasion from Guatemala.

POLITICAL UPHEAVAL IN THE CARIBBEAN

■ Members of Commonwealth

BAHAMAS

CUBA

Spread of communist influence

MEXICO

BELIZE (independent 1981)

JAMAICA independent 1962

D.R.

HAITI 'Baby Doc' overthrown 1986

PUERTO RICO (U.S.)

ANGUILLA BARBUDA
ST. KITTS ANTIGUA
NEVIS
MONTSERRAT
DOMINICA

West Indies Federation

?

ST. LUCIA
ST. VINCENT

BARBADOS

GUAT-EMALA HONDURAS

Caribbean Sea

GRENADA

Civil War in El Salvador 1980

Sandinista guerrillas took control in 1979

NICAR-AGUA

TOBAGO

TRINIDAD

independent 1962

PANAMA CANAL

COSTA RICA PANAMA

Canal Zone

VENEZUELA

GUYANA

SURINAM

In 1978 the U.S. Senate approved a treaty giving Panama control of and responsibility for the canal in the year 2000.

COLOMBIA

109

50: The developing realms: Canada, Australia and New Zealand

A realm

A realm accepts the Queen not only as symbolic Head of the Commonwealth but also as Head of State; whereas a Commonwealth republic accepts the Queen only as symbolic head of the Commonwealth.

World War II

These three realms, Britain's oldest Dominions, made an immense contribution to victory in World War II. They set up a Commonwealth Air Training scheme in December 1939; they sent their finest fighting men all over the world—a tremendous gesture when one remembers how relatively underpopulated these countries are even today. Among 'The Few' who fought and won the Battle of Britain (1940) were 103 New Zealanders, 90 Canadians and 21 Australians. Forty-eight of these Commonwealth fighter pilots died during the Battle. Hundreds of Commonwealth aircrew served in Bomber and Coastal Commands. The Commonwealth Navies served in all parts of the world—the New Zealand light cruiser HMNZS *Achilles* winning undying fame for the part she played in the defeat of the German surface raider *Graf Spee* during the Battle of the River Plate (December 1939). In the Middle East, the crack New Zealand Division was Rommel's implacable foe; in New Guinea the Australians bore the brunt of the jungle war; and after D-Day in 1944 the intensity of the Canadian effort may be judged from one German officer's ironical comment: 'The British are fighting to the last drop of Canadian blood'. Apart from the loss in lives the war had a great impact on these Commonwealth countries. The presence of Allied troops and the demand for foodstuffs and raw materials boosted their economies and also underlined the influence of the U.S.A.

American influence

At first Canada resisted this influence. One Canadian grievance was that, ever since she became a dominion in 1867, she had failed to incorporate Newfoundland within her frontiers. So she was highly irritated when, in 1940, Britain gave America some bases there. However, after the war the Royal Canadian Mounted Police uncovered a communist spy ring in Ottawa—it had been seeking atomic bomb secrets. This helped to bring home to Canadians that they had common defence and security interests with the U.S.A. Also Canada's own economic wealth became more apparent after the war. Oil strikes were made near Leduc; an atomic plant opened at Chalk River; the St. Lawrence Seaway was completed; and partly as a result of immigration, Canada's population increased. All of this convinced Canada that she would be able to direct her own future as an ally and partner of the U.S.A., a belief reinforced after Newfoundland became a Canadian province in 1949. Australia and New Zealand have also drawn closer to the U.S.A. since 1945, largely because of their common interests in the Pacific and South East Asia. The war against Japan had shown how dangerous the rise of an Asiatic aggressor could be—especially after Japanese 'planes had bombed Northern Australia. This partly explains why both Australia and New Zealand sent contingents to fight in Viet Nam; and why in 1951 they signed the A.N.Z.U.S. (Australia, New Zealand, United States) Pact which integrated their defence with the U.S.A.

Living standards

To many British people Australia and New Zealand have always seemed a haven, a refuge from the 'stop-go' economy of overcrowded Britain. There are plenty of attractive features in Australia: it's the 'land of opportunity', 'equality' and 'wide open spaces'. Many Britishers and Western Europeans have emigrated there since 1945 and have found that most Australians—and most immigrants—live in big cities. Even the educational opportunities are not always equal. Free enterprise is limited by powerful companies, many of them foreign, which control Australia's industry. For example, her motor industry is dominated by Volkswagen–Audi, Chrysler, Ford and General Motors-Holden. New Zealand is still largely dependent on the import of foreign manufactured goods and still sends half of her exports to Britain. She supported the 1950 Colombo Plan largely in the hope that a rise in the living standards of S.E. Asia would result in nearer and increasing markets for her dairy products. After 1975 Australia admitted Vietnamese boat people and became a truly multicultural country. But she still neglected the 'First Australians' who began to show their teeth in 1966. That year the Gurindji Tribe of aborigines caused some consternation in the Northern Territory by walking off the Wave Hill cattle station and beginning the first systematic native strike action!

The Developing Realms: CANADA, AUSTRALIA and NEW ZEALAND

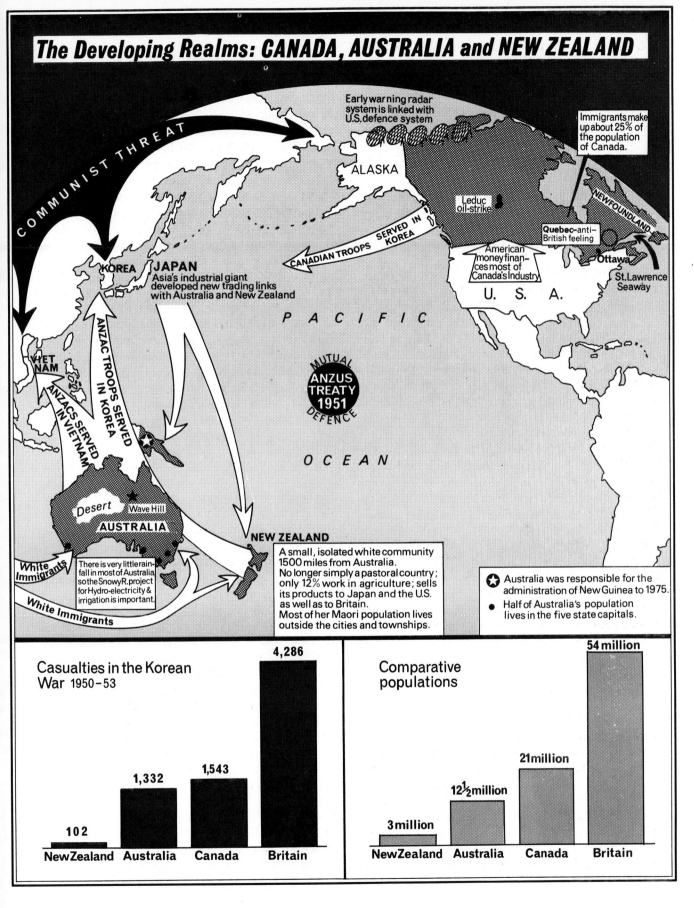

Early warning radar system is linked with U.S. defence system

COMMUNIST THREAT

ALASKA

Immigrants make up about 25% of the population of Canada.

Leduc oil-strike

NEWFOUNDLAND

CANADIAN TROOPS SERVED IN KOREA

Quebec-anti-British feeling

Ottawa

American money finances most of Canada's Industry

St.Lawrence Seaway

U. S. A.

KOREA

JAPAN
Asia's industrial giant developed new trading links with Australia and New Zealand

PACIFIC

ANZAC TROOPS SERVED IN KOREA

VIET NAM

ANZACS SERVED IN VIETNAM

MUTUAL ANZUS TREATY 1951 DEFENCE

OCEAN

Desert   Wave Hill
AUSTRALIA

NEW ZEALAND

White Immigrants

There is very little rainfall in most of Australia so the Snowy R. project for Hydro-electricity & irrigation is important.

White Immigrants

A small, isolated white community 1500 miles from Australia.
No longer simply a pastoral country; only 12% work in agriculture; sells its products to Japan and the U.S. as well as to Britain.
Most of her Maori population lives outside the cities and townships.

⭐ Australia was responsible for the administration of New Guinea to 1975.

● Half of Australia's population lives in the five state capitals.

Casualties in the Korean War 1950–53

- New Zealand: 102
- Australia: 1,332
- Canada: 1,543
- Britain: 4,286

Comparative populations

- New Zealand: 3 million
- Australia: 12½ million
- Canada: 21 million
- Britain: 54 million

111

The 'third force'

At the end of World War II Russia and America were the two greatest powers on earth. Their wealth, resources and military might made them 'superpowers'. Unfortunately they were diametrically opposed in their political views and offered to the rest of the world a future based either on Russian communism or American capitalism. Such a prospect made little appeal to the first of the 'new nations' who emerged after the war and it was natural that these should seek a third path towards peace and prosperity in the divided world. They tried to devise a 'third force'—a group of nations uncommitted either to the Russians or the Americans. The first inkling of this 'third force' had come in 1945 when the Arab League was formed. The Arabs united because of their common religion and culture, because they disliked the growing power of the Jews in Palestine (Israel) and because both Britain and the superpowers coveted the precious oil reserves of the Middle East. Then from India came the idea that neutral countries had a new and vital role to play in world affairs. Men such as Pandit Nehru saw India as the great mediator in disputes between communist and non-communist countries. And India did in fact play such a role during the war in Korea (1950–53).

Bandung

Just before this war Sukarno had emerged as the 'strong man' in Indonesia, whilst in 1954 Colonel Nasser had seized power in Egypt. Thus by 1955 there were three important 'neutral' centres of power—geographically they stretched across the world from the Mediterranean to the Pacific, from Egypt, through India to Indonesia. These three, together with delegates from 26 other nations, met at the historic Bandung Conference in 1955. Here they uttered impassioned pleas for the abolition of nuclear weapons, accused the communists of committing 'imperialist' crimes and bitterly attacked the ambitions of the Jews in Israel. The Conference ended, however, with a statement of intent; in Nehru's words the Afro-Asian countries 'meant no ill to anybody'.

Disintegration

Unfortunately, the hope that Bandung might lead to a third 'neutral' force in the world evaporated in the next eleven years. Firstly, neither the western nor the communist camps maintained their unity and solidarity: in the West N.A.T.O. suffered with the withdrawal of France; in the East communism polarized into two distinct groupings—Russian communism* and Chinese communism. Secondly, despite the increasing numbers of independent states, Afro-Asian unity disappeared. This was partly due to their own national selfishness and jealousies; and partly to the policies of the British and United States governments. Egypt's attempt, for example, to form a United Arab Republic with Syria and the Yemen was a total failure; and now Egypt, still retaining the title of the U.A.R., enjoys the unenviable distinction of having killed Yemeni tribesmen with Russian napalm. India soon betrayed her pacifism: Nehru ejected the Portuguese from Goa in 1961 while his successor, Shastri, went to war with Pakistan over Kashmir in 1965. This led to an event which amazed the world: in 1966 Soviet Russia's Mr. Kosygin mediated between the two warring nations at the famous Tashkent Conference. Meanwhile, in S.E. Asia Indonesia had fought Malaysia in the 'confrontation' which ended in 1966.

Neutralism

So the 'third force' had barely materialized by the end of 1967. But this does not mean that the new nations are under the sway of the superpowers. Some have chosen to combine features of both systems in order to construct novel forms of society: in Tanzania Julius Nyerere has begun to build his 'egalitarian society'. Basing his ideas on the teachings of East and West he is trying to create an African socialism which encourages private enterprise. And it is important to remember that several countries of long standing have maintained a fairly neutral position since 1945. Most famous are Sweden and Switzerland while Finland, Yugoslavia and Austria try to follow independent policies of their own.

* Because the Czech people and their leaders tried to throw off rigid communist control, the Russians sent Warsaw Pact troops to occupy Czechoslovakia in 1968.

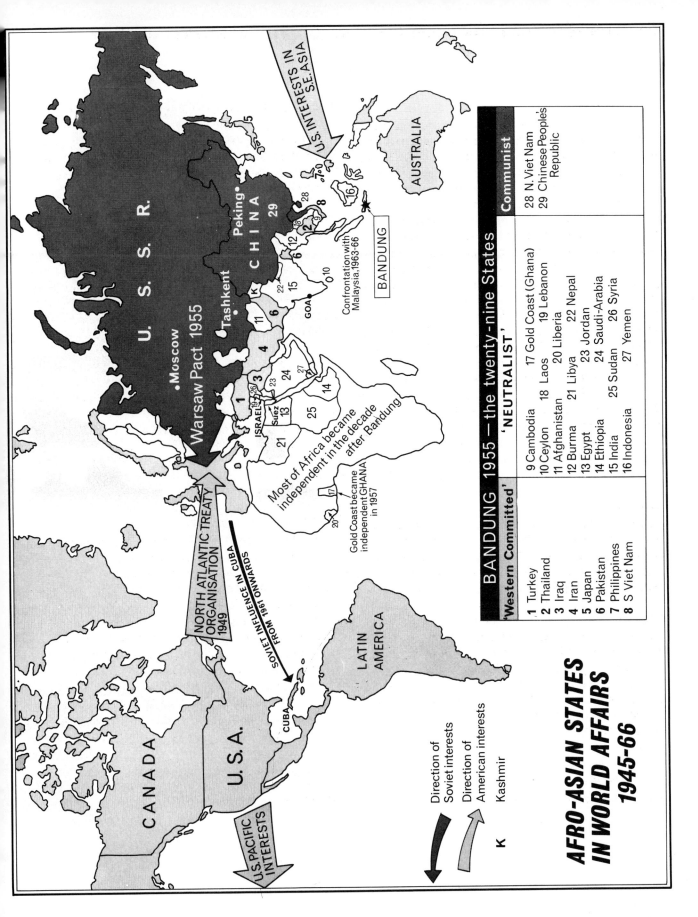

AFRO-ASIAN STATES IN WORLD AFFAIRS 1945-66

CANADA

U.S.A.

CUBA

LATIN AMERICA

U.S. PACIFIC INTERESTS

Direction of Soviet interests

Direction of American interests

K Kashmir

U. S. S. R.

•Moscow

Warsaw Pact 1955

•Tashkent

Peking•

CHINA

AUSTRALIA

U.S. INTERESTS IN S.E. ASIA

NORTH ATLANTIC TREATY ORGANISATION 1949

SOVIET INFLUENCE IN CUBA FROM 1961 ONWARDS

ISRAEL

Suez

GOA

BANDUNG

Confrontation with Malaysia, 1963-66

Most of Africa became independent in the decade after Bandung

Gold Coast became independent GHANA in 1957

BANDUNG 1955 – the twenty-nine States

'Western Committed'	'NEUTRALIST'		Communist
1 Turkey	9 Cambodia	17 Gold Coast (Ghana)	28 N. Viet Nam
2 Thailand	10 Ceylon	18 Laos	19 Lebanon	29 Chinese Peoples' Republic
3 Iraq	11 Afghanistan	20 Liberia	
4 Iran	12 Burma	21 Libya	22 Nepal	
5 Japan	13 Egypt	23 Jordan	
6 Pakistan	14 Ethiopia	24 Saudi-Arabia	
7 Philippines	15 India	25 Sudan	26 Syria	
8 S Viet Nam	16 Indonesia	27 Yemen	

113

52: Oil and Arab Nationalism: to the outbreak of the 1973 Arab-Israeli War

The oil industry

Oil is one of the world's indispensable commodities; a quarter of the world's supplies comes from the Middle East. To this part of the world, oil men have brought their money and their expertise; they have accelerated progress in the Arab lands and this in turn has fostered demands for national independence. As the original demand for oil sprang from Europe and the United States, it is mainly money from these areas which finances the expensive technology behind the oil industry. First in the field was the British Anglo-Iranian Oil Company which, in 1954, was replaced by an international 'consortium' of British, French, Dutch and American companies. These companies are in the main on good terms with the Arab governments. They are generous employers. They have helped to raise living standards. Despite this, the Arabs are jealous of the foreigners on whom their wealth depends; and yet at the same time they realize that they cannot finance the oil wells, refineries and tanker fleets involved in the biggest international industry in the world *unless* they have some outside assistance.

Abadan Crisis

This was well illustrated when in 1951 the aged but determined Dr. Mussadiq of Iran (Persia) nationalized the Anglo-Iranian Oil Company and evicted the British from the huge Abadan refineries. Britain appealed to the International Court of Justice which ruled that it could do nothing as nationalization was an internal matter, of concern only to the government of Iran. Frustrated, the oil companies developed oil reserves elsewhere —notably in Kuwait. Soon Mussadiq's actions brought Iran to the edge of bankruptcy for the Persians had lost all means of marketing the oil they refined. In 1953 Mussadiq fell from power and the international consortium took over the affairs of the Anglo–Iranian Oil Company.

Political upheaval

Iran's experience was a warning to other Arab countries, who are now unlikely to imitate Dr. Mussadiq. But they found plenty of other sources of national unrest and the ten years which followed the 1956 Suez fiasco saw no end to the confusion and strife in the Middle East. Fearing Soviet intervention in the Middle East, President Eisenhower offered aid to all Arab states who wished to combat the menace of communism. But the Arabs were reluctant to accept this 'Eisenhower doctrine' and so in 1957 the U.S. 6th Fleet appeared off the coast of Lebanon. Jet fighters screamed over the beaches in a show of American might; Lebanon asked for aid and Jordan soon followed suit. Next year, President Nasser formed his ill-fated United Arab Republic; Jordan and Iraq formed the Arab Federation. These moves failed to lead to stability and the period 1958–1963 was one of revolution in the Middle East. Governments were overthrown in the Lebanon and Iraq (1958), the Yemen (1962) and in Syria and Iraq again (1963). To add to this bewildering situation, the Arab states began to take sides in the Yemen Civil War, and the fighting spilled over into the Federation of South Arabia. Aden joined the Federation in 1963 and British troops stationed there fought Arab nationalists operating in the Radfan Mountains as well as inside the British base itself. By the end of 1966 it was clear that the Arab peoples had suffered from this wasteful concentration on national jealousies and constant warfare. The waste of money, the loss of life and a growing shortage of food was one price to pay. Another was the unexpected defeat suffered by the armed forces of Egypt, Syria and Jordan at the hands of the Israelis in the remarkable 'Six Days War' of June 1967.

A danger to world peace

During this lightning war, Israeli troops captured the Holy City of Jerusalem together with all Egyptian territory as far as the east bank of the Suez Canal. Their continued occupation of Jerusalem infuriated the Jordanians; President Nasser tried to use threats to persuade the Israelis to leave Egypt. But the Arab states were powerless to drive out the Israelis. Russia quickly replaced the Egyptian tanks and aircraft lost in the June fighting; America supplied Israel with the latest 'Phantom' jets. But neither superpower managed to control the actions of its protégé; the frontiers of Israel became the scene of continued artillery duels and guerrilla strikes until, in October 1973, the Arab states launched a concerted attack upon Israeli-occupied territories.

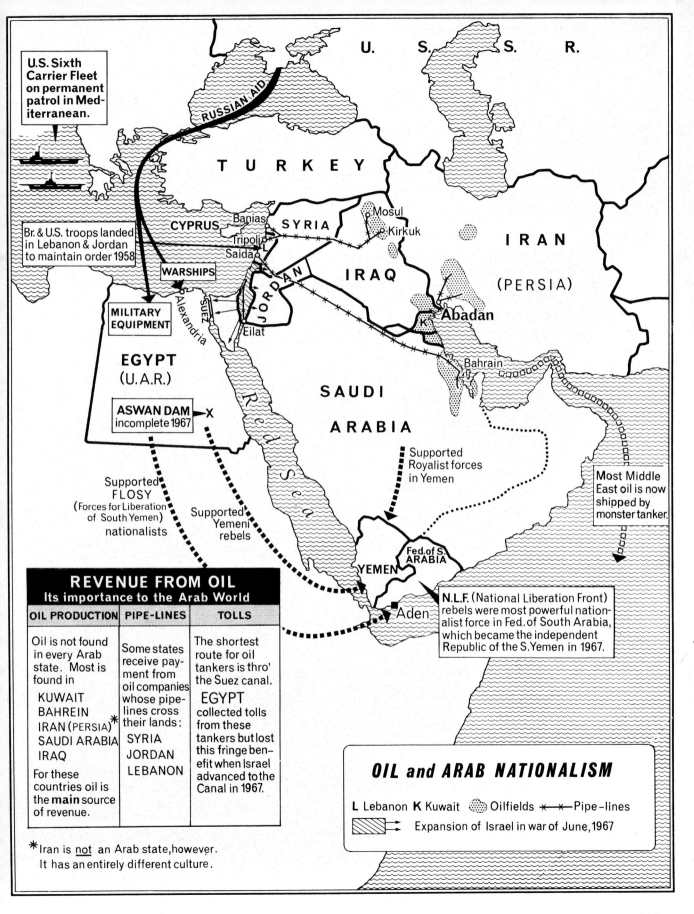

U.S. Sixth Carrier Fleet on permanent patrol in Mediterranean.

U. S. S. R.

RUSSIAN AID

TURKEY

Br. & U.S. troops landed in Lebanon & Jordan to maintain order 1958

WARSHIPS

MILITARY EQUIPMENT

CYPRUS

Banias
Tripoli
Saida
L

SYRIA

Mosul
Kirkuk

IRAQ

IRAN
(PERSIA)

K Abadan

JORDAN

SUEZ
Alexandria
Eilat

Bahrain

EGYPT
(U.A.R.)

ASWAN DAM incomplete 1967 —X

Red Sea

SAUDI

ARABIA

Supported Royalist forces in Yemen

Most Middle East oil is now shipped by monster tanker.

Supported **FLOSY** (Forces for Liberation of South Yemen) nationalists

Supported Yemeni rebels

Fed. of S. ARABIA

YEMEN

Aden

N.L.F. (National Liberation Front) rebels were most powerful nationalist force in Fed. of South Arabia, which became the independent Republic of the S.Yemen in 1967.

REVENUE FROM OIL
Its importance to the Arab World

OIL PRODUCTION	PIPE-LINES	TOLLS
Oil is not found in every Arab state. Most is found in **KUWAIT BAHREIN IRAN** (PERSIA)* **SAUDI ARABIA IRAQ** For these countries oil is the **main** source of revenue.	Some states receive payment from oil companies whose pipelines cross their lands: **SYRIA JORDAN LEBANON**	The shortest route for oil tankers is thro' the Suez canal. **EGYPT** collected tolls from these tankers but lost this fringe benefit when Israel advanced to the Canal in 1967.

* Iran is **not** an Arab state, however. It has an entirely different culture.

OIL and ARAB NATIONALISM

L Lebanon **K** Kuwait Oilfields ✕—✕ Pipe-lines

 ➝ Expansion of Israel in war of June, 1967

Part 5 – Book List

36. *Cold War*	D. Heater	OUP	
37. *United Nations*	C. Boyd	Pelican	
Agony of the Congo	R. Calder	Gollancz	
United Nations	C. Coyle	Mentor	
38. *United Nations*	C. Coyle	Mentor	pp 19–20
39. *United Nations*	C. Coyle	Mentor	pp 21–30
40. *United Nations*	C. Coyle	Mentor	pp 72–74
41. *African Nationalism*	N. Sithole	Oxford	
42. *Rise of Modern Asia*	I. Thompson	Murray	
This Modern World	D. Wood	Heinemann	pp 131–140; 247–261
43. *This Modern World*	D. Wood	Heinemann	pp 261–275
44. *This Modern World*	D. Wood	Heinemann	pp 275–293
45. *Rise of Modern Asia*	I. Thompson	Murray	
46. *Battle of Dien Bien Phu*	J. Roy	Faber	
47. *Black and White in South Africa*	G. H. Le May	MacDonald	
A Plague of Europeans	David Killingray	Penguin	
	(Topics in History)		
48. *History of Latin America*	G. Pendle	Pelican	
49. *Jamaica – Search for an identity*	K. Norris	OUP	
50. *History of New Zealand*	K. Sinclair	Penguin	
51. *India*	T. Zinkin	OUP	
52. *Suez – Ten Years After*		BBC Publication	

PART 6

The dangerous years
From 1945 to the end of American
involvement in Viet Nam,
January 1973

During these twenty-eight years there was a great deal of friction between the two superpowers, Russia and the United States. Their uneasy coexistence was complicated by the rise of a much more fanatical brand of communism inside the Chinese People's Republic. Distrust and rivalry—these were the characteristics of these dangerous years. The Communists were dedicated to the extension of their principles and to the overthrow of western capitalism. In the West, the democracies were determined to defend their principles and to resist any communist attempt to encroach upon their territories and their peoples. This, in the words of President Kennedy, was the 'great issue' which divided the modern world.

Divided Berlin and divided Germany were examples of this great issue. Others such as Korea and Viet Nam led to years of fighting and literally millions of casualties. The great issue drew an Iron Curtain across Europe and, in the atomic age, it left mankind with the knowledge that each and every one of these conflicts has held, or still holds, the danger of escalation: that from small beginnings a war could grow until, in the jargon of the military strategist, there would occur a 'nuclear exchange'.

At least the War in Viet Nam ended without a nuclear exchange. During 1972 American and North Vietnamese representatives finally hit on a solution which enabled the United States to withdraw from the conflict without too much loss of face. But with the Americans out of the way (January 1973), there was little to stop the North Vietnamese from overrunning the south. By April 1975 their tanks and infantry were in Saigon—which they promptly renamed Ho Chi Minh City. US ships and aircraft evacuated all American citizens who had stayed on in the south, together with numbers of Vietnamese children, an event which President Ford described as closing 'a chapter in the American experience'.

53: The problem of preserving world peace

The two armed camps

In 1945, for the first time in history, scientists had made weapons capable of mass destruction; now any war involving these weapons just had to be avoided. Yet since the atomic bombs exploded over Hiroshima and Nagasaki there have been many dangerous moments in world history. Most have arisen out of the division of the world into communist and non-communist blocs. Within these are several alliance systems but the two most important are the North Atlantic Treaty Organisation (N.A.T.O.) formed in 1949 and the Warsaw Pact, formed in 1955. Of course, alliances do not of themselves cause war; the danger lies in the possible failure to *resolve peacefully* the various disputes between the two armed camps. So since 1945 various devices have been used to settle international disputes: the United Nations; summit meetings; and 'brinkmanship'.

U.N. and the Congo

U.N.O. was the most obvious means of guaranteeing world peace in 1945. But the U.N. did not represent the entire world; Communist China was debarred from membership until as late as 1971. Nor could the U.N. settle disputes in those parts of the world which were already the direct concern of the superpowers—for example, partitioned Germany and partitioned Viet Nam. These divided states were not even members of the U.N.* Therefore the U.N. tended to involve itself in those trouble-spots where the superpowers were not directly concerned. One example of this was the 1956 Suez Crisis; another was the Congo problem 1960–64. Here, where the Belgian government had ruled for fifty years, rebellion broke out in 1959. Almost immediately the Belgians offered the Congolese their independence, and in June 1960 they left the young republic to be governed by President Kasavubu. Within a month his army had mutinied, and when the Belgians returned to protect civilian families and property he appealed to the U.N. for help. In the midst of this chaos, Tshombe, governor of Katanga Province, declared that Katanga was independent and that he was its new head

* When hostilities officially ceased (January 1973) neither North nor South Viet Nam were U.N. members; but in September 1973 both East and West Germany joined the U.N.

of state. Civil war followed and in 1961 the U.N. intervened; during September it was at war with Tshombe's mercenary soldiers in Katanga. In an attempt to arrange a cease-fire with Tshombe, the U.N. Secretary-General flew out to Africa, but his plane crashed at Ndola and he was killed. Thus Dag Hammarskjold died in the cause of world peace. Eventually the U.N. troops pulled out of the Congo in 1964 having failed to restore complete law and order to this troubled region. Nevertheless they had, by their very presence, denied both superpowers the chance of exploiting the Congo crisis.

Summit meetings

Summit meetings, usually between American and Russian leaders, are held to discuss some major issue—frequently a longstanding one such as disarmament or the German problem. There have been memorable summits, such as when the Russians turned down Eisenhower's 'open skies policy' (unrestricted reconnaissance flights over one another's territories) at the 1955 Geneva Summit. Then five years later the Paris Summit was wrecked when Khrushchev told a very embarrassed Eisenhower that a U.S. spy-plane (Gary Power's famous U-2) had been shot down by a Russian guided missile over the middle of the U.S.S.R. And at the 1961 Vienna Summit, Kennedy and Khrushchev failed to agree over the East German refugee problem which the Russians promptly settled by ordering the construction of the Berlin Wall.

Brinkmanship

'Brinkmanship' is the most dangerous method of resolving a crisis. Here one superpower will push its demands to the brink of war and then either retreat from the very edge of disaster or trust that the other side will have the good sense to back down. Such a 'war of nerves' was played by Kennedy and Khrushchev in the 1962 Cuban nuclear missile crisis and, eleven years later, by Nixon and Brezhnev in 'the week in which the world was taken close to the nuclear brink'** during the fourth Arab-Israeli War.

** The Times 27 October 1973

PEACE-KEEPING: Some problems, 1945-62

CANADA

U.S.A.

North Pole

Hiroshima
Nagasaki   1945

U.S.S.R.

CHINA

New York
H.Q. of United
Nations

CUBA
1962

U.2 incident
1960

Peshawar

PAKISTAN
INDIA

EASTERN
EUROPE

Paris

Geneva
Vienna

Warsaw Pact countries
N.A.T.O. countries
□ Vienna   Summit meeting

CONGO
U.N. OPERATIONS, 1960-64

SUDAN

ETHIOPIA

CENTRAL AFRICAN
REPUBLIC

Paulis

GABON

REPUBLIC OF THE CONGO

CONGOLESE
Stanleyville

REPUBLIC

RWANDA

KENYA

BURUNDI

CONGO

Leopoldville

TANZANIA

KATANGA
Elizabethville

Portuguese
ANGOLA

Ndola
Copper belt

ZAMBIA

MALAWI

MOZAMBIQUE

U.N. FORCES came from Eire;
Malaya; Nigeria; Liberia;
Sudan; Tunisia; Ethiopia;
Morocco; India; Switzerland;
Canada; Pakistan.
Belgian troops helped to crush
rebellions in Stanleyville and
Paulis after U.N. withdrew in 1964.

Regmarad

54: Flashpoint: Germany!

The root of the cold war in Europe

The German problem is the root of the cold war in Europe. During 1945 Stalin had absorbed the eastern areas of Germany within the Polish and Russian frontiers. The rest of Germany was then divided into four occupation zones as was the capital, Berlin. But then no-one could agree on what to do with defeated Germany. The western allies wanted to 'denazify' the Germans and then allow them to hold free elections so that a new, united, peace-loving Germany could take its place in post-war Europe. But the Russians had very recent, bitter memories of German cruelty. They were not prepared to tolerate the rise of another united Germany unless it was under communist rule. Many times since 1945 the allies have tried to make the Russians change their minds, but as Khrushchev so plainly said in 1955: 'We shall never, never, never change our minds about the German problem. We shall never change our policy'.

The Berlin Airlift

In 1945 the Germans were in a pitiable state. They had no government, hardly any jobs or homes; their menfolk languished in P.O.W. camps; refugees flooded in from the east to escape the avenging Red Army. Money was virtually useless. On the Black Market (where one could illegally obtain rationed goods in short supply) cigarettes were the best currency. In the western zones, the allies did send in some supplies; but in the east the Russians were demanding 10,000 million dollars' worth of reparations to help *their* starving families. Eventually the western allies welded their three zones into a single economic unit during 1948—and Stalin replied by forbidding all trade between his zone and the west. He barred all road and rail links with Berlin. Doubtless he was trying to starve the Berliners into joining the Soviet sector, but although all the roads and railway routes were blocked by the Russians, roaring along the three air corridors came hundreds of Allied planes bringing food, clothing and even coal to the beleagured West Berliners. This 'Berlin Airlift' was kept up throughout the winter of 1948–49 until Stalin conceded defeat and lifted the blockade in May 1949. Within a few days of this the allies announced that their three zones would now form the Federal German Republic (West Germany); Stalin's retort was to proclaim the German Democratic Republic (East Germany).

Berlin Crises

Since then, in a divided Germany, Berlin has seen three crises which have brought the world close to war. The first was in 1956 when the West Berliners were enraged with Russian efforts to stamp out the Hungarian Uprising in Budapest—and equally infuriated with the Anglo-French attack on Suez. They stormed through the streets, wrecked British and French cars and then tried to invade the Russian sector in order to burn down the Soviet embassy. Fortunately, they were turned back at the Brandenburg Gate. Then in 1958 Khrushchev threatened to sign a *separate* peace treaty with East Germany. This would have given the East Germans control over their own borders and air space, a situation which the western allies would refuse to accept. For two years neither side would give way until Khrushchev withdrew his threats at the time of the U-2 crisis in 1960. The next year saw the third Berlin crisis when the communists built a wall across Berlin to prevent East German refugees from escaping to the west. At once a tough U.S. battle-group raced to Berlin and a crisis ensued when a 'Vopo' (East German policeman) tried to stop an allied official from entering the Russian sector. Tension reached its height when, at the Friedrichstrasse 'Checkpoint Charlie' Russian and American tanks trained their guns on one another. Fortunately, the crisis passed without further incident. During 1963 President Kennedy praised the West Berliners: 'All free men wherever they may be are citizens of Berlin and thus I take pride in saying: Ich bin ein Berliner'.

Ostpolitik

Ten years later, the German problem remained unsolved. By then both East and West Germany were prosperous countries, drawing closer together only as far as their commercial and cultural interests were concerned. This was due largely to Chancellor Willy Brandt's gestures of friendship towards East Germany—referred to as his *Ostpolitik*—and which led to the *Treaty on the Bases of Relations* (1973). But Chancellor Brandt emphasized that this meant co-operation *not* re-unification: 'At the moment nothing indicates that the fragmented German state could be restored in its old form . . .'

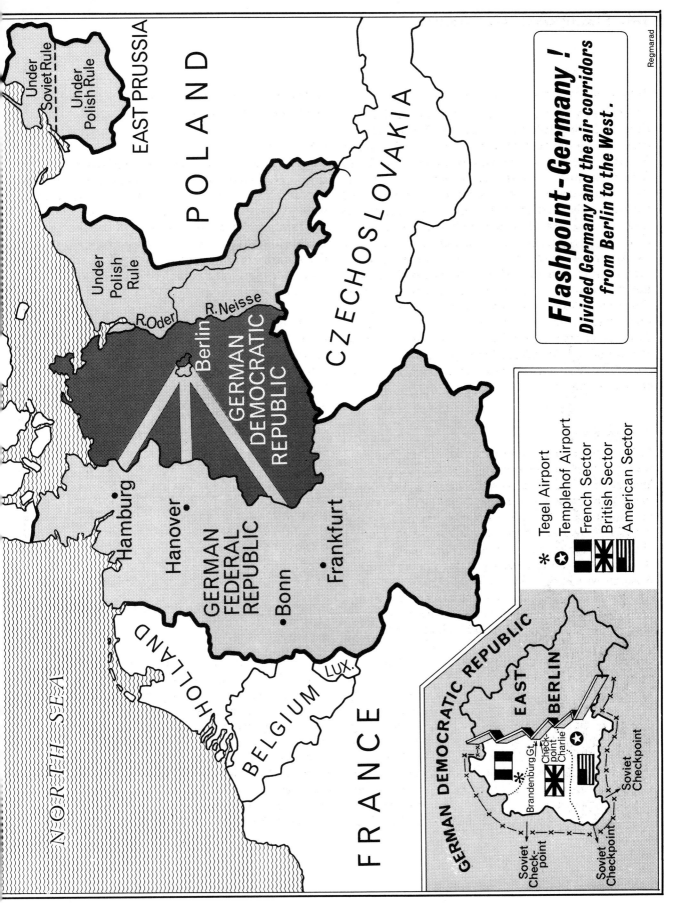

Flashpoint - Germany !
Divided Germany and the air corridors from Berlin to the West.

Regmarad

UNDER Soviet Rule

Under Polish Rule

EAST PRUSSIA

P O L A N D

Under Polish Rule

C Z E C H O S L O V A K I A

R. Oder

R. Neisse

Berlin

GERMAN DEMOCRATIC REPUBLIC

NORTH SEA

Hamburg

Hanover

GERMAN FEDERAL REPUBLIC

Bonn

Frankfurt

HOLLAND

BELGIUM

LUX.

F R A N C E

* Tegel Airport
✪ Templehof Airport
French Sector
British Sector
American Sector

GERMAN DEMOCRATIC REPUBLIC

EAST BERLIN

Brandenburg Gt.

Check-point Charlie

Soviet Check-point

Soviet Checkpoint

Soviet Checkpoint

55: Flashpoint—Korea! The war in Korea 1950–1953

Korea 1910–1949

From 1910 onwards Korea had been a Japanese colony until, in the last few hours of World War II, it was invaded by Russian troops. After the Japanese surrender in August 1945 American troops also arrived and Korea was split into two occupation zones. During 1947 the U.N. tried to hold free elections so that the Korean people could choose their own form of government in a united republic but the Russians would not let the U.N. election teams enter their zone. So separate elections were held in the south with the result that the 'Republic of Korea' was set up in 1948. In the north the communists created their 'Korean Peoples' Republic'. The frontier between them was the 38th Parallel. By the end of 1948 the Russians had evacuated their zone; during 1949 the Americans left the south.

North Korea invades

This left the two republics, both of whom claimed the whole of Korea, facing each other. Almost immediately border incidents occurred but a year was to pass before the U.N. received news that was destined to involve them in war. On 25 June 1950 North Korean soldiers, supported by Russian-built T-34 tanks and aircraft, invaded South Korea. On 26 June the U.N. Security Council ordered the North Koreans to withdraw—significantly the Russian delegate was absent from this session and thus unable to veto these instructions. The next day the Council asked member states of the U.N. to send aid to South Korea—the Russian delegate was still absent.

U.N. v. China

So, under the banner of the United Nations, troops from sixteen countries came to South Korea—and in the nick of time for the communists were already threatening Pusan! Most of the U.N. soldiers were American; the U.N. commander was the famous U.S. General MacArthur. He decided to strike the communists in the rear and ordered the successful Inchon landings in September. Soon the U.N. troops had captured Seoul amidst hideous slaughter and they reached the 38th Parallel. Their task, it seemed, was accomplished. The communists had been contained. But the Americans were determined to destroy the aggressor state; only with the destruction of North Korea, they

argued, could the people of Korea be united under a single government. The General Assembly of the U.N. gave its blessing and soon, despite warnings from Communist China, the Americans were forging towards the Yalu River—some actually reached it during November 1950. Then came the catastrophe. Thousands of Chinese 'volunteers' surged between the U.N. armies who were forced to retreat to the south. By the spring of 1951 it seemed that the communists would win the war in Korea, but U.N. counter-attacks drove the Chinese back to a position roughly corresponding with the 38th Parallel.

The limited war

Now both sides began peace talks at Panmunjom whilst the armies settled down to a static, 'limited' war. While the peace delegates hurled charges of 'germ-warfare' and counter-charges of 'brain-washing' at one another the killing went on in a pointless but costly fashion. Chinese infantry dug deep into the Korean hillsides, only to emerge in fanatical infantry charges reminiscent of World War I. Over them screamed American 'Shooting Star' jets, depositing their tankloads of napalm on the hillsides. High above the battlefields droned the B.29 bombers, en route to North Korean reservoirs and hydro-electric plants. Near their own border Chinese pilots flying MiG-15 jets fought the American F-86 Sabres. Eventually on 17 July 1953 both sides agreed to an armistice. They also agreed to settle the Korean problem within the next few months.

The long armistice

By 1986 the Korean problem remained unsolved and the armistice—one of the longest in modern history—was still in force. British veterans revisiting the battlefields in 1981 saw plenty of evidence of the tension that still existed in this divided peninsula. Thousands of U.S. troops were on stand-by alert and Republic of Korea soldiers constantly patrolled the D.M.Z. (Demilitarized Zone) where the 'static war' had once been fought. In 1978 they discovered that the North Koreans were burrowing *under* the D.M.Z. in order to infiltrate the south. So the South Koreans built their own tunnels to intercept the communists and prevent them from making any more headway underground!

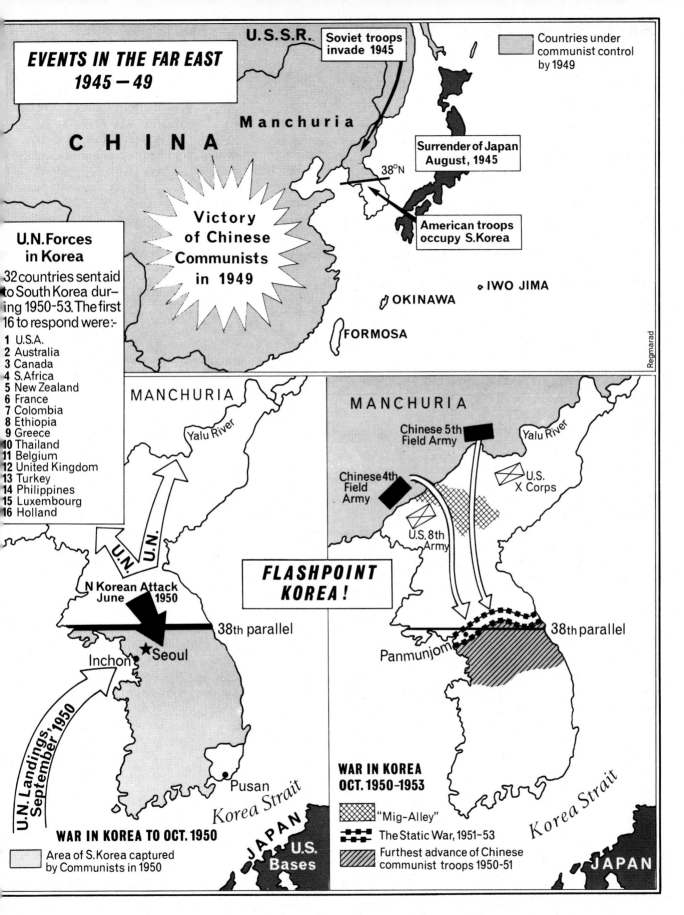

EVENTS IN THE FAR EAST 1945 – 49

U.S.S.R.

Soviet troops invade 1945

Countries under communist control by 1949

M a n c h u r i a

C H I N A

Surrender of Japan August, 1945

38°N

American troops occupy S.Korea

Victory of Chinese Communists in 1949

⚬ IWO JIMA

⌀ OKINAWA

FORMOSA

Regmarad

U.N. Forces in Korea

32 countries sent aid to South Korea during 1950-53. The first 16 to respond were:-

1 U.S.A.
2 Australia
3 Canada
4 S.Africa
5 New Zealand
6 France
7 Colombia
8 Ethiopia
9 Greece
10 Thailand
11 Belgium
12 United Kingdom
13 Turkey
14 Philippines
15 Luxembourg
16 Holland

MANCHURIA

Yalu River

U.N. U.N.

N Korean Attack June 1950

FLASHPOINT KOREA!

38th parallel

★Seoul

Inchon

U.N. Landings September 1950

Pusan

Korea Strait

JAPAN U.S. Bases

WAR IN KOREA TO OCT. 1950

Area of S.Korea captured by Communists in 1950

MANCHURIA

Chinese 5th Field Army

Yalu River

Chinese 4th Field Army

U.S. X Corps

U.S. 8th Army

38th parallel

Panmunjom

WAR IN KOREA OCT. 1950–1953

"Mig-Alley"

The Static War, 1951–53

Furthest advance of Chinese communist troops 1950-51

Korea Strait

JAPAN

Overthrow of Batista

Freed from Spanish rule after the Spanish-American War of 1898, the island of Cuba became dominated by U.S. financial and military interests. Sugar was its main export; the U.S.A. its main buyer. U.S. Marines were permanently stationed at their base at Guantanamo. Cubans who demanded complete independence were treated as rebels; and the U.S.A. accepted any Cuban government *as long as it supported American interests*. One such government was led by ex-army Sgt. Batista who organised a reign of terror in Cuba between 1952 and 1958. He exiled or executed his enemies; he misused dollar aid from the U.S.; he stole government funds. Under Batista Cuba became bankrupt. Many young Cubans fought a guerrilla war in the mountains against him and, led by Fidel Castro (born 1927), overthrew him in 1959. Thousands of Batista's followers fled to the U.S.A. and the Cuban people welcomed Castro as their liberator.

Castro's problems

Castro formed his new Cuban government in 1959; his first task was to put his bankrupt house in order. But no-one would lend him any money! The U.S.A. and the International Monetary Fund refused him. So Castro approached the communist countries and began to nationalize American-owned industries. These activities smacked of communism to President Eisenhower and the thought of a communist state 90 miles from the U.S. mainland was intolerable. Secretly he allowed Batista supporters to train for an invasion of Cuba, while he applied pressure on Castro by refusing to buy Cuban sugar in 1960. But then the Russians said they would buy it instead. By the end of the year the Russians had loaned Cuba money and technicians.

The missiles

Kennedy became President of the U.S.A. in 1961. He inherited Eisenhower's scheme to invade Cuba and in April 1961 he authorised the attack. 1,500 Cubans came ashore at the Bay of Pigs, supported by *Douglas Invader* bombers. Castro's jets shot them out of the air and the invasion force surrendered after three days. After the fiasco of the Bay of Pigs, Castro understandably sought aid from Russia. In August 1962, 30 Russian ships arrived with mysterious cargoes. Now Kennedy ordered constant air surveillance and his U-2s brought back air photographs which showed that Castro was armed with I.R.B.M.s—Intermediate Range Ballistic Missiles. *If* they had nuclear warheads, every U.S. city within the missile range of 2,500 miles was in danger of atomic attack. On 22 October 1962 Kennedy ordered a *quarantine* or blockade of Cuba:

> This secret, swift and extraordinary build-up of communist missiles in an area well known to have a special and historical relationship to the United States... is a deliberately provocative change in the status quo which cannot be accepted by this country... To halt this offensive build-up a strict quarantine on all offensive military equipment under shipment of Cuba is being initiated.

Chairman Khrushchev of the U.S.S.R. protested:

> Your rockets are in Turkey. You are worried by Cuba. You say that it worries you because it is 90 miles from the American coast. But Turkey is next to us!

While the two leaders argued, Russian ships were steaming towards Cuba. What would happen when these ships were intercepted by the U.S. Navy? Fortunately, Khrushchev was not prepared to risk nuclear war—which was what Kennedy had threatened. The Russian ships turned back and on 27 October 1962 Khrushchev sent Kennedy a letter:

> We agree to remove those weapons from Cuba which you regard as offensive.

So, although relations between Cuba and America did not improve, the immediate risk of nuclear war in 1962—the first nuclear crisis in world history—was averted.

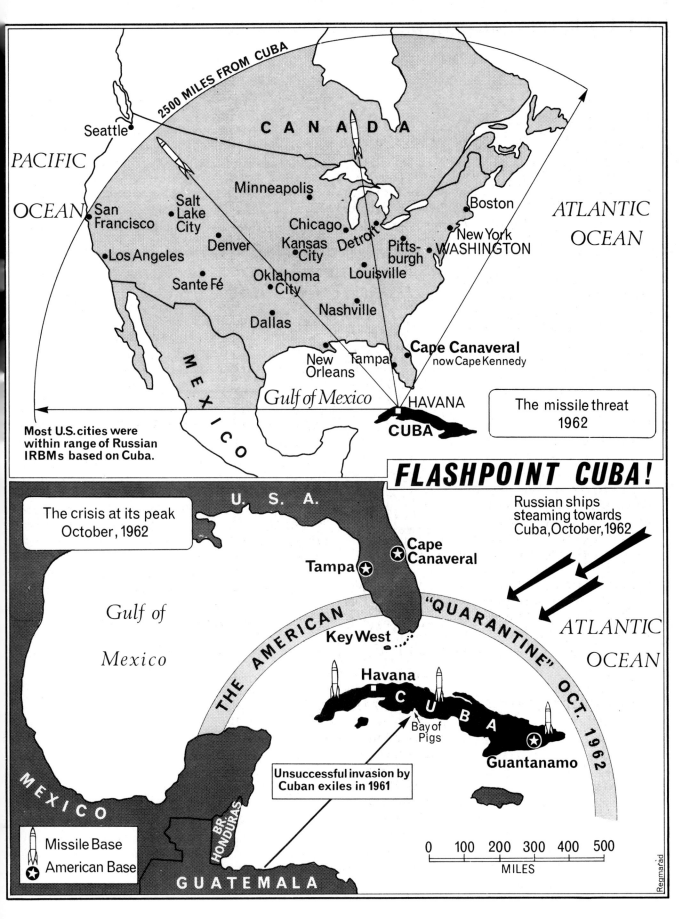

2500 MILES FROM CUBA

C A N A D A

Seattle

PACIFIC

OCEAN

San
Francisco

Salt
Lake
City

Minneapolis

Los Angeles

Denver

Santé Fé

Oklahoma
City

Dallas

Chicago

Kansas
City

Detroit

Pittsburgh

Louisville

Nashville

Boston

New York
WASHINGTON

ATLANTIC

OCEAN

New
Orleans

Tampa

Cape Canaveral
now Cape Kennedy

M E X I C O

Gulf of Mexico

HAVANA

CUBA

**The missile threat
1962**

**Most U.S. cities were
within range of Russian
IRBMs based on Cuba.**

FLASHPOINT CUBA!

**The crisis at its peak
October, 1962**

U. S. A.

Russian ships
steaming towards
Cuba, October, 1962

Gulf of

Mexico

Cape
Canaveral

Tampa

ATLANTIC

OCEAN

THE AMERICAN "QUARANTINE" OCT. 1962

Key West

Havana

C U B A

Bay of
Pigs

Guantanamo

M E X I C O

B R.
HONDURAS

**Unsuccessful invasion by
Cuban exiles in 1961**

Missile Base
American Base

GUATEMALA

0   100   200   300   400   500
MILES

Regmar'ad

57: Flashpoint—Viet Nam!

Geneva

Events in Germany and Korea had shown what scant hopes there were of ever unifying the communist and non-communist zones of a partitioned country. So the decisions reached at the 1954 Geneva Conference (a) that within two years there should be free elections in Viet Nam and (b) that the country should be reunited after these elections seemed at the best to be wishful thinking.

The Viet Cong

The partition of Viet Nam had immediate serious results. Firstly, it cut off North Viet Nam from her essential rice supplies in the Mekong Delta. Secondly, lots of Viet Minh now found themselves living in the south. Many of these were communists; others were Buddhist nationalists. All hated the new Saigon government, led by Premier Diem, a bigoted Roman Catholic who was constantly at loggerheads with the Buddhist priests. These facts helped to spark off guerrilla risings during 1955–56. The rebels styled themselves the Viet Cong (Vietnamese Communists) and claimed to be fighting for a free and united Viet Nam. But Diem justly claimed that his was the legal—if far from efficient—government in the South and promptly asked the U.S.A. for help. In 1956 the U.S. sent in about 16,000 'military advisers' to help the South form an 'Army of the Republic of Vietnam' (Arvins) to crush the communists. But all the U.S. advisers and Arvin operations failed to defeat the barefooted men and women of the Viet Cong who ambushed and raided from their hideouts in the forests and paddy-fields. By 1961 the Viet Cong controlled more than half of Viet Nam's 43 provinces; and by 1963 the Arvin officers had tired of Diem's inadequate leadership. They staged a revolution and killed him.

American fears

Now came a bewildering procession of Saigon governments. Frantically the U.S.A. supported every one: General Minh, General Khanh, a civilian leader Phan Khac Suu, Marshal Ky, and President Thieu. This was America's desperate attempt to contain communism in S.E. Asia, for now the war in Viet Nam was the 'great issue'. If the Saigon government fell and South Viet Nam succumbed to communism, the same fate would befall Laos, Cambodia, Thailand, Burma, India and Pakistan; this was America's 'domino theory'.

Escalation

In August 1964 the war suddenly escalated. Communist torpedo boats attacked U.S. warships in the Gulf of Tonking; as a reprisal U.S. carrier planes bombed North Vietnamese naval bases. Then the Viet Cong retaliated by raiding the U.S. base at Bien-Hoa where they tossed hand grenades amidst parked B.57 Canberra jets. American troops then began to arrive by the thousand; more and more communist soldiers swarmed down the 'Ho Chi Minh Trail' from Hanoi. Soon the war was being fought out between crack U.S. combat units and Viet Cong at battalion strength armed with such sophisticated weapons as recoilless rocket launchers. In an effort to stop the flow of men and munitions from North Viet Nam the U.S. began to bomb above the 17th Parallel, only to face heavy losses as a result of attacks from the new MiG-21s and the ground-to-air missiles.

Impasse

The Vietnamese people tried to live normal lives in the midst of this fighting. More than 3000 peasants died every month in the south, victims of the Viet Cong and the murderous American firepower. Thousands more died in the north during the relentless U.S. air strikes which began in 1965. Both sides claimed to be fighting for the 'hearts and minds' of the Vietnamese people, most of whom equated all forms of government with tyranny and preferred to be left alone. Hanoi demanded the end of U.S. air attacks; the Americans promised to stop the bombing if Hanoi would terminate aid to the Viet Cong in the south. Fighting became even fiercer when the Viet Cong launched their *Tet Offensive* in January 1968 and although peace negotiations began in Paris the years passed and Viet Nam seemed far from a settlement.

Peace

When Richard Nixon became President in 1968 he promised to take America out of the war in Viet Nam. Gradually the American soldiers pulled out of their main bases and ARVIN troops moved in to take their place. There was near disaster when North Vietnamese units began their massive attacks across the 17th Parallel in 1972. Nixon blockaded Haiphong and stepped up the B-52 attacks—but was soon able to announce that Henry Kissinger (U.S.A.) and Le Duc Tho (North Viet Nam) had signed the *Paris Peace Agreement*. The American involvement in Viet Nam ended on 27 January 1973.

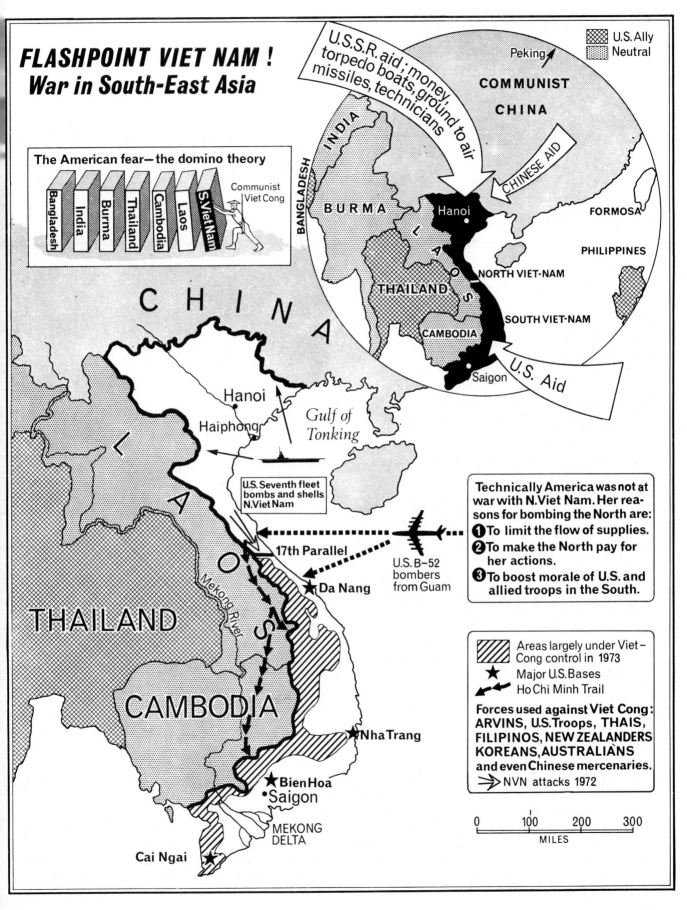

FLASHPOINT VIET NAM !
War in South-East Asia

The American fear— the domino theory

Bangladesh | India | Burma | Thailand | Cambodia | Laos | S.Viet Nam

Communist Viet Cong

U.S.S.R. aid ; money, torpedo boats, ground to air missiles, technicians

U.S. Ally
Neutral

Peking →

COMMUNIST CHINA

INDIA

BANGLADESH

BURMA

Hanoi

CHINESE AID

FORMOSA

THAILAND

L A O S

PHILIPPINES

NORTH VIET-NAM

CAMBODIA

SOUTH VIET-NAM

Saigon

U.S. Aid

C H I N A

Hanoi

Haiphong

Gulf of Tonking

L A O S

Mekong River

U.S. Seventh fleet bombs and shells N.Viet Nam

17th Parallel

U.S. B–52 bombers from Guam

★ Da Nang

Technically America was not at war with N.Viet Nam. Her reasons for bombing the North are:
❶ To limit the flow of supplies.
❷ To make the North pay for her actions.
❸ To boost morale of U.S. and allied troops in the South.

THAILAND

CAMBODIA

★ Nha Trang

★ Bien Hoa
• Saigon

MEKONG DELTA

Cai Ngai ★

Areas largely under Viet – Cong control in 1973
★ Major U.S. Bases
Ho Chi Minh Trail

Forces used against Viet Cong:
ARVINS, U.S.Troops, THAIS, FILIPINOS, NEW ZEALANDERS KOREANS, AUSTRALIANS and even Chinese mercenaries.
⟹ NVN attacks 1972

0   100   200   300
MILES

Part 6 – Book List

The people of North Viet Nam suffered heavier bombing attacks than did the Germans and Japanese in World War II. These Haiphong civilians are taking cover in one-man shelters built in tens of thousands in North Vietnamese urban areas. (*Eupra Press Service*)

PART 7

Internal problems of the
modern states

Even the most advanced communities are not free from their own internal difficulties. In the United States, the richest and most powerful country in the world, there exists one of the most dangerous issues of all: a racial problem. Twenty million negroes form a very large minority who, because they do not enjoy the same opportunities as do other US citizens, have come to constitute a major social and political problem.

The Soviet Union too has its own problems. Certainly communism is becoming easier to live with inside Russia. More and more consumer goods have begun to appear in the state shops and there has been a general increase in the Russian people's standard of living. Nevertheless the Russians have had to face serious agricultural shortages, a change in political leadership and, since 1956, the growing possibility of friction with that other centre of communism: China.

In Europe completely new political and economic organisations were developed. British governments—both Conservative and Labour—sought to join Europe so that British industry might share in the expanding economies of the Common Market countries. In 1973 Britain gained entry to the European Economic Community, a radical change that was bound to effect the relationship between the United Kingdom and the other Commonwealth countries.

58: The United States of America: racialism and the 'American poor'

Origins

The U.S.A. has created the world's most powerful economy. She makes nearly half of the world's steel, nearly half of the world's oil is drilled in America. She has become the richest nation in the world and yet her 'Great Society' of 190 million people faces two serious internal problems: racial discrimination and the growth of poverty. Many different races make up the American people and most live side by side fairly harmoniously—*if they are white*. But for thousands of Puerto Ricans, Mexicans, Orientals *and* 20 million negroes there exists a great deal of racial discrimination. Americans honour Abraham Lincoln who set the American negro free during the 1861–5 Civil War. However, he well knew that 'freedom' was not necessarily the same as 'equality' and he even toyed with the idea of transporting the 4 million negroes back to Africa. Finally he decided upon amalgamation or 'integration' and so, in a sense, he began the struggle for negro 'Civil Rights' more than a hundred years ago. In 1870 the Americans amended their constitution:

The rights of the citizens of the United States to vote shall not be denied or abridged by the United States or by any state on account of race, colour, or previous condition of servitude. (Fifteenth Amendment ratified 1870)

But in the South where 90% of the negroes lived, efforts were made both to terrorise and disfranchise them. White Americans founded the Ku Klux Klan in 1865 to preach terrorism and racial hatred. Between 1896 and 1904 several states introduced literacy and property tests which the negroes had to pass before receiving the vote. This reduced the 130,000 negro voters in Louisiana to less than a thousand. And such moves were perfectly legal because they didn't contravene the words of the Fifteenth Amendment.

Civil Rights

In 1939 the negroes were a poor, depressed minority but then World War II gave many a chance to find better jobs in industry and the army. In 1948 President Truman abolished racial discrimination in the armed services; in 1954 the U.S. Supreme Court declared that 'educational segregation' (separate schools and colleges for blacks and whites) was illegal and that American educational institutions must integrate. Many states in the south disliked this and in 1957 President Eisenhower had to call out troops to protect negroes entering Little Rock schools. Kennedy had to do the same thing when in 1963 Governor Wallace of Alabama personally barred the entry of two negro students into the State university. Gradually negro protest and white sympathy grew. Demonstrators demanded the right to eat in the same restaurant, to ride on the same bus, as white people. Groups such as S.N.I.C.K. (Students' Non-Violent Co-ordinating Committee) and C.O.R.E. (Congress on Racial Equality) organised 'sit-ins' at luncheon counters and 'freedom-rides' on interstate coaches. After 1955 Dr. Luther King led his Civil Rights demonstrations; the Rev. Hosea Williams led more violent acts that led to the Selma race riots of 1965. But despite the efforts of Kennedy and Johnson to prevent discrimination the problem grew worse. In 1966 and 1967 many northern towns were torn by racial violence. In 1968, King, the champion of non-violence, was assassinated.

The Size of the Problem

Despite these troubles many negroes have secured skilled jobs and entered the professions. Some hold high posts in the government and armed services. Yet many in the 'Deep South' and more and more in the northern cities know what it is to be 'Last to be hired and first to be fired'. Unemployment, poverty, racialism—these can't be separated. About 4 million of America's labour force of 73 million are unemployed. But about 40 million men, women and children are classified as poor. Some are poor Appalachian farmers, others are teenagers and old people—and many are negroes. In the northern cities, where negroes congregate in 'black ghettoes' the advent of automation is accentuating all of these problems. America's task is a giant one: the construction of a multi-racial, industrialized, poverty-free American society by means not of bloodthirsty revolution but by legislation and goodwill.

Viet Nam

Many young Americans were drafted to fight in the war in Viet Nam where the 46,000 U.S. casualties exceeded the number lost in the Korean War. The American 'draft' or 'call-up' had operated on a selective basis; wealthy students who could afford to pursue their studies could get deferment and perhaps escape the draft forever. So most GIs came from the poorer levels of society and naturally many of them were negroes. In Viet Nam, negroes suffered a disproportionately high percentage of casualties. When the American people elected President Nixon in 1968 they hoped for a rapid end to the war in Viet Nam. Nixon achieved this in 1973; now millions of dollars could be diverted to improving living and working conditions for the American poor.

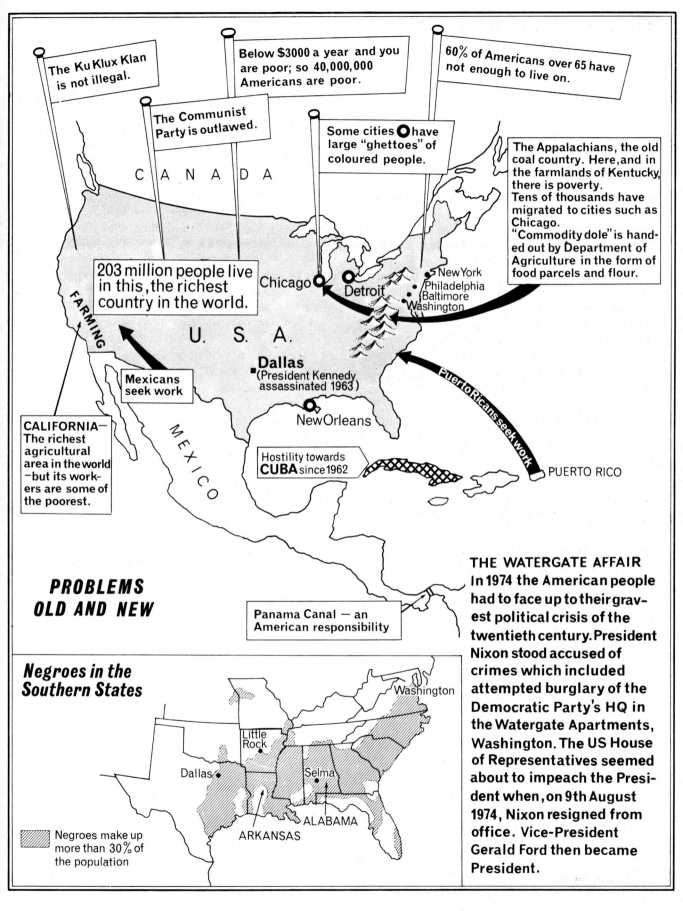

The Ku Klux Klan is not illegal.

The Communist Party is outlawed.

Below $3000 a year and you are poor; so 40,000,000 Americans are poor.

60% of Americans over 65 have not enough to live on.

Some cities have large "ghettoes" of coloured people.

The Appalachians, the old coal country. Here, and in the farmlands of Kentucky, there is poverty.
Tens of thousands have migrated to cities such as Chicago.
"Commodity dole" is handed out by Department of Agriculture in the form of food parcels and flour.

CANADA

203 million people live in this, the richest country in the world.

Chicago

Detroit

New York
Philadelphia
Baltimore
Washington

FARMING

U. S. A.

Dallas
(President Kennedy assassinated 1963)

Mexicans seek work

Puerto Ricans seek work

MEXICO

New Orleans

CALIFORNIA—
The richest agricultural area in the world –but its workers are some of the poorest.

Hostility towards **CUBA** since 1962

PUERTO RICO

PROBLEMS OLD AND NEW

Panama Canal — an American responsibility

Negroes in the Southern States

Washington

Little Rock

Dallas

Selma

ALABAMA

ARKANSAS

Negroes make up more than 30% of the population

THE WATERGATE AFFAIR
In 1974 the American people had to face up to their gravest political crisis of the twentieth century. President Nixon stood accused of crimes which included attempted burglary of the Democratic Party's HQ in the Watergate Apartments, Washington. The US House of Representatives seemed about to impeach the President when, on 9th August 1974, Nixon resigned from office. Vice-President Gerald Ford then became President.

59: The Union of Soviet Socialist Republics: competing with America 1945–1964

Stalin's Russia

The U.S.S.R. is three times as big as America and covers one sixth of the land area of this planet. More than 230 million people live in this vast country, whose mineral wealth and industrial resources rival those of the U.S.A. But unlike the U.S.A., Russia suffered hideously at the hands of the German Wehrmacht. 20 million Russians died in World War II. Much of the livestock vanished and, as the bitter fighting spread over western Russia, thousands of towns and villages were devastated. When the war ended in 1945, 25 million Russians were without adequate food and shelter.

Stalin was adamant: Russia must rise again. He took what he could from defeated Germany and Manchuria; he began another Five Year Plan in 1946; he had the secret of the atom bomb by 1949; in 1950 the production figures for heavy industry were double those of 1945.

Khrushchev's agricultural policies

Stalin died in 1953; his successor, Nikita Khrushchev, talked of 'coexistence with the west', of 'commercial rivalry':

> We want to compete with the capitalist countries in peaceful endeavour ... let us see who produces more per head of population, who provides a higher material and cultural standard for the people.

He had thrown down the gauntlet; he was promising Russians a higher standard of living than America's. But he also disclosed that he was facing a difficult problem. All was not well with agriculture: there was a shortage of grain. He said he had the answer—the huge collectives and state farms must become more efficient and grow more grain whilst in the Virgin Lands there were 100 million acres awaiting the plough. Here the first harvests were brought in during 1956; 1957 and 1958 were bumper years. And then came disaster. Erosion wrecked the topsoil and Khrushchev was left with a giant dustbowl in the middle of Siberia. He blamed the weather, the misuse of fertilizers and Soviet farming generally. Many Russians chose to blame the collective system for all their troubles—it is still disliked in Russia. But Khrushchev was doubly unfortunate that these Russian shortages should coincide with a general lack of grain in the communist camp. Hungary and the G.D.R. had to buy grain from Western Europe; in 1963 Russia imported wheat from Canada and Australia; in 1964 Khrushchev had to buy American grain. Undoubtedly this helped to keep the cost of Russian foodstuffs high and this may have contributed to Khrushchev's downfall in 1964. Said one collective farm-manager: 'Good riddance!! What did he want to stick his nose into farming for? A statesman's job is to look after defence and foreign affairs—and not to tell us how to farm!' So Khrushchev's efforts to overtake American farming were unsuccessful.

Russia's potential

When Khrushchev fell from power, production figures for Russian consumer goods bore little comparison with those of America. In 1964 Russia made 3 million TV sets; America produced 8 million. Russia made 5 million radios; America built 19 million. Russia manufactured 185,000 cars. American factories turned out 7 million. As far as such statistics are valuable, it is obvious that Russia was lagging far behind the *material standards* enjoyed in the U.S.A. But Russia's *potential* in, for example. Siberia is fantastic. Here grow a quarter of the world's forests. There is abundant oil and so much coal that it is estimated at 75 times the British coal reserves. Siberia's mineral wealth includes copper, gold, uranium, lead and tungsten. There are diamonds—and 150,000 *million* tons of iron ore. Stalin used to say: 'Life has improved, comrades—it has become more joyous'. With Russia's potential it will no doubt get much better—but it will take time.

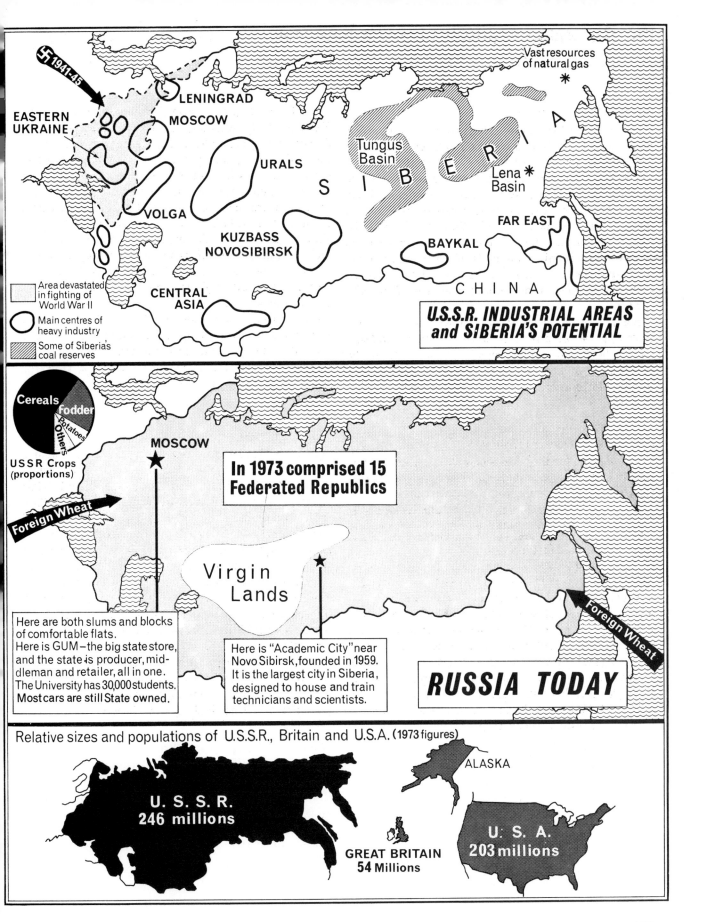

U.S.S.R. INDUSTRIAL AREAS and SIBERIA'S POTENTIAL

1941-45

EASTERN UKRAINE

LENINGRAD

MOSCOW

URALS

Tungus Basin

Vast resources of natural gas

S I B E R I A

Lena Basin

VOLGA

KUZBASS NOVOSIBIRSK

FAR EAST

BAYKAL

CENTRAL ASIA

C H I N A

- Area devastated in fighting of World War II
- Main centres of heavy industry
- Some of Siberia's coal reserves

RUSSIA TODAY

Cereals
Fodder
Potatoes
Others

USSR Crops (proportions)

Foreign Wheat

MOSCOW

In 1973 comprised 15 Federated Republics

Virgin Lands

Foreign Wheat

Here are both slums and blocks of comfortable flats.
Here is GUM – the big state store, and the state is producer, middleman and retailer, all in one.
The University has 30,000 students.
Most cars are still State owned.

Here is "Academic City" near Novo Sibirsk, founded in 1959. It is the largest city in Siberia, designed to house and train technicians and scientists.

Relative sizes and populations of U.S.S.R., Britain and U.S.A. (1973 figures)

ALASKA

U. S. S. R.
246 millions

GREAT BRITAIN
54 Millions

U. S. A.
203 millions

133

60: The growing power of the Chinese People's Republic 1949–1970

China extends her frontiers

Fear is often based upon ignorance; and the western world has been woefully ignorant of events in China since 1949. This fear has caused Americans, for example, to speak of a 'new Frankenstein' being 'congealed and coalesced' in China. Certainly China has acted aggressively—sometimes with good cause—since 1949. She fought the U.N. in Korea; annexed Tibet in 1950; Wa in 1960. She challenged Indian sovereignty in the Himalayas and in 1962 this led to serious fighting on 'the roof of the world'. For years China had stationed troops there so the communists were acclimatised but the Indian soldiers were not. Ill-equipped to fight at such altitudes, they discovered that excessive effort rapidly led to congestion of the lungs, which could prove fatal within a few hours. So the Indians retreated and Communist China claimed another 15,000 square miles of territory.

Sino-Soviet split

It is clear that China would like to foster the spread of communism over the whole of S.E. Asia, where millions of Chinese have gone to live. But her aggressive policy and her noisy contempt for 'the American way of life' have not been entirely supported by the Soviet Union, who has tended towards a policy of 'peaceful coexistence' with the West. In 1960 China and Russia openly disagreed on the meaning of communism and their quarrel, known as the 'Sino-Soviet split', gradually worsened. Both sides stationed troops and aircraft along the borders of Kazakh Province and Sinkiang, where some serious clashes have occurred. The Russians have moved mobile missile launchers into Mongolia. During 1968 and 1969 small-scale frontier incidents along the Ussuri River led to a furious propaganda war between the two communist giants. The Russians regarded the aggressive Mao as a re-incarnation of Hitler; while the Chinese shouted about the 'anti-China atrocities of the new Czars . . . their Fascist heel tramples on the Motherland!' However, most western observers agreed that the Sino-Soviet split was a political and ideological quarrel rather than a serious military confrontation.

The Cultural Revolution

Perhaps the most mystifying event inside China has been Mao Tse-tung's 'proletarian cultural revolution', designed to 'purify' the bureaucracy that had grown up inside China since 1949, and to prevent the Chinese adopting 'soft' western capitalist styles and ideals. One of Mao's instruments has been the 'Red Guards—young people who, in 1966, were given a year's holiday from schools and colleges so that they could force prominent communists to confess their sins, rename streets with revolutionary titles and drive out western influences. Infant schoolchildren sang 'I love China, I love Chairman Mao', but outsiders believed that these events obscured a power struggle inside China. Mao appeared to emerge from this struggle victorious and appointed Marshal Lin Piao as the future ruler of Communist China. In the event Lin fell into disgrace and died in an air crash in 1971. Mao himself died in 1976 and the new leader of China was the former Vice-Premier Hua Kuo-feng.

The 'Great Leap Forward'

It seemed likely that the Cultural Revolution would limit China's economic progress which had been phenomenal since 1949. This 'Great Leap Forward' had led to the growth of new industries—including car and aircraft manufacture; the state farms or 'communes' had doubled the crops and livestock produced; millions of acres of reclaimed land grew food to feed China's increasing population. The communists tackled one of China's biggest problems: the lack of contact between the Mandarin speaking North and the Cantonese speaking South. Major improvements in road, rail and air transport plus the simplification of Chinese script and the spread of education are helping to give the Chinese people a new sense of national unity in the modern world. However, rice was still rationed in Peking at the beginning of the Seventies; there were no *private* cars on the busy streets: £20 was the *average monthly wage* though there was a substantial pay increase on 1 October 1977. The years 1976–7 were especially bad for agriculture—the Chinese had to contend with floods, frosts, typhoons, plant diseases and even earthquakes. Yet though the standard of living was not high, China was sufficiently advanced to develop hydrogen bombs at her Lop Nor test site, to begin the construction of a missile force and to maintain the biggest land forces in the world.

FOOD

U.S.S.R.

MONGOLIA

Peking ★

Little food produced. Mainly pastoral farming. "A region of difficulty."

WHEAT

RICE

Tropic of Cancer

PEOPLE

U.S.S.R.

MONGOLIA

Peking ★

Over 600 per sq.m.
60–600 per sq.m.
Under 60 per sq.m.

Tropic of Cancer

CHINA

U.S.S.R

MONGOLIA

Border incidents along Ussuri R. (Damansky I.) 1969

Chinese armies fought in N. Korea 1950-53

Peking ★

KAZAKH PROVINCE

SINKIANG

Lop Nor

Communist CHINA

China claims N. Kashmir

Absorbed by China 1950

TIBET

1962, fighting in Himalayas with India

W. PAKISTAN

INDIA

WA absorbed by China 1960

Chinese aid to N. Viet Nam

NATIONALIST CHINA

E. PAKISTAN

BURMA

China aided Malayan Communist Party 1949-57

PHILIPPINE ISLANDS

■ Large Chinese communities living abroad

CHINA and Asia 1949-70

Rebuilding post-war Europe

The old Europe had died in 1945. No longer were its nations 'world powers'. No longer would their alliances and armies control world affairs. Europe was overshadowed by the two superpowers. Now the war-torn European countries desperately needed money so that they might rebuild their shattered industries and restart their trade. In 1947 the U.S. Secretary of State George Marshall had come to their aid, saying that it was 'logical to do whatever the United States is able to do to assist in the return of the normal economic health of the world'. During 1948 dollar aid began to flow into the Organization for European Economic Co-operation (O.E.E.C.) which was formed to supervize the building of the new Europe. In March 1948 Belgium, the Netherlands and Luxemburg formed their famous economic union called Benelux; in 1949 the North Atlantic Treaty Organization (N.A.T.O.) welded most of Western Europe into a tight military alliance.

New attitudes

Whilst all this was happening the old wartime passions were gradually fading in Europe. In France, men such as the Foreign Minister Robert Schuman believed that if West Germany (the Federal German Republic formed in 1949) were made an equal partner in a great European system, then the threat of another German war would disappear forever and Europe as a whole would gain great economic benefits. So in 1951 six European countries—France, Italy, West Germany and the Benelux countries—formed a common market in iron and steel. Four years later the 'Six' met in Messina to discuss ways of improving upon this highly successful economic union. They set up an investigating committee under Paul-Henri Spaak who reported back in 1956 that Europe should set up within the next twelve years a tariff-free system of trading within the frontiers of the 'Six'. And so at Rome on 24 March 1957 the 'Six' signed the treaty which set up this European Economic Community (E.E.C.)—better known as the Common Market.

The Common Market

What did it mean to be a member? It meant that E.E.C. industrialists had a new market of 170 million potential customers; it meant that E.E.C. workers could seek jobs in six countries; it meant the chance of building a completely new Europe—perhaps a 'United States of Europe'. The Germans in particular jumped at this chance. Living in a divided country and uncertain of their political future, the 57 million West Germans had experienced their worst war in history—but, more recently, had been receiving more dollar aid than anyone else. Through hard work and sound labour relations, good planning and plenty of financial aid the West Germans carried out their Wirtschaftswunder— their 'economic miracle'. From the depths of despair in 1945 the West Germans advanced to a point 20 years later when their standard of living was, for Europe, slightly above average. Compared with Britain, who had originally refused to join the Common Market, her achievement was impressive. Britain and West Germany are about the same size; Britain has a slightly smaller population. By 1964 the West Germans were building twice as many houses as did Britain; they had fewer unemployed, barely any industrial strikes; they enjoyed higher wages and slightly shorter working hours.

Britain and Europe

The undoubted success of the E.E.C. spurred the British government, rather belatedly, to devise a trading rival and in December 1959 Britain, Norway, Sweden, Portugal, Austria, Denmark and Switzerland formed the European Free Trade Association (E.F.T.A.). Within two years Britain was trying to persuade the Six to allow the E.F.T.A. partners and the British Commonwealth to join the Common Market. But President de Gaulle vetoed these proposals. Then in 1966 negotiations with the Six began again and in 1967 the Prime Minister, Harold Wilson, was able to announce his 'historic decision': Britain had made formal application to join the Common Market, but again de Gaulle stood in the way. But during 1968–69 the General's popularity declined in France after a series of strikes and riots. In April 1969 the French people rejected his policies and he was forced to resign. His successor was President Pompidou. These events made the British Labour government* more hopeful of entry into the E.E.C.—especially after the pro-British Willy Brandt became Chancellor of West Germany.

---

*Labour lost the 1970 General Election. The new Conservative government, led by Edward Heath, took Britain into the Common Market.

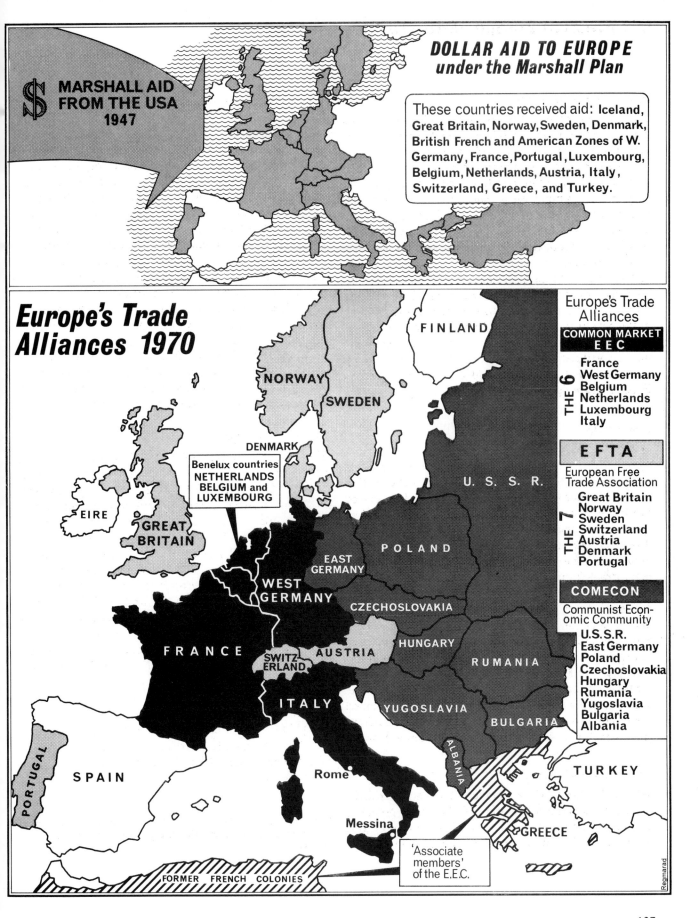

DOLLAR AID TO EUROPE
under the Marshall Plan

$ MARSHALL AID FROM THE USA 1947

These countries received aid: Iceland, Great Britain, Norway, Sweden, Denmark, British French and American Zones of W. Germany, France, Portugal, Luxembourg, Belgium, Netherlands, Austria, Italy, Switzerland, Greece, and Turkey.

Europe's Trade Alliances 1970

FINLAND

NORWAY

SWEDEN

DENMARK

Benelux countries
NETHERLANDS
BELGIUM and
LUXEMBOURG

U. S. S. R.

EIRE

GREAT BRITAIN

POLAND

EAST GERMANY

WEST GERMANY

CZECHOSLOVAKIA

HUNGARY

FRANCE

SWITZERLAND

AUSTRIA

RUMANIA

ITALY

YUGOSLAVIA

BULGARIA

ALBANIA

PORTUGAL

SPAIN

Rome

TURKEY

Messina

GREECE

'Associate members' of the E.E.C.

FORMER FRENCH COLONIES

Europe's Trade Alliances

COMMON MARKET E E C

THE 6
France
West Germany
Belgium
Netherlands
Luxembourg
Italy

E F T A

European Free Trade Association

THE 7
Great Britain
Norway
Sweden
Switzerland
Austria
Denmark
Portugal

COMECON

Communist Economic Community

U.S.S.R.
East Germany
Poland
Czechoslovakia
Hungary
Rumania
Yugoslavia
Bulgaria
Albania

Regmarad

62: Britain and the inflationary spiral 1945–1970

The Age of Austerity

In 1945 the British people returned a Labour government to power in the first election held for a decade. Labour set out to create a Welfare State which would care for the interests of the British citizen 'from the cradle to the grave'. There was a spate of legislation (the 1944 Education Act setting up state primary and secondary schools where education was to be given according to the age, aptitude and ability of the child, had been passed by the wartime coalition government.) In 1946 civil aviation was nationalized and the National Insurance Act passed. Next year saw the nationalization of the mines, railways, canals, road haulage and electricity. In 1948 gas was nationalized and the National Health Services began. All of this costly legislation coincided with the gloomy years of post-war shortages. Too few houses meant that families squatted in disused army-camps; food was still rationed due partly to the world shortage of food and partly to the lack of supply ships after the dreadful wartime losses (25%) suffered by the British mercantile marine. But there was fairly full employment and wages were going up; unfortunately, so were prices and taxation. The post-war inflationary spiral had begun.

Thirteen years of Conservative rule

Depressed by these austere conditions, the British began to lose faith in Labour government. The Labour Party just managed to scrape home in the 1950 elections but lost to the Conservatives the following year. Meanwhile, a quarter of a million disenchanted Britishers had emigrated in search of a better life. But now Britain began to share in Western Europe's growing prosperity. Harold Macmillan, Conservative Prime Minister from 1957 to 1963, borrowed an American phrase to tell the country that it had 'never had it so good'. Certainly fewer Britishers were doing manual jobs as more machinery replaced muscle power. There were more homes and cars. Washing machines, vacuum cleaners, T.V. sets and holidays abroad came within the reach of far more people. But this pursuit of all the pleasures that money could buy led to a rapid shortage of cash; and it was the custom for most families to use hire-purchase and credit deals when buying consumer goods. During these years taxation rose, price increases and wage demands became common and the purchasing power of the £ declined.

Britain's financial commitments

Her problems were basically due to a national and private willingness to buy what was wanted without having the money to pay for it. So Britain's debts mounted. Governments were too ready to invest in unprofitable activities: the African groundnuts scheme, the Blue Streak missile and the TSR-2 project are only a few of the more notorious examples. At the same time Britain retained many of the characteristics of a great and prosperous nation. She possessed conventional defence forces and a nuclear striking force; she maintained a costly but desirable programme of overseas aid; she undertook military commitments which involved her armed forces (nearly 500,000 in 1966) in costly local wars all over the globe. In financial terms, the most costly would be the Falklands campaign (1982) and the 'Fortress Falkland' policy followed by Margaret Thatcher's government.

The economy

All these government services have to be paid for through taxation. As the wealth of Britain depends on the success of its export trades, governments resort to many devices to encourage exports. They raise Bank interest rates, H.P. deposits; they impose import tariffs—all these things are designed to reduce home spending and to increase national exports. When these exports exceed in value the imports, then Britain enjoys a favourable balance of trade. This is shown in the regularly published trade figures. But when 'trade figures are down', Britain may have to meet her overseas debts and this will cause her gold bullion and dollar reserves to dwindle. When the Labour government was elected in 1964 its main aim was to limit the inflationary spiral and in 1966 it decided to 'freeze' prices and incomes and to impose a new tax (the Selective Employment Tax) in a major effort to increase the nation's 'productivity' by act of parliament. But on two occasions since 1945 even drastic economies and austerities have proved insufficient. In 1949 and again in 1967 Labour Governments had to devalue the £ sterling in a desperate effort to boost British exports (which appear cheaper abroad after devaluation). Once more the British people lost faith in Labour leadership and, in 1970, returned the Conservative Party to power.

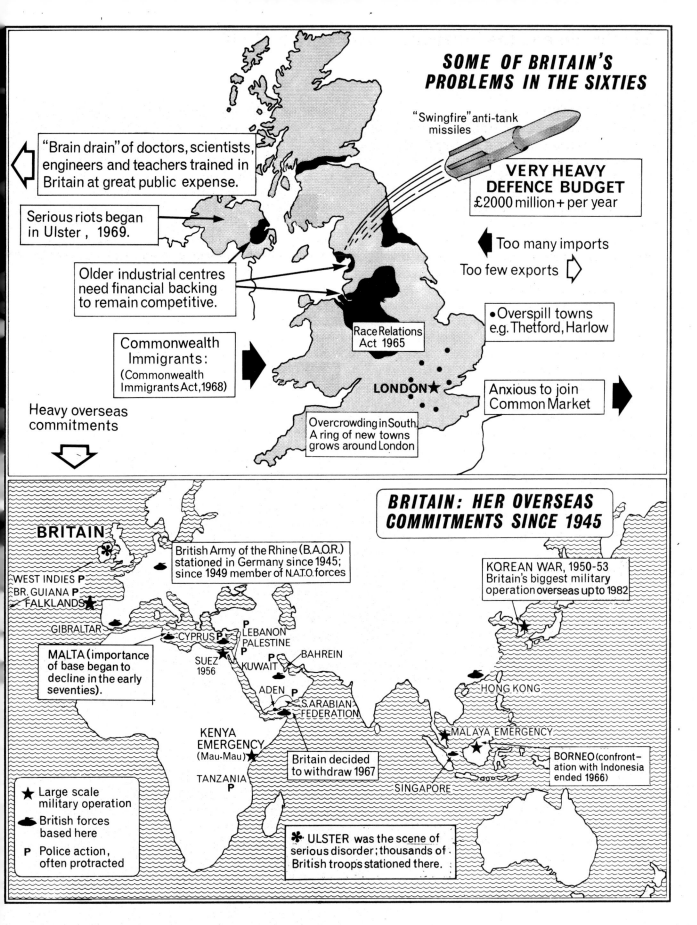

SOME OF BRITAIN'S PROBLEMS IN THE SIXTIES

"Swingfire" anti-tank missiles

VERY HEAVY DEFENCE BUDGET
£2000 million + per year

"Brain drain" of doctors, scientists, engineers and teachers trained in Britain at great public expense.

Serious riots began in Ulster, 1969.

Older industrial centres need financial backing to remain competitive.

Too many imports

Too few exports

Commonwealth Immigrants: (Commonwealth Immigrants Act, 1968)

Race Relations Act 1965

• Overspill towns e.g. Thetford, Harlow

Heavy overseas commitments

LONDON ★

Anxious to join Common Market

Overcrowding in South. A ring of new towns grows around London

BRITAIN: HER OVERSEAS COMMITMENTS SINCE 1945

BRITAIN

WEST INDIES **P**
BR. GUIANA **P**
FALKLANDS ★

GIBRALTAR

British Army of the Rhine (B.A.O.R.) stationed in Germany since 1945; since 1949 member of N.A.T.O. forces

KOREAN WAR, 1950-53 Britain's biggest military operation overseas up to 1982

MALTA (importance of base began to decline in the early seventies).

CYPRUS **P**
SUEZ 1956
P LEBANON
PALESTINE **P**
KUWAIT
P BAHREIN

ADEN **P**
S. ARABIAN FEDERATION

HONG KONG

KENYA EMERGENCY (Mau-Mau) ★

Britain decided to withdraw 1967

MALAYA EMERGENCY ★

TANZANIA **P**

BORNEO (confront- ation with Indonesia ended 1966)

SINGAPORE

★ Large scale military operation

◣ British forces based here

P Police action, often protracted

✳ ULSTER was the scene of serious disorder; thousands of British troops stationed there.

139

63: The Commonwealth to 1979

What is the Commonwealth?

All the present members of the Commonwealth were once ruled by the Parliament at Westminster; all were once members of the British Empire. But now there are so few colonies awaiting independence that the Colonial Office in London has closed. It is difficult to define the new Commonwealth except in vague terms. The 1931 Statute of Westminster enacted that Great Britain and the Dominions were 'equal in status, in no way subordinate one to another in any aspect of their domestic or foreign affairs, though united by a common allegiance to the Crown'. By 1979 the Commonwealth had grown into a free association of forty independent states owing allegiance to Queen Elizabeth II who, at her coronation in 1953, was described as 'Head of the Commonwealth'. But even here there is no single rule. Some Commonwealth countries such as Canada, Australia and New Zealand recognize the Queen as *their* Queen; but republics such as Ghana, India and Ceylon* accept the Queen *not* as their Head of State but only as Head of the Commonwealth.

Strength and weaknesses of the Commonwealth

It has often been said that the Commonwealth will only break up when it ceases to be useful. Militarily, the contribution of the Commonwealth forces to victory in two world wars needs no emphasis. Economically, the Commonwealth trading agreements are beneficial to all members. Britain imports much of her food and raw materials from the Commonwealth which in turn buys British exports. Britain helps the more needy members with economic aid. The Commonwealth Prime Ministers' Conference provides a fair sample of world opinion. For instance, Commonwealth pressure on South Africa caused that country, condemned for its policy of apartheid, to resign her membership in 1961. However, it has also been said that the Commonwealth has no role to play in the modern world; that Britain, geographically a part of the European Community, cannot expect to maintain her world-wide interests at the same time. This point was highlighted when in 1973 Britain gained entry to the European Economic Community. Moreover, some critics think that, because some emergent African member states (e.g. Kenya and Tanzania) have not adopted the 'Westminster' style of government, the spirit of Commonwealth unity is dying. Of course there is disagreement within the Commonwealth. Many members were

*Since 1972, the Republic of Sri Lanka.

hostile in their reactions to the British attack on Suez in 1956. Zambia and others bitterly attacked Britain's lack of action over the Rhodesian crisis.

Rhodesia 1923–1979

In October 1923 Southern Rhodesia became a self-governing colony within the British Empire. In 1961 Britain granted her a new constitution which gave the African people some representation in the white dominated Rhodesian parliament. In 1964 the Commonwealth Prime Ministers agreed that Southern Rhodesia 'would attain full sovereignty as soon as her governmental institutions were sufficiently representative'. Then the Rhodesian Prime Minister, Ian Smith, made two trips to London (September 1964 and October 1965) to negotiate the grant of independence. Britain refused this, insisting that the white Rhodesians give some guarantee that the African people would have political rights. Ian Smith replied by issuing his Unilateral Declaration of Independence on 11 November 1965. The colony's governor, Sir Humphrey Gibbs, dismissed Smith—but he defiantly carried on with the government of Rhodesia. Some Commonwealth countries demanded armed action—but Britain refused. Guyana cynically observed that when she (as British Guiana) committed 'illegal acts', Britain soon sent out troops. However, Britain chose to try other ways of restoring 'the rule of law'. She imposed economic sanctions; and most countries agreed not to sell Rhodesia oil or buy Rhodesian tobacco. A year after U.D.I., Harold Wilson, the British Prime Minister, held talks with Smith aboard H.M.S. *Tiger* but they reached no settlement. In 1968 further talks held aboard H.M.S. *Fearless* were equally unproductive. Ten years later, black and white Rhodesians formed their first biracial government. But the Rhodesian *Patriotic Front* refused to recognize its legality and intensified the guerrilla war against the government of Zimbabwe-Rhodesia.

Britain's 'Six Principles'

Britain always insisted that *Six Principles* must be the basis of any settlement of the Rhodesian problem: the majority of the Rhodesian people must play a part in government; the constitution must not be altered *retrogressively*; Africans must enjoy a higher political status; there must be no racial discrimination; and there must be no oppression of the majority by the minority—*or* of the minority by the majority.

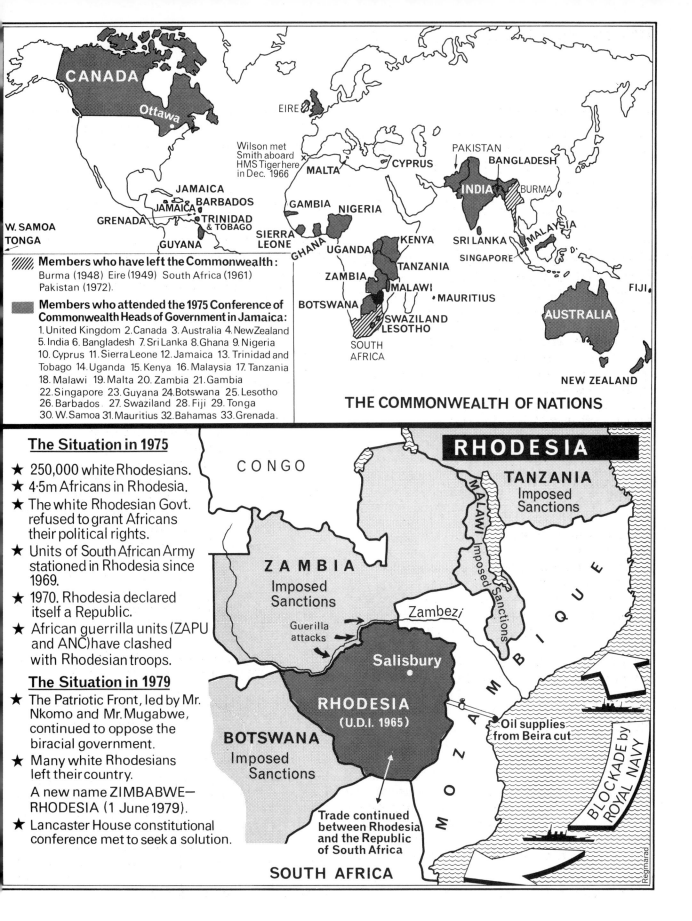

THE COMMONWEALTH OF NATIONS

CANADA
Ottawa

EIRE

Wilson met
Smith aboard
HMS Tiger here
in Dec. 1966

MALTA
CYPRUS

PAKISTAN
BANGLADESH
INDIA
BURMA

W. SAMOA
TONGA

JAMAICA
BARBADOS
GRENADA
TRINIDAD & TOBAGO
GUYANA

GAMBIA
NIGERIA
SIERRA LEONE
GHANA
UGANDA

KENYA
SRI LANKA
SINGAPORE
MALAYSIA

FIJI

TANZANIA
ZAMBIA
MALAWI
MAURITIUS
BOTSWANA
SWAZILAND
LESOTHO
SOUTH AFRICA

AUSTRALIA

NEW ZEALAND

//// **Members who have left the Commonwealth:**
Burma (1948) Eire (1949) South Africa (1961)
Pakistan (1972).

■ **Members who attended the 1975 Conference of
Commonwealth Heads of Government in Jamaica:**
1. United Kingdom 2. Canada 3. Australia 4. New Zealand
5. India 6. Bangladesh 7. Sri Lanka 8. Ghana 9. Nigeria
10. Cyprus 11. Sierra Leone 12. Jamaica 13. Trinidad and
Tobago 14. Uganda 15. Kenya 16. Malaysia 17. Tanzania
18. Malawi 19. Malta 20. Zambia 21. Gambia
22. Singapore 23. Guyana 24. Botswana 25. Lesotho
26. Barbados 27. Swaziland 28. Fiji 29. Tonga
30. W. Samoa 31. Mauritius 32. Bahamas 33. Grenada.

The Situation in 1975

★ 250,000 white Rhodesians.

★ 4·5m Africans in Rhodesia.

★ The white Rhodesian Govt. refused to grant Africans their political rights.

★ Units of South African Army stationed in Rhodesia since 1969.

★ 1970. Rhodesia declared itself a Republic.

★ African guerrilla units (ZAPU and ANC) have clashed with Rhodesian troops.

The Situation in 1979

★ The Patriotic Front, led by Mr. Nkomo and Mr. Mugabwe, continued to oppose the biracial government.

★ Many white Rhodesians left their country.

A new name ZIMBABWE–RHODESIA (1 June 1979).

★ Lancaster House constitutional conference met to seek a solution.

RHODESIA

CONGO

TANZANIA
Imposed
Sanctions

MALAWI Imposed Sanctions

ZAMBIA
Imposed
Sanctions

Guerilla
attacks

Zambezi

MOZAMBIQUE

Salisbury

RHODESIA
(U.D.I. 1965)

BOTSWANA
Imposed
Sanctions

Oil supplies
from Beira cut

BLOCKADE by
ROYAL NAVY

Trade continued
between Rhodesia
and the Republic
of South Africa

SOUTH AFRICA

Regmarad

The power blocs

At the height of the Cold War in 1949, the United States formed the North Atlantic Treaty Organisation to meet the threat of a Soviet strike in the West. In 1955 the Russians organised their East European satellite states into the Warsaw Pact. Both military alliances were still in being at the end of the sixties although by then they were showing signs of wear and tear.

General de Gaulle and NATO

Ever since the General had regained power in France (1958) he had made no secret of his resentment of American influence in Europe. His attitude was a constant embarrassment to the western allies, especially as NATO's HQ was in Paris. Frequently the General would warn the Americans: 'You will be seeing less and less of us in NATO'. He argued that the main French commitment in Europe was the defence of West Germany; and he had already guaranteed this when he signed the Franco-German Treaty of 1963. Eventually, he took the plunge; in July 1966 France withdrew from the NATO command. However, he kept his promise to West Germany; he assured Chancellor Kiesinger that France would continue to offer military protection. De Gaulle's decision forced NATO to shift its HQ from Paris to Brussels and to seek new bases for its 'planes and personnel. Canada's jets were normally based in France; now they transferred to Zweibrucken and Söllingen. American 'Hercules' transports moved to Mildenhall; 'Voodoo' jets arrived in Upper Heyford; while supersonic 'Phantoms' flew from Alconbury in Huntingdonshire.

Czechoslovakia and the Warsaw Pact

While NATO adjusted to the mood of the General (who resigned from the Presidency of France in April 1969), the Warsaw Pact countries faced a unique problem within their own community. One Iron Curtain country, Czechoslovakia, began to introduce genuine democratic reforms to its citizens during 1968. A delighted people experienced free speech on radio, television and in the press. Censorship disappeared—for the first time for twenty years—and Roman Catholics enjoyed religious toleration. Most of the credit for these dramatic changes went to Alexander Dubcek, who had become First Secretary of the Czechoslovak Communist Party in

January 1968. In what he called 'a socialist democratic revolution' he transformed his people's way of life. Happiness seemed complete when, in March 1968, a wartime hero named General Svoboda (his name meant 'freedom'!) replaced the unpopular President Novotny. Dubcek's reforms met disapproval in the other Warsaw Pact countries. President Ulbricht of East Germany and President Gomulka of Poland loudly condemned Czechoslovakia's imitation of the 'Western imperialists'. They accused Dubcek of exposing an important section of the Iron Curtain frontier to western attack; and at a communist summit meeting held in Warsaw during July they issued a strong warning:

. . . we cannot agree to have hostile forces push your country away from the road of socialism and create a danger of Czechoslovakia being severed from the socialist camp. . . .

But though Dubcek went to meet the Russians in Cierna, he remained intransigent. He would not abandon his policy of reform. The Russians had already decided to resolve the issue by force—just as they had done in East Berlin (1953) and Hungary (1956). They appointed General Shtemenko as Chief of Staff of the Warsaw Pact armies. Significantly, he had helped to win the greatest tank battle in history—the Battle of Kursk 1943. He prepared an armoured invasion of Czechoslovakia and chose the cities of Prague, Brno and Bratislava as his main targets.

The invasion of Czechoslovakia 1968

Spearheaded by Soviet tanks, the forces of five Warsaw countries invaded Czechoslovakia on 20 August 1968. They met no armed opposition but found, to their amazement, that the civilian population resented their presence. There were several ugly incidents; Russian tanks burned and Czech patriots died. Thousands fled to Austria; secret radio and TV stations kept the outside world informed of events especially in the main centre of resistance—Wenceslas Square, Prague. The Russians had now precipitated a worse crisis—and they settled it by taking Dubcek to Moscow and there persuading him to abandon his liberal projects. The Russians forced a new constitution on Czechoslovakia in January 1969. In April 1969 Dubcek resigned from the leadership of the Czechoslovak Communist Party. His attempt to liberalise a Warsaw Pact country ended in total failure.

CANADA

UNITED STATES

FINLAND

NORWAY

SWEDEN

THE

SOVIET

UNION

Moscow

UNITED KINGDOM

DENMARK

Alconbury
Upper Heyford
Mildenhall

HOLLAND

Söllingen

E. GERMANY

POLAND

Warsaw

1968

Brussels

Paris

NATO moves HQ to Brussels

Zweibrucken

1968

WEST GERMANY

Prague • Brno
Bratislava

Cierna

1966

1966

De Gaulle withdraws from NATO command 1966

SWITZ-ERLAND

AUSTRIA

HUNGARY

1968

RUMANIA

ITALY

YUGOSLAVIA
Communist, but independent of Russia and the Warsaw Pact

BULGARIA

PORTUGAL

SPAIN

ALBANIA

1968

GREECE

TURKEY

Communist, but a supporter of China in the Sino-Soviet split

CONCLUSIONS

1. The Dubcek reforms did not really endanger the security of the Warsaw Pact, but the Russians were not prepared to risk a country which bordered on the West.

2. The Czechoslovak crisis underlined the determination of the Russians never to allow free criticism of the communist régime.

3. The movement of the communist armour—over great distances and on a large scale—caught the NATO defence forces napping. Hurriedly, they sent troops to the West German frontier, and thus lent substance to the earlier charges that hostile forces threatened the Iron Curtain frontier!

EUROPE and the SUPERPOWERS
1966 – 1969

- Warsaw Pact country
- Warsaw Pact invasion of Czechoslovakia, 1968
- Boundary between Czech and Slovak republics imposed by Russia, 1st. January, 1969
- The Iron Curtain
- NATO Power
- U.S. Air Force Base
- Canadian Air Force Base
- NATO HQ moves to Brussels

Part 7 – Book List

General reference: Keesings Contemporary Archives

58. *U.S.A.–Twenties to Viet Nam* D. Snowman   Batsford
59. *The U.S.S.R.*   C. Wright Miller OUP
60. *China*   Ping-chia Kuo   OUP
61. *The Post War World*   R. H. Thomas   Philip
62. *Life Since 1900*   C. Furth   Allen & Unwin
63. *The Post War World*   R. H. Thomas   Philip
64. *Czechoslovakia 1968*   P. Windsor &   Chatto & Windus
                                   A. Roberts.

Throughout the Sixties, young people all over the world saw themselves as the agency of social and political change. These West Berlin demonstrators carry pictures of political leaders whose thoughts and actions enjoy massive support: Lenin, Marx and Mao Tse-Tung. (*Deutsche Presse Agentur*)

PART 8

Your World

Progress, change and advance: humanity's efforts in the twentieth century have led to a divided world, a world split into East and West, Communist and non-Communist blocs. For a generation these two divisions have managed to preserve world peace by means of the nuclear deterrent. In 1975 they emerged from the Cold War to settle international frontiers at the Helsinki Conference on European Security. Their scientists showed how they could work together in the International Geophysical Year without worrying about international frontiers and ideological differences. In 1975 America and the Soviet Union provided a dramatic example of international co-operation in their Apollo–Soyuz Test Project when the Apollo spacecraft docked with the Soyuz capsule 140 miles (224 km) above the earth and astronaut Stafford shook hands with cosmonaut Leonov. But after the 1975 link-up Soviet spacemen concentrated on developing their orbiting laboratories and involving representatives from socialist bloc countries in their experiments—the first of whom was Czech cosmonaut Vladimir Remek who visited the Salyut 6 space station in 1978. America had launched her two Voyager space probes in 1977 and these beamed back detailed photographs of Jupiter and Saturn during 1980–81; while the space shuttle Columbia made its two famous flights from Cape Canaveral in April and November 1981 to demonstrate that space-ships were re-usable.

After the beginning of the space age in 1942, scientists developed electronic computers (1946), transistors (1948), satellites (1957), silicon chips (1962) and electrostatic word processors (1963). Between them, they laid the foundations of a communications revolution—the 'information technology' that has already had an impact upon everybody's way of life. Information Technology (IT) is a term covering all micro-electronic devices that can produce, store, obtain and transmit data in the form of words, pictures and numbers.

But while some nations could afford to fund expensive projects such as these, others couldn't even afford to feed their own people. In 1980 Willy Brandt, the former Federal German Chancellor, published a report on the dangers facing the human race when half the world suffered poverty and disease that the other half—if it wished—could put right. Twenty-two nations met at Cancun in Mexico during 1981 to try to formulate a plan that would help less developed countries—but there was little positive action that year, and while such summits were being held new crises appeared to threaten international peace. Africa and the Middle East were still rent by wars and assassinations; international arms control agreements were not implemented; and in Afghanistan (1979) and Poland (1981) the hopes and aspirations of ordinary people were blocked either by outright military invasion or by the imposition of martial law.

65: Instruments of international destruction

The 'Black Portent'

Once the horror of Hiroshima and Nagasaki became known in 1945, President Truman realized that possession of the bomb was 'a grave responsibility for any nation to bear alone'. Was the world, he wondered, responsible enough to share the secrets of nuclear fission—for peaceful purposes? At the U.N., Bernard Baruch put the issue more bluntly as he unfolded his plan for an International Atomic Agency:

> Fellow citizens of the world! We are here to make a choice between the quick and the dead; that is our business. Behind the black portent of the atomic age lies a hope which, if seized upon with faith, can work our salvation. If we fail we have damned every man to be the slave of fear. Let us not deceive ourselves—we must elect world peace, or world destruction.

But because of the distrust generated by the Cold War, America would share her secrets only with Britain, whose scientists had worked closely on the original weapons. Despite this, the Russians exploded a nuclear device in 1949 and between 1954–55 both sides developed hydrogen weapons. Within ten years of Hiroshima, the 'black portent' had grown far more alarming.

Principle of Deterrence

Many International Disarmament Conferences were held in Geneva during this period in an effort to reduce the risk of nuclear war, but the years 1956–1962 saw the 'arms race' worsen. After the 1961 Berlin Wall crisis, Russia and America tested colossal weapons. By 1962 both sides possessed enough bombs and warheads to destroy one another—and probably the whole of planet Earth. Both justified this state of affairs, saying that large armaments deterred the other side from beginning a war. This was the 'policy of the deterrent', history's most awe-inspiring method of preserving world peace.

Partial Test Ban Treaty

'Deterrence' also meant keeping up with the other side's research developments, so there was no end to the escalation of costly, sophisticated devices. In the Sixties, the U.S.A. had its Strategic Air Command of subsonic B-52 bombers on constant patrol; dozens of Polaris submarines and Minuteman ICBMs (Intercontinental Ballistic Missiles) standing by. The U.S.S.R. had fewer but equally powerful equivalents. And apart from the cost of these weapons, continual atomic tests produced radio-active 'fall-out' which endangered world health. Fission products such as strontium-90 and cesium-37 collected in bones and tissues and could cause serious harm. Research showed that in 1962 the fall-out danger had not reached alarming proportions, but indicated that further tests might prove dangerous. This encouraged Russia and America to draw together in 1963; to establish a 'hot-line' (direct telephone link) between the White House and the Kremlin; and to sign the Partial Test Ban Treaty which prohibited all nuclear explosions except those carried out underground. Two nuclear powers, China and France, refused to sign, but the treaty did bring some measure of world relief.

'Proliferation' and 'Deterrent Balance'

Two other dangers remained. The first was the fear that nuclear weapons would 'proliferate' i.e. that more countries would acquire nuclear capability; this problem hadn't been solved by the end of 1966. Then there was the permanent problem of maintaining the deterrent balance between the superpowers. In 1964 it appeared that Russia might have some advantage when she revealed her new 'A.B.M.' (Anti-ballistic missile). This, she claimed, would enable her to destroy U.S. missiles in mid-air! This prompted the Americans to contemplate the building of the enormously expensive and complicated Nike-X computer-controlled A.B.M. system; and to instal Poseidon MIRV missiles in their nuclear submarines.

By the end of the Sixties both superpowers understood the urgent need to limit the extraordinary nuclear armouries they had acquired. They began their S.A.L.T. talks (Strategic Arms Limitation Talks) at Helsinki and Vienna and negotiated agreements* on their A.B.M. systems. Unfortunately, both France and China still jeopardized world health with their nuclear tests at Muroroa Atoll and at Lop Nor. These tests were a constant source of anxiety. Russia feared the growth of Chinese nuclear power and reinforced her armies along the Sino-Soviet frontiers. In the Pacific, both Australia and New Zealand protested against the French tests— and for a time a New Zealand warship patrolled the test area around Muroroa in an effort to deter the French from exploding their nuclear devices.

*See page 148.

A DANGEROUS WORLD

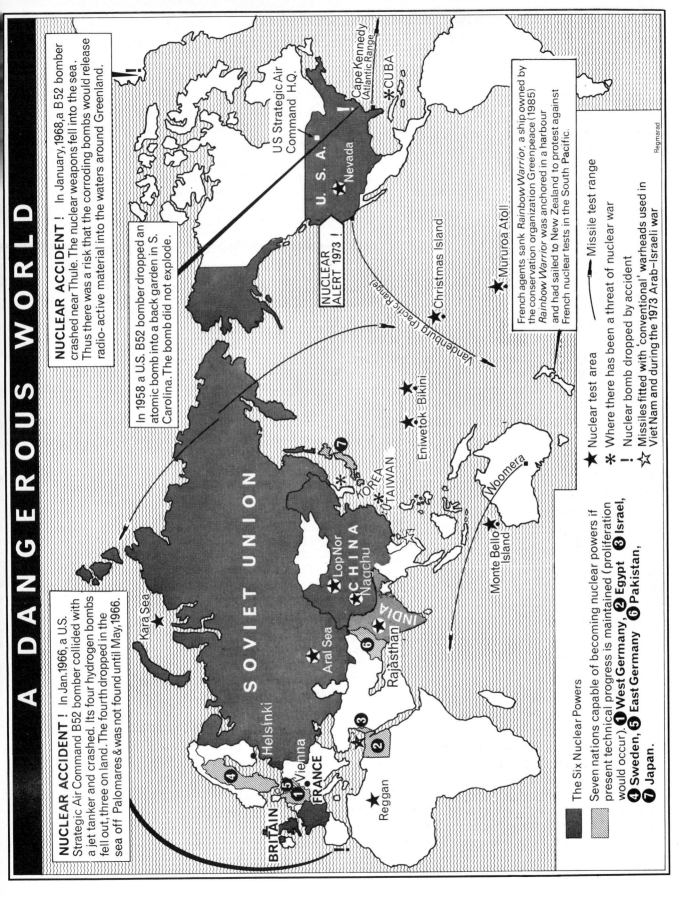

NUCLEAR ACCIDENT! In Jan.1966, a U.S. Strategic Air Command B52 bomber collided with a jet tanker and crashed. Its four hydrogen bombs fell out, three on land. The fourth dropped in the sea off Palomares & was not found until May,1966.

NUCLEAR ACCIDENT! In January, 1968, a B52 bomber crashed near Thule. The nuclear weapons fell into the sea. Thus there was a risk that the corroding bombs would release radio-active material into the waters around Greenland.

In 1958 a U.S. B52 bomber dropped an atomic bomb into a back garden in S. Carolina. The bomb did not explode.

US Strategic Air Command H.Q.

Cape Kennedy (Atlantic Range)

*CUBA

U. S. A.
☆ Nevada

NUCLEAR ALERT 1973 !

Mururoa Atoll

French agents sank *Rainbow Warrior*, a ship owned by the conservation organization Greenpeace (1985) *Rainbow Warrior* was anchored in a harbour and had sailed to New Zealand to protest against French nuclear tests in the South Pacific.

Christmas Island

Landenburg (Pacific Range)

Eniwetok · Bikini

Kara Sea ★

S O V I E T   U N I O N

Helsinki

Vienna

BRITAIN

④

⑤ ● ①

FRANCE

③

② ★

Reggan

Aral Sea ★

Rajāsthan ⑥ ★

INDIA

Lop Nor ★
C H I N A
★ Nagchu

KOREA
☆ TAIWAN

Monte Bello ★
Island

Woomera ■

The Six Nuclear Powers

Seven nations capable of becoming nuclear powers if present technical progress is maintained (proliferation would occur). ① **West Germany,** ② **Egypt** ③ **Israel,** ④ **Sweden,** ⑤ **East Germany** ⑥ **Pakistan,** ⑦ **Japan.**

★ Nuclear test area

* Where there has been a threat of nuclear war

! Nuclear bomb dropped by accident

☆ Missiles fitted with 'conventional' warheads used in VietNam and during the 1973 Arab–Israeli war

— Missile test range

Regmarad

66: Instruments of international co-operation

The 1963 *Partial Test Ban Treaty* proved that the leading powers of the world could come to an understanding for the sake of mankind; the United Nations specialized agencies had long dedicated themselves to the same end. But there have been other events that augur well for the future.

Sputnik

During 1957 and 1958, scientists from 67 nations co-operated in an 'International Geophysical Year' (IGY) designed to discover more about the world we live in. These scientists proved that, even in our divided world, they could maintain their long tradition of sharing knowledge without undue concern for national and political bias. All over the world, scientific teams studied solar flares, explored the ocean bed, examined volcanic formations, recorded radio-active fall-out and sent the first earth satellites into space. For 1957 was the 'year of the Sputnik', the year in which Russia astounded the world with her scientific achievements. It was the Russian 'Sputniks' and the American 'Explorers' and 'Pioneers' that hurtled our world into the Space Age.

Antarctica

During the IGY ten nations set up bases in the Antarctic, a lonely continent where the Ice Age still exists. Here teams of experts tested the thickness of the ice, kept meteorological records and explored mountain ranges where, at heights of 13,000 feet above sea level, the temperature would drop to 110 degrees below zero. As one map-maker remarked after 28 months in the Antarctic:

> The most difficult part was not the weather itself but the effort of maintaining consistently accurate observations under such miserable conditions.

During 1957–58 a Commonwealth expedition made a successful crossing of Antarctica where Captain Scott and his companions had died in 1912. The only hint of international disagreement came when various nations quarrelled over the ownership of tracts of this vaste waste of ice. Then in 1959 came the signing of the *Antarctic Treaty* which ruled that Antarctica was to be used for peaceful purposes only and that national claims to this region should not interfere with scientific research. In the words of one of the most distinguished of the IGY scientists, the Canadian Professor Tuzo Wilson, 'The Treaty makes Antarctica the first truly international territory.' This marked yet another step forward in peaceful international co-operation.

Outer Space Treaty

Seven years after the Antarctic Treaty came an unusual, but vital, international agreement—the *Outer Space Treaty* of December 1966. It ruled that the moon and all the planets were to be used for peaceful purposes only; that no country on Earth may lay claim to ownership of the moon or any other celestial body. The treaty defined astronauts as 'envoys of mankind in outer space' and urged all nations to help spacemen in distress. Most significant of all was Article 4 of the Treaty:

> States parties to the Treaty undertake NOT to place in orbit round the earth any objects carrying nuclear weapons or any other kinds of weapons of mass destruction, install such weapons on celestial bodies, or station such weapons in outer space in any other manner.

Equally significant over the last two decades have been the moves to use nuclear power for peaceful purposes. Many countries now have nuclear research stations and Britain led the way in large scale production of electricity at reactor plants such as Calder Hall and Winfrith Heath. And nuclear power was used for propelling not only Polaris submarines but also icebreakers such as Russia's *Lenin* and merchant ships such as America's *Savannah*.

The prevention of nuclear war

During May 1972 President Nixon made his historic visit to the Soviet Union. In Moscow he signed the very important *Treaty on the Limitation of antiballistic missile systems*. Just over a year later, Chairman Brezhnev arrived in Washington where he initialled an agreement (June 1973) to prevent the outbreak of nuclear war. As Brezhnev commented. 'One can hardly over-estimate its significance for the peaceful life of our peoples and for the future of all mankind.' The 1972 treaty became known as the Strategic Arms Limitation Treaty—or S.A.L.T. 1. It was due to be renewed in 1977. However, because of the breakdown in friendly relations between the U.S.S.R. and America, S.A.L.T. wasn't signed until 1979.*

*See pages 162–3.

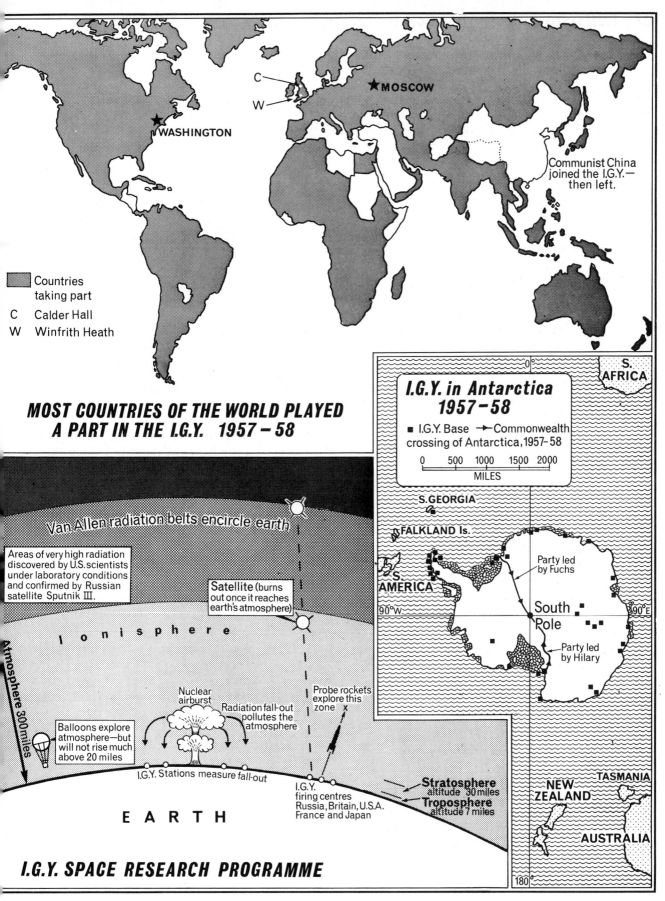

C   Calder Hall
W   Winfrith Heath

Countries taking part

★MOSCOW

C
W
★WASHINGTON

Communist China joined the I.G.Y. — then left.

MOST COUNTRIES OF THE WORLD PLAYED A PART IN THE I.G.Y. 1957–58

I.G.Y. in Antarctica 1957–58

■ I.G.Y. Base   → Commonwealth crossing of Antarctica, 1957–58

0   500   1000   1500   2000
MILES

S. AFRICA

S. GEORGIA

FALKLAND Is.

S. AMERICA

90°W

Party led by Fuchs

South Pole

90°E

Party led by Hilary

NEW ZEALAND

TASMANIA

AUSTRALIA

180°

Van Allen radiation belts encircle earth

Areas of very high radiation discovered by U.S. scientists under laboratory conditions and confirmed by Russian satellite Sputnik III.

Satellite (burns out once it reaches earth's atmosphere)

I o n i s p h e r e

Atmosphere 300 miles

Nuclear airburst

Radiation fall-out pollutes the atmosphere

Probe rockets explore this zone

Balloons explore atmosphere—but will not rise much above 20 miles

I.G.Y. Stations measure fall-out

I.G.Y. firing centres Russia, Britain, U.S.A. France and Japan

Stratosphere altitude 30 miles
Troposphere altitude 7 miles

E A R T H

I.G.Y. SPACE RESEARCH PROGRAMME

67: The exploration of space

The German V-2

On Peenemünde Island (Hitler's research centre for work on radar, jets and atomic weapons) a group of German scientists had gathered to watch the firing of the first A/4 rocket, commonly called the V.2. As it soared into the air General Dornberger, the German commander, remarked, 'Today the space age is born'. It was 1942.

After Germany's surrender in 1945, most of these scientists went to work in the U.S.A. where they and their American colleagues developed the V.2 into a vehicle capable of carrying instruments into outer space. Meanwhile, scientists in the Soviet Union were concentrating on building monster rockets capable of lifting heavy payloads. The remarkable success of the Russians in this field was due, not to captured German brains as some have suggested, but to their own technical brilliance.

Man in Space

The Space Age truly began with the launching of Sputnik 1 during the International Geophysical Year, although the first manned exploration of space came when Major Yuri Gagarin orbited the earth in his Vostok spacecraft on 12 April 1961. Next month America fired Alan Shepard on a ballistic flight which took him to a height of 113 miles; and in July Virgil Grissom repeated the experiment. America's first orbital flight occurred when in February 1962, nearly a year after Gagarin's success, Colonel John Glenn circled the earth three times. The next four years saw many spectacular manned space flights. In 1962 Russia sent up two spaceships which orbited only a few miles apart; in 1963 Valentina Tereshkova became the first woman astronaut and completed 48 orbits. By the end of 1966, America had completed the Gemini programme of manned flights with the remarkable achievements of the two astronauts, Aldrin and Lovell. During their four-day flight they docked with their Agena target and Aldrin carried out the longest 'space-walk' then recorded.

Unmanned probes

Unmanned probes were equally impressive. Again Russia had led the way when in 1959 she released three Luniks to explore the moon. Lunik 1 missed the moon and became the sun's first artificial planet; Lunik 2 made a direct hit on the moon in September; while Lunik 3 photographed the far side of the moon in October and relayed the pictures back to earth. In

1964 America's Ranger 7 managed to hit the moon within six miles of its target and, before it crashed, transmitted pictures of the lunar surface from a height of 1000 feet. By the end of 1966 Russian and American probes had made 'soft landings' on the moon so that TV cameras were able to relay pictures of the lunar landscape from a height of four feet. The long-distance probes to Venus and Mars carried out by Russia in 1961 and 1962 both suffered from instrument failures, while the American Mariner probes to Mars in 1964–65 were erratic and difficult to control.

The first men on the Moon

Now America began her spectacular Apollo programme—the manned exploration of the Moon*. At Christmas 1968 three astronauts orbited the Moon and returned safely to Earth. Then on 16 July 1969 a million people at Cape Kennedy watched a Saturn rocket lift-off Apollo XI. Riding inside were three astronauts: Neil Armstrong, the Flight Commander; Michael Collins, Command Module Pilot; Edwin Aldrin, Lunar Module Pilot. Their destination was the surface of the Moon. Four days later the Lunar Module *Eagle* landed in the south-west corner of the Sea of Tranquillity. Armstrong and Aldrin stepped down to the surface of the moon— and about one fifth of the world's population watched the moon-walk on television. *Eagle* then blasted off and docked with the Command Module *Columbia* which had remained in orbit round the Moon. The three astronauts successfully re-entered the Earth's atmosphere and splashed down in the Pacific on 24 July 1969. It had been a triumph of training, timing and technology.

The hazards

Before 1967 neither Russia nor America had lost a single astronaut in this hazardous business of space exploration. Then in January that year, tragedy struck the Apollo launching pad at Cape Kennedy. Three astronauts, Grissom, White and Chaffee, died when fire charred their capsule as it sat on top of its Saturn rocket. And in April Colonel Komorov** died when his spaceship's parachutes failed to function after re-entry. In 1986 all seven crew died when the space shuttle Challenger disintegrated 12 seconds after launch. Such is the sacrifice men and women have made in the job which carries the highest risk in the world.

*Successfully completed by Apollo 17 (December 1972).
**Three more Soviet cosmonauts died in 1971—on board Soyuz 11.

SKETCH MAPS OF THE MOON

The reverse side first seen in 1959

Where the first men landed 20 July, 1969

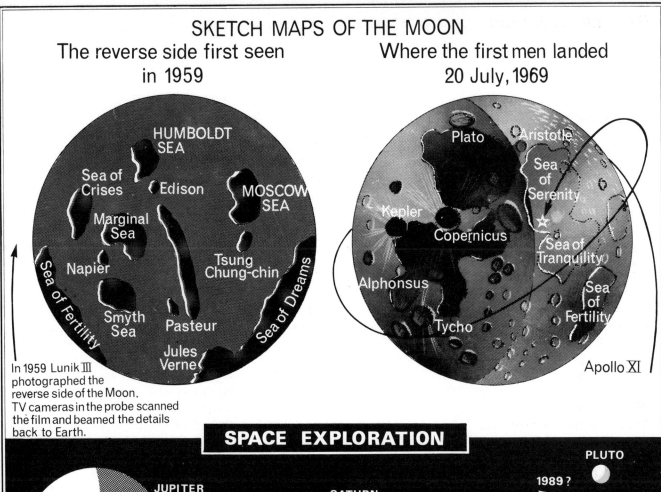

HUMBOLDT SEA

Sea of Crises

Edison

MOSCOW SEA

Marginal Sea

Tsung Chung-chin

Napier

Sea of Fertility

Smyth Sea

Pasteur

Sea of Dreams

Jules Verne

In 1959 Lunik III photographed the reverse side of the Moon. TV cameras in the probe scanned the film and beamed the details back to Earth.

Plato

Aristotle

Sea of Serenity

Kepler

Copernicus

Sea of Tranquility

Alphonsus

Sea of Fertility

Tycho

Apollo XI

SPACE EXPLORATION

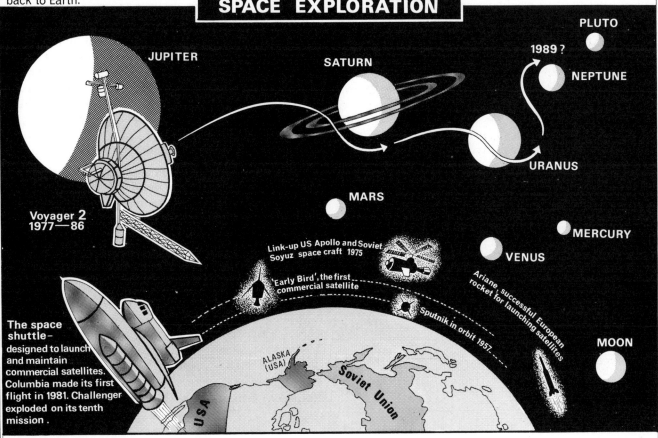

PLUTO

JUPITER

SATURN

1989 ?

NEPTUNE

URANUS

MARS

MERCURY

VENUS

MOON

Voyager 2 1977—86

Link-up US Apollo and Soviet Soyuz space craft 1975

'Early Bird', the first commercial satellite

Ariane successful European rocket for launching satellites

Sputnik in orbit 1957

The space shuttle – designed to launch and maintain commercial satellites. Columbia made its first flight in 1981. Challenger exploded on its tenth mission.

ALASKA (USA)

Soviet Union

USA

Voyager 1 and Voyager 2 were American space probes that began their journeys into space during 1977. Voyager 2 was a spectacular success, diving through Saturn's rings in 1981, photographing Uranus in 1986 and then continuing towards its next destination, Neptune, scheduled for 1989.

68: The continued quest for peace and national liberation 1968–1975

International détente

In December 1968 President Nixon appointed to his staff a man destined to help heal some of the wounds existing between America and the communist world. He was Dr. Henry Kissinger and it was largely through his efforts that President Nixon was able to visit Peking and Moscow in 1972—visits which led to new understandings between America and her Cold War enemies. In fact, the Russians seemed only too happy to refer to 'the end of the Cold War'—a feeling that was, to a limited extent, borne out by developments in the traditional trouble-spots of the world.

The old flash-points

i) *Divided Germany*: as the leaders of East and West Germany became more friendly towards one another they tried, in their *Basic Treaty* of July 1973*, to 'make the best of a sterile and dangerous situation'. Both countries joined the U.N. in September 1973 and thousands of Germans exchanged visits between East and West. But the two hundred who had tried illegally to cross the Berlin Wall or the death strips during 1971–2 met their fate at the hands of the border guards or trod on anti-personnel mines. However, a cordial atmosphere developed in which even the Russians now joined. In 1971 they invited Chancellor Brandt to the USSR and two years later they were supplying the West Germans with natural gas in exchange for high quality steel piping.
ii) *Divided Korea*: twenty years after the armistice had been signed at Panmunjom, the D.M.Z. remained tightly sealed as far as North and South Korea were concerned. Nevertheless, North and South representatives visited one another's capitals during 1972 and agreed to work for peaceful re-unification, for the establishment of a 'hot-line' between Pyongyang and Seoul and for a reduction in the armed forces—though Kim Il Sung was adamant that all U.S. troops must leave the peninsula before this could happen.
iii) *Cuba*: apart from occasional scares that Soviet submarines were using Cuban bases, international tension virtually disappeared from the Caribbean during the ten years following the 1962 Cuban missile crisis.
iv) *Divided Viet Nam*: as far as the Americans were concerned peace came to Viet Nam in 1973. Dr. Kissinger had had many conversations with North Vietnamese

*See page 120.

representatives in Paris and on 28 January 1973 a cease-fire officially came into operation. More accurately, this meant that *Americans* were no longer involved in the fighting for, as President Thieu later admitted, 'there has been no cease-fire at all . . . a full-scale war may soon be rekindled.' It was. In April 1975 President Thieu fell from power as the armed forces of North Viet Nam occupied the south to reunite it under communist rule.

National liberation movements

i) *The Frelimos*: one European country, Portugal, still controlled large areas of colonial Africa. Technically, the Portuguese defined their African territories as provinces rather than colonies, but this fine distinction escaped the thousands of guerrilla fighters operating in Angola, Mozambique and Portuguese Guinea. The most publicised guerrilla units were the Frelimos who waged a vicious war against the Portuguese army in Mozambique. When Frelimos attacked targets such as the Cabora Bassa dam project, thousands of Portuguese conscripts took part in anti-guerrilla operations comparable with those in Viet Nam. They frequently behaved in a ruthless fashion and during 1973 were accused of the Wiriyamu massacre. In 1974 the army seized power in Portugal and conceded political and military defeat in the colonies. Portuguese Guinea became independent Guinea-Bissau in 1974; Angola and Mozambique became independent in 1975.
ii) *Palestinian guerrillas*: today no nation is free from the threat of guerrilla attack now that revolutionaries and terrorists are prepared to murder innocent civilians during their hi-jacking and bombing campaigns. Various Palestinian Liberation groups have adopted unprecedented forms of attack. In May 1972 they used Japanese gunmen to kill 28 people in the Lod airport massacre. Four months later Black September terrorists murdered 11 Israeli athletes during the Munich Olympics. Since then the Israelis have carried out equally reprehensible attacks. In February 1973 their jet fighters shot down a Libyan Boeing 727 and killed 104 people. Two months later their so-called 'commandos'—some disguised as hippies—entered some apartment blocks in Beirut and gunned down the top Palestinian guerrilla leaders. It was not long before the Arabs and Israelis were at one another's throats in a full-scale war.

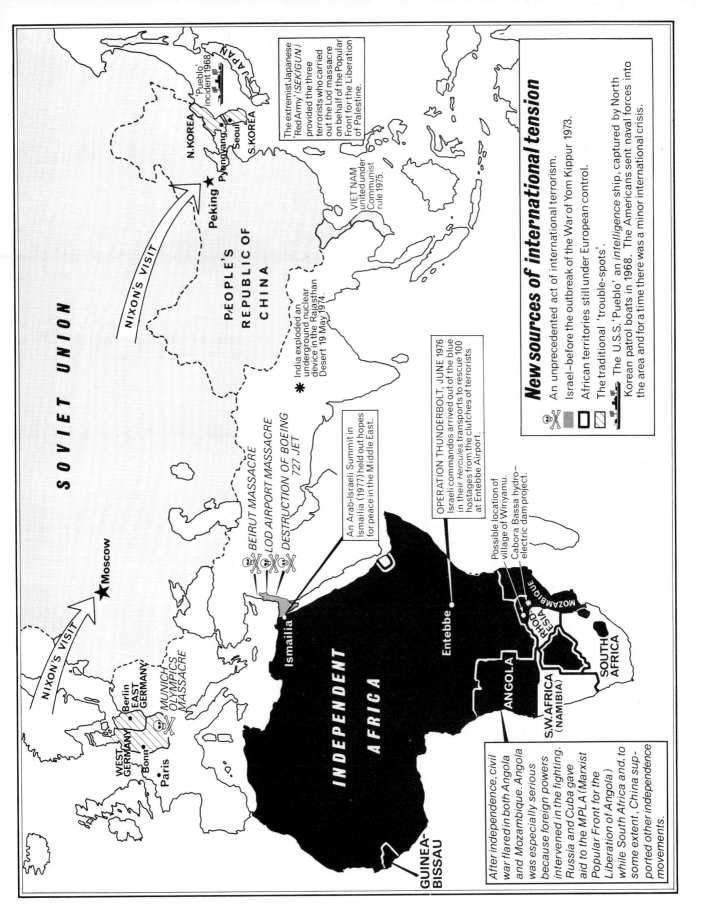

New sources of international tension

An unprecedented act of international terrorism.

Israel—before the outbreak of the War of Yom Kippur 1973.

African territories still under European control.

The traditional 'trouble-spots'.

The U.S.S. 'Pueblo' an *intelligence* ship, captured by North Korean patrol boats in 1968. The Americans sent naval forces into the area and for a time there was a minor international crisis.

'Pueblo' incident 1968

The extremist Japanese 'Red Army' (*SEKIGUN*) provided the three terrorists who carried out the Lod massacre on behalf of the Popular Front for the Liberation of Palestine.

VIET NAM united under Communist rule 1975.

India exploded an underground nuclear device in the Rajasthan Desert 19 May 1974.

NIXON'S VISIT

SOVIET UNION

PEOPLE'S REPUBLIC OF CHINA

JAPAN

N.KOREA

Pyongyang

Seoul

S.KOREA

Peking

Moscow

BEIRUT MASSACRE

LOD AIRPORT MASSACRE

DESTRUCTION OF BOEING 727 JET

An Arab-Israeli Summit in Ismailia (1977) held out hopes for peace in the Middle East.

OPERATION THUNDERBOLT, JUNE 1976 Israeli commandos arrived out of the blue in their *Hercules* transports to rescue 100 hostages from the clutches of terrorists at Entebbe Airport.

Possible location of village of Wiriyamu.

Cabora Bassa hydro–electric dam project.

MUNICH OLYMPICS MASSACRE

Berlin

EAST GERMANY

WEST GERMANY

Bonn

Paris

Ismailia

INDEPENDENT AFRICA

Entebbe

ANGOLA

S.W.AFRICA (NAMIBIA)

MOZAMBIQUE

RHODESIA

SOUTH AFRICA

GUINEA-BISSAU

After independence, civil war flared in both Angola and Mozambique. Angola was especially serious because foreign powers intervened in the fighting. Russia and Cuba gave aid to the MPLA (Marxist Popular Front for the Liberation of Angola) while South Africa and, to some extent, China supported other independence movements.

153

69: The Yom Kippur War 1973

The Arab attacks

Quite secretly and throughout the summer of 1973 the Egyptian and Syrian armed forces planned their surprise attacks upon the lands wrested from them by Israel back in 1967. On 6 October 1973 (it was *Yom Kippur* in the Jewish calendar—the Day of Atonement) a thousand field guns lashed the Israeli reservists holding the Bar-Lev line; specially trained engineers and assault troops slithered down the sandy slopes of the Suez Canal and rushed the enemy defences. Simultaneously, 1,200 Syrian tanks poked their gun muzzles over the Golan Heights to begin, they hoped, an Arab *blitzkrieg*.

Initial Arab successes

Bombarded by hundreds of SAM missiles, the ill-prepared Israeli troops reeled under this unprecedented form of attack. They fell back, desperately radioing for help from their fighter-pilots. But as soon as the *Phantoms* and *Skyhawks* appeared they fell flaming from the skies as deadly SAM-7 *Strela* heat-seeking missiles homed in on the Israeli jets. Above the Golan Heights the Israelis suffered heavy losses in this new form of combat, losses which forced the survivors to change their tactics and to fit their planes with anti-missile missiles. Then they took off to fly mission after mission against the Syrian armour and within a week they had destroyed nearly a thousand enemy tanks. Israeli ground troops pushed the Syrians back and even preempted an Iraqi attack by dropping paratroopers on a column of unsuspecting Arab reinforcements. By 13 October the Israeli army stood poised for an advance on Damascus, the Syrian capital.

Tank battles in Sinai

Meanwhile, the Israelis 'in Africa' (the expression used by troops stationed in Sinai) were desperately trying to contain the thousands of Egyptians who had swarmed across the Suez Canal. Squadrons of Egypt's Russian-built *T.55s* and *T.64s* clashed with Israel's British *Centurions* and American *M.48s*. These tank battles were on a scale greater than any of those in the Western Desert during World War II and were probably equal in size and intensity to the clash between Russian and German armour at Kursk, thirty years earlier.

Israeli counter-attack

Now that they had defeated the Syrians in the north, the Israelis were ready to take the offensive in Sinai. On 15 October three tank brigades commanded by General Sharon discovered a weak spot in the Egyptian line just south of Ismailia. With typical Israeli *panache* these brigades smashed a path between Egypt's Second and Third Armies and even managed to get a few tanks across the Canal. They then held the Egyptian forces at the *Battle of Chinese Farm** so that Israeli engineers could push pontoon bridges across to the west side of the Canal. This daring attack not only cut the enemy forces in half; it also managed—by 24 October—to encircle the entire Third Army around Suez. And now that many of the SAM missile sites had been overrun the Israeli jets could at last come into their own. Almost every *MiG* sent in by the Egyptians fell victim to Israeli pilots flying *Mirage* interceptors.

The 'cease-fire crisis'

Individually and collectively, the great powers in the United Nations made frantic efforts to end the Yom Kippur War. Americans and Russians used their new-found friendship to solve the problem—though at first matters didn't look too promising when the Russians declared that the first requirement was the withdrawal of Israeli forces from the territories they had occupied during the Six Days War in 1967. Dr. Kissinger flew to see Mr. Brezhnev; Mr. Kosygin went to Cairo to talk to a militant President Sadat. Eventually a cease-fire was agreed for 22 October. But then the Israelis resumed the fighting—they were determined to encircle the Third Army—and although a second cease-fire was imposed two days later the Egyptians appealed for Russian and American help. Fearing that Brezhnev might send Russian troops to the Middle East, Nixon put U.S. armed forces on nuclear alert! Suddenly, without warning, the world seemed to be as close to disaster as it had been during the 1962 Cuban missile crisis. Fortunately, the Russians favoured the second cease-fire and on 31 October the U.S. President cancelled the nuclear alert. After this harrowing experience it was a very grateful world that watched the ubiquitous Dr. Kissinger bring to the conference table at Geneva those Arab representatives who were willing to discuss the subject of military disengagement with Israel's Foreign Minister, Abba Eban.

---

*So named because Chinese agricultural experts had been working in the area just before hostilities began.

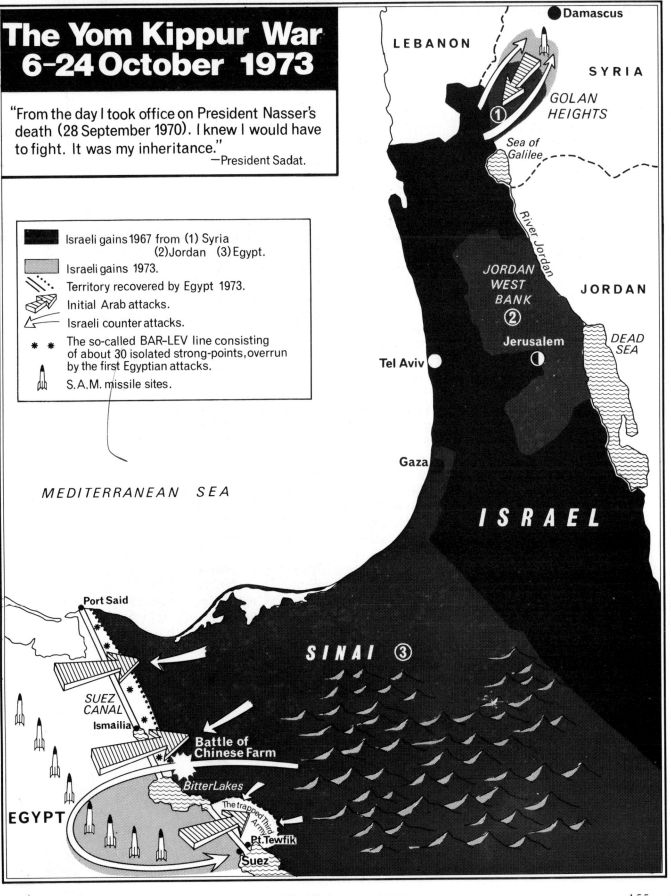

The Yom Kippur War 6–24 October 1973

"From the day I took office on President Nasser's death (28 September 1970). I knew I would have to fight. It was my inheritance."
—President Sadat.

Israeli gains 1967 from (1) Syria (2) Jordan (3) Egypt.

Israeli gains 1973.

Territory recovered by Egypt 1973.

Initial Arab attacks.

Israeli counter attacks.

The so-called BAR–LEV line consisting of about 30 isolated strong-points, overrun by the first Egyptian attacks.

S.A.M. missile sites.

LEBANON

Damascus

SYRIA

GOLAN HEIGHTS

①

Sea of Galilee

River Jordan

JORDAN WEST BANK

②

Jerusalem

JORDAN

DEAD SEA

Tel Aviv

Gaza

ISRAEL

MEDITERRANEAN SEA

Port Said

SUEZ CANAL

Ismailia

Battle of Chinese Farm

Bitter Lakes

The trapped Third Army

Pt. Tewfik

EGYPT

Suez

SINAI

③

155

70: The World Energy Crisis 1972–1973

Early warning signs

During the winter of 1972–3 a sudden shortage of heating oil forced many schools and factories in America to close. In Colorado motorists arrived at their filling stations to find 'No Gas' notices on the forecourt. Experts were soon arguing about the causes of this unexpected shortage. They all knew that fossil fuels would be exhausted one day—but *surely* that day was many years in the future? It seemed that there were several factors to consider:

i. Because the U.S.A. used oil for 45% of its energy needs (and this percentage was rising annually) there were insufficient refineries in the country to process the increasing imports of crude oil. This appeared to be the root cause of the shortages.

ii. However, the recent oil price increases had forced several petrol distributors out of business—so there was less fuel on the American market.

iii. Moreover, as the Americans were no longer self-sufficient (this in itself came as a major shock to most people) they had to import crude oil from the Middle East. This was an open invitation to Arab countries who resented America's support of Israel to interrupt oil supplies to the United States.

This last view came across very strongly in September 1973 when King Faisal of Saudi Arabia gave an interview on N.B.C. Television. He confirmed that oil deliveries from his country would depend upon U.S. policies overseas. Simultaneously, 76 "non-aligned" countries meeting in Algiers heard Yugoslavia's President Tito underline the new strength of the Third World—a strength that would increase once advanced nations such as America understood that their standard of living depended upon the poorer countries who were lucky enough to possess enormous energy reserves.

The catalyst

Events soon proved how right Tito had been. Having failed to gain their objectives by attacking the Israelis in the Yom Kippur War, the Arabs decided to push the Israelis back to their pre-1967 frontiers by using oil as an international sanction—just as Britain had been trying to do over Rhodesia for years. As most of the Arab oil-producing states agreed to cut-back oil supplies to nations—such as Holland and America—who favoured Israel, it would be true to say that the Yom Kippur War acted as the catalyst in the world energy crisis.

Immediate effects

The decision had a catastrophic effect upon the industrial nations. They had no other sources of supply simply because the world was already desperately short of oil. Neither Nigeria nor Indonesia could increase production for several years. Venezuela's rich deposits were rapidly drying up* and she was already exporting 50% of her production to Britain and America. Consequently, Rotterdam's huge refinery had its crude oil imports reduced and as the Dutch supplied most of Western Europe with petrol there were instant shortages there. Britain was unlucky in that the oil embargo coincided with other crises in her energy industries. The Japanese were appalled by the Arab decision—they were almost totally dependent upon imported oil. Their Deputy Prime Minister hurried to the Middle East to plead for the resumption of supplies while, back home, Japanese housewives with memories of wartime shortages began hoarding consumer goods and even resorted to riot in some city supermarkets! Even the Comecon countries—ironically, including Yugoslavia—suffered from the Arab cut-back. Was there an alternative energy source?

A difficult problem

America and Canada have rich reserves of oil shale and tar sands—but to obtain a million tons of oil from shale it is necessary to shift two million tons of rock! Some countries—especially Britain**—could increase coal production. Nuclear power, tidal and solar energy could all be developed. But these alternatives would take time and a great deal of investment capital. Perhaps it was just as well that the Western world had been forced to grasp the fact that it had been wasting Planet Earth's fossil fuels for most of the twentieth century, that energy was now going to be *very* expensive and that it no longer had the right to develop its technology at the expense of the poor countries who happen to be sitting on large reserves of oil.

* Venezuelans expect their oil deposits to dry up around 1988. They are wondering how to develop an alternative economy.
** Britain proposed to open up a new coal seam at Selby, Yorkshire and to speed up development of the North Sea oilfields, the first of which came 'on stream' in 1975.

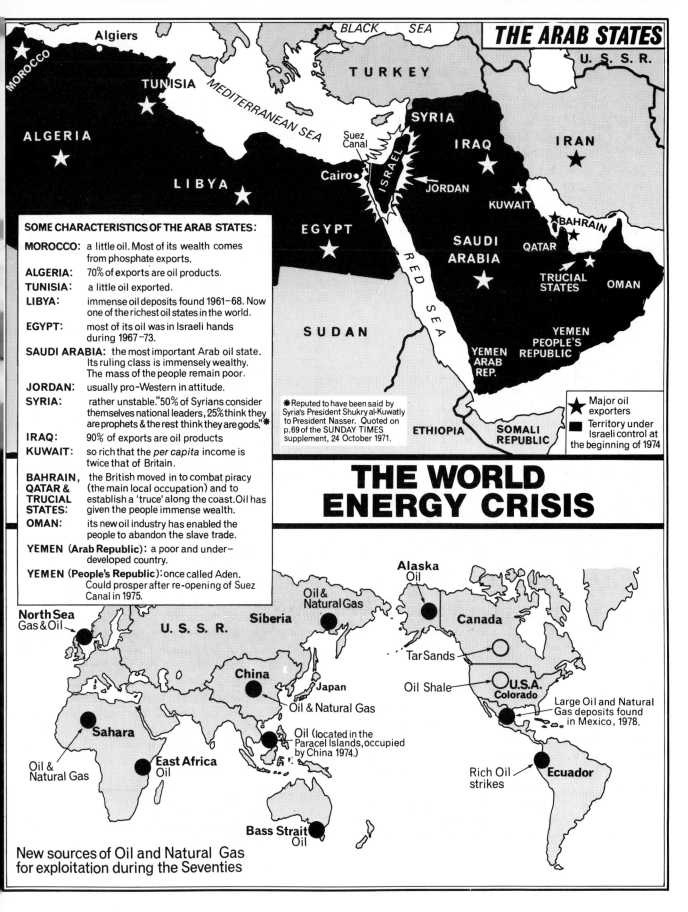

THE ARAB STATES

BLACK SEA

U.S.S.R.

MOROCCO

Algiers

TUNISIA

MEDITERRANEAN SEA

TURKEY

SYRIA

IRAQ

IRAN

ALGERIA

Suez Canal

Cairo

ISRAEL

JORDAN

KUWAIT

BAHRAIN

LIBYA

EGYPT

SAUDI ARABIA

QATAR

TRUCIAL STATES

OMAN

RED SEA

SUDAN

YEMEN PEOPLE'S REPUBLIC

YEMEN ARAB REP.

ETHIOPIA

SOMALI REPUBLIC

SOME CHARACTERISTICS OF THE ARAB STATES:

MOROCCO: a little oil. Most of its wealth comes from phosphate exports.

ALGERIA: 70% of exports are oil products.

TUNISIA: a little oil exported.

LIBYA: immense oil deposits found 1961–68. Now one of the richest oil states in the world.

EGYPT: most of its oil was in Israeli hands during 1967–73.

SAUDI ARABIA: the most important Arab oil state. Its ruling class is immensely wealthy. The mass of the people remain poor.

JORDAN: usually pro-Western in attitude.

SYRIA: rather unstable. "50% of Syrians consider themselves national leaders, 25% think they are prophets & the rest think they are gods."✱

IRAQ: 90% of exports are oil products

KUWAIT: so rich that the *per capita* income is twice that of Britain.

BAHRAIN, QATAR & TRUCIAL STATES: the British moved in to combat piracy (the main local occupation) and to establish a 'truce' along the coast. Oil has given the people immense wealth.

OMAN: its new oil industry has enabled the people to abandon the slave trade.

YEMEN (Arab Republic): a poor and under-developed country.

YEMEN (People's Republic): once called Aden. Could prosper after re-opening of Suez Canal in 1975.

✱ Reputed to have been said by Syria's President Shukry al-Kuwatly to President Nasser. Quoted on p.69 of the SUNDAY TIMES supplement, 24 October 1971.

★ Major oil exporters

■ Territory under Israeli control at the beginning of 1974

THE WORLD ENERGY CRISIS

North Sea
Gas & Oil

U.S.S.R.

Siberia

Oil & Natural Gas

Alaska
Oil

Canada

Tar Sands

China

Japan

Oil & Natural Gas

Oil Shale

U.S.A.
Colorado

Large Oil and Natural Gas deposits found in Mexico, 1978.

Sahara

Oil &
Natural Gas

East Africa
Oil

Oil (located in the Paracel Islands, occupied by China 1974.)

Rich Oil strikes

Ecuador

Bass Strait
Oil

New sources of Oil and Natural Gas
for exploitation during the Seventies

157

71: The West Europeans 1972–1975

The enlarged community

In January 1973 three new member countries—Denmark, Ireland and the United Kingdom—joined the European Economic Community. Their entry was not without drama. During May 1972 the Irish government had held a referendum to test whether or not its people wished to join the E.E.C. The Irish voted overwhelmingly in favour of entry. Yet when the Norwegian government asked its people the crucial question: 'Do you think Norway should join the European Communities?' the Norwegians turned the Common Market down*. Though there had never been any provision within the Norwegian constitution for holding such a referendum, Prime Minister Bratteli thought it advisable to give the electorate a chance to participate in the vital decision. Naturally, once Norway had voted *against* entry, there was great interest in the next country to hold a referendum. In October 1972 63.3% of the Danish voters *favoured* entry. 'We wish,' they said, 'to participate in the construction of Europe and to contribute what we have to offer to that Europe.' Perhaps the British would have echoed these sentiments—but they never had the chance. Prime Minister Heath—a convinced Marketeer**—believed that a referendum was unnecessary.

Problems for the British

To mark Britain's entry into the E.E.C., the British government had planned an elaborate 'Fanfare for Europe'. But even before the first year of membership was over, the celebrations died away. The British became engrossed in their own problems. Severe economic crises forced the Conservative government to pass successive stages of legislation in order to limit free, collective wage bargaining. It hoped that a policy of strict wage controls would reduce inflation. After all, argued the government, high wages simply pushed up manufacturing costs and it wouldn't be long before British goods priced themselves out of the market. Many Trade Unionists opposed these arguments and challenged the justice of Stage III—at least as far as the mining industry was concerned. Unfortunately, these difficulties coincided with the 1973 Middle East crisis, the oil shortage and the world-wide increase in oil prices. In an effort to conserve energy, Prime Minister Heath declared a *State of Emergency* which, by January 1974, had entered its third month—the longest State of Emergency since the year of the General Strike (1926). Emergency measures included a three-day working week for industry which, by the beginning of 1974, placed millions of workers on short time. These events were decisive factors in the defeat of the Conservative Party in the 1974 General Election.

Europe and America

Chancellor Brandt's dreams of a 'United States of Europe'*** would obviously take many years to come true. Nevertheless, the E.E.C. discussed collective security and, spurred on by the Arab oil cut-back, a common foreign policy. When the Community expressed alarm over President Nixon's nuclear alert (October 1973), Dr. Kissinger accused the West Europeans of acting selfishly simply to ingratiate themselves with Arab oil producers. 'Some of our European allies', he said, 'saw their interests so different from those of the United States that they are prepared to break rank with the U.S. on a matter of very grave international consequence.'

Europe's law and order problems

Undoubtedly, the most lawless area in the E.E.C. was Ulster where, for a time, Britain had to suspend democratic government and rule the province directly from Westminster. While 12,000 troops tried to pacify troubled Ulster, units of the Royal Navy engaged Icelandic gunboats in the rather ridiculous *Cod Wars*. Far more serious was the emergence of the international terrorist. Britain had known the occasional Irish Republican Army bomb outrage during the Thirties; but the modern terrorist attacked targets all over the world to draw maximum attention to his cause. Europe in the Seventies became the scene of car bombs, letter bombs, hijacking and political assassination. Early in 1974 police and troops had to set up a security alert at London Airport in case Palestinian guerrillas attacked civil aircraft with SAM-7 missiles. Governments had a duty to take such precautions after the horrifying Rome Airport massacre in December 1973.

---

*The Norwegians held their referendum in September 1972.
**He led Britain's original application 1961–63. See p. 136. Britain did hold a referendum in 1975 and voted to stay in the Common Market.

***Willy Brandt didn't just want economic and monetary union in Western Europe; his aim was political union.

THE WEST EUROPEANS

ICELAND

The 1973 and 1975-6 'COD WARS'

ICELAND (joined E.F.T.A. in 1970)
- Areas where fishing is limited
- Conservation areas

Rich reserves of natural gas and oil that exist in the North Sea are of enormous value to E.E.C. members.

FINLAND

NORWAY

SWEDEN

DENMARK

ULSTER remained the most lawless area in Europe 1970-5; the 1975 'cease-fire' was a dismal failure.

Murder of Lord Louis Mountbatten, Sligo Bay, 1979.

EIRE

UNITED KINGDOM

London

NETHERLANDS

BELGIUM

LUX.

WEST GERMANY

COMECON COUNTRIES

1971-73 A growing terrorist problem in Britain

1. The 'Angry Brigade' 1971.
2. I.R.A. bombs.
3. Letter bombs.
4. Two Pakistanis shot while attacking Indian High Commission 1973.
5. Threats from Palestinian guerrillas.

AUSTRIA

FRANCE

SWITZERLAND

ITALY

Assassination of Spanish Prime Minister, Admiral Blanco – 20 Dec. 1973.

PORTUGAL

Madrid

S P A I N

Rome

GREECE

Rome Airport Massacre
Even after the end of the War of Yom Kippur the Palestinian guerrillas kept up their terror attacks. Their worst exploit in 1973 was the attack upon a Pan-American jet at Leonardo da Vinci International Airport, Rome, Dec 1973.
The terrorists hurled fire bombs into the aircraft's fuselage and roasted 32 people to death.

THE ENLARGED COMMUNITY JAN. 1973
1. France
2. West Germany
3. Italy
4. Belgium
5. Netherlands
6. Luxembourg
7. Denmark
8. Eire
9. United Kingdom

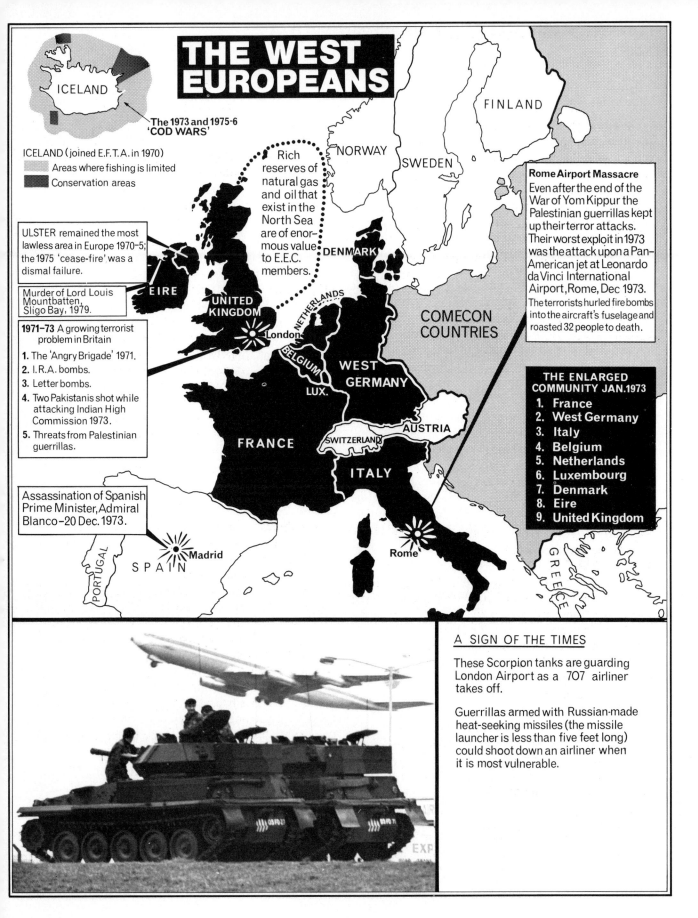

A SIGN OF THE TIMES

These Scorpion tanks are guarding London Airport as a 707 airliner takes off.

Guerrillas armed with Russian-made heat-seeking missiles (the missile launcher is less than five feet long) could shoot down an airliner when it is most vulnerable.

72: Africa and the Middle East since 1974

Black majority rule

By the end of 1980 all but two major areas of southern Africa (Namibia and the Republic of South Africa) had secured independent black majority rule. Portugal had withdrawn from the struggle against the guerrilla armies operating in Angola and Mozambique (1975), an event that heartened the *Patriotic Front* guerrillas waging war against the illegal Smith régime in Rhodesia. The 1979 Commonwealth Conference in Lusaka urged Britain to find a peaceful solution to the fourteen-year-old problem. In 1980 Rhodesia's black citizens, now proudly calling themselves Zimbabweans, voted in a free democratic election supervised by British and Commonwealth troops and policemen. Robert Mugabe's *Zimbabwe African People's Union* (Z.A.P.U.) won the election and in April 1980 he became Prime Minister of an independent Zimbabwe.

The Republic of South Africa

Isolated from the rest of Africa, the white Afrikaner government continued its policy of *apartheid* ('separateness') and refused to grant black majority rule except in those African homelands defined as 'independent Bantustans'. Transkei became the first of these in 1976; followed by Bophuthatswana (1977), Venda (1979) and Ciskei (1981). But these Bantustans became dumping grounds for black people who weren't needed for work in the white areas, and, inevitably, the poverty of the Bantustans caused malnutrition, disease and hopelessness among thousands of black families, often separated from their menfolk. There was protest: from children in Soweto who protested against the use of Afrikaans in their lessons and who sparked off the riots described as the 'whirlwind before the storm'*; and from guerrillas based in Zimbabwe who led raids across the border as part of their effort to transform white-dominated South Africa into an independent black 'Azania'.

Namibia

South Africa had ruled the former German colony of *Sud-West Afrika* since the First World War. In 1966 the South Africans extended their apartheid laws into the territory. The U.N. progressively retaliated by ending South Africa's mandate there; by defining the area as 'Namibia'; and by recognizing S.W.A.P.O. (*South West African People's Organization*) as the true representatives of the Namibian people. South Africa feared the

creation of yet another hostile black state along her frontier and countered S.W.A.P.O. guerrilla raids by hitting S.W.A.P.O. bases in Angola. These offensive sweeps reached a climax during 1981 when South African troops drove deep into Angola to fight S.W.A.P.O., Angolan and eastern bloc forces.**

Other confrontations

Throughout the 1970s, Africa was a divided continent. Its O.A.U. (*Organization for African Unity*) was unable to stop the fighting between Polisario guerrillas and Moroccan troops in the Western Sahara (1976–82); unable to settle the conflict between Ethiopia and Somalia over the Ogaden (1977–78); and helpless when faced by a civil war in Chad—a war that led to the Libyan occupation of that country during 1979–81. Africa's new nation-states seemed united on one issue only: South Africa's racial policies.

Events in the Middle East

Up to 1977 the Muslim world had been unanimous in its condemnation of Israel's very existence. Then came President Sadat's courageous visit to Jerusalem in 1977. In turn, this led to his meeting with Prime Minister Begin and President Carter at Camp David in 1978; and then to the 1979 peace treaty between Israel and Egypt. This was signed in the spirit of the Camp David Agreements: recognition of the state of Israel; autonomy for Palestinians living on the West Bank and in the Gaza strip; and gradual Israeli evacuation of Sinai. This peace treaty split the Muslim world, already threatened by the Soviet invasion of Afghanistan (1979) and the outbreak of the Gulf War between Iran and Iraq (1980). So the main effort against Israel came from the Arab-backed *Palestine Liberation Organization* (P.L.O.) in the Lebanon, where the U.N. struggled to keep apart the armies of Israel, Syria and the bellicose Christian groups of that perpetually disturbed country. Meanwhile, Israel honoured her promise to evacuate the Sinai, and mourned the loss of President Sadat, shot by his own soldiers at a military parade in Cairo during 1981. Yet Israel's sense of security in the south seemed to encourage a new aggressiveness towards other members of the Muslim world. In June 1981 her newly supplied American warplanes attacked an Iraqi nuclear reactor near Baghdad, and in December 1981 Prime Minister Begin annexed the Golan Heights.

---

*'The storm has not struck yet. We are only experiencing the whirlwinds that go before it.' Prime Minister Vorster of South Africa (31 December 1976).

**They killed several Russian advisers and captured a Soviet sergeant-major.

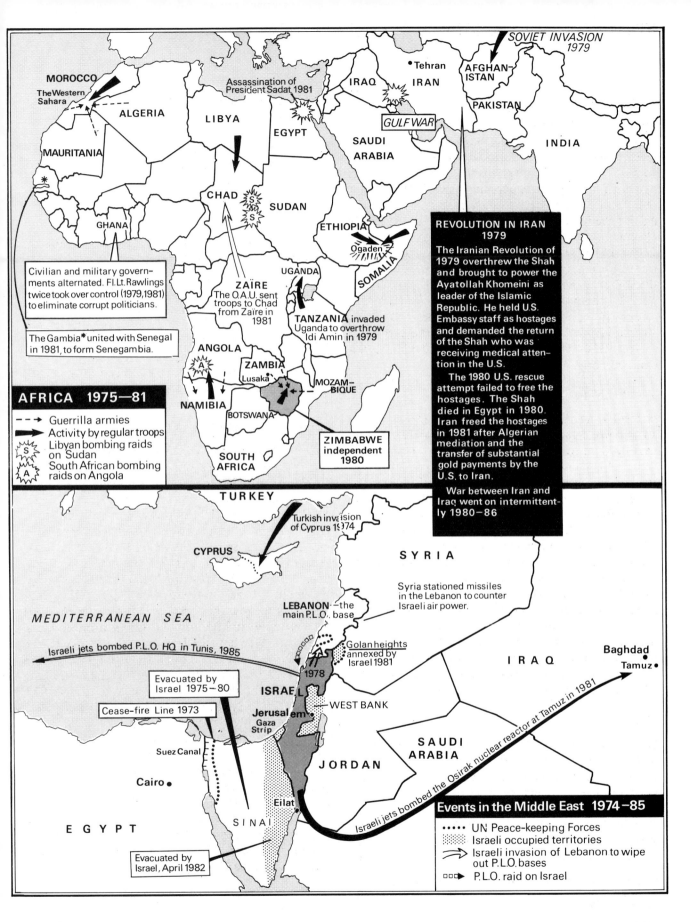

MOROCCO

The Western
Sahara

ALGERIA

MAURITANIA

LIBYA

EGYPT

Assassination of
President Sadat 1981

IRAQ **IRAN**

SOVIET INVASION
1979

**AFGHAN-
ISTAN**

• Tehran

PAKISTAN

GULF WAR

**SAUDI
ARABIA**

INDIA

GHANA

CHAD

S
S
S

SUDAN

ETHIOPIA

Ogaden

SOMALIA

Civilian and military governments alternated. Fl.Lt.Rawlings
twice took over control (1979,1981)
to eliminate corrupt politicians.

The Gambia* united with Senegal
in 1981, to form Senegambia.

ZAÏRE
The O.A.U. sent
troops to Chad
from Zaire in
1981

UGANDA

TANZANIA invaded
Uganda to overthrow
Idi Amin in 1979

ANGOLA

A

NAMIBIA

ZAMBIA
Lusaka •

**MOZAM-
BIQUE**

BOTSWANA

AFRICA 1975—81

- - → Guerrilla armies
── → Activity by regular troops
S Libyan bombing raids
on Sudan
A South African bombing
raids on Angola

**SOUTH
AFRICA**

ZIMBABWE
independent
1980

REVOLUTION IN IRAN
1979

The Iranian Revolution of
1979 overthrew the Shah
and brought to power the
Ayatollah Khomeini as
leader of the Islamic
Republic. He held U.S.
Embassy staff as hostages
and demanded the return
of the Shah who was
receiving medical atten-
tion in the U.S.

The 1980 U.S. rescue
attempt failed to free the
hostages. The Shah
died in Egypt in 1980.
Iran freed the hostages
in 1981 after Algerian
mediation and the
transfer of substantial
gold payments by the
U.S. to Iran.

War between Iran and
Iraq went on intermittent-
ly 1980—86

TURKEY

CYPRUS

Turkish invasion
of Cyprus 1974

MEDITERRANEAN SEA

SYRIA

Syria stationed missiles
in the Lebanon to counter
Israeli air power.

Israeli jets bombed P.L.O. HQ in Tunis, 1985

LEBANON — the
main P.L.O. base

Golan heights
annexed by
Israel 1981

1978

I R A Q

Baghdad
Tamuz •

Evacuated by
Israel 1975–80

Cease-fire Line 1973

ISRAEL

Jerusalem •
Gaza
Strip

— **WEST BANK**

Suez Canal

Israeli jets bombed the Osirak nuclear reactor at Tamuz in 1981

Cairo •

Eilat •

E G Y P T

S I N A I

Evacuated by
Israel, April 1982

**SAUDI
ARABIA**

JORDAN

Events in the Middle East 1974—85

••••• UN Peace-keeping Forces
▒ Israeli occupied territories
⇗ Israeli invasion of Lebanon to wipe
out P.L.O. bases
□□□▶ P.L.O. raid on Israel

73: The uneasy peace 1972–1985

The road to détente

During the 1970s the world witnessed some of the military spin-off from technological advances in space exploration and the invention of micro-electronic circuitry. Nuclear missiles became smaller and more mobile; they also became far more accurate and deadly. Nixon and Brezhnev had already signed their 1972 *Strategic Arms Limitation Treaty* (S.A.L.T 1) in an effort to limit the number of missiles held by the two superpowers; while the two Germanies, conscious that they would be in the front-line of any future conflict, patched up old quarrels and recognized one another's frontiers in their *Basic Treaty* of the same year. It was now desirable to draw into this stabilizing process (usually called *détente*) as much of Europe and North America as possible.

The Helsinki Agreements 1975

Thirty-five countries—all of Europe (except Albania), Canada, the U.S.S.R. and the U.S.A.—met at the 1975 *Helsinki Conference*. There they recognized the legality of existing European frontiers and agreed to respect human rights and fundamental freedoms: 'The participating states recognize the universal significance of human rights and fundamental freedoms, respect for which is an essential factor for the peace, justice and well-being necessary to ensure the development of friendly relations and co-operation among themselves as among all states . . .' But the problem was how to reconcile respect for human rights with the 1968 *Brezhnev Doctrine*, outlined by the Russian leader after Soviet tanks had invaded Czechoslovakia. Brezhnev had argued that when a 'fraternal socialist country' seems to be menaced by enemies inside or outside its frontiers it is quite proper for other socialist countries to lend military assistance.* Of course, the arrival of a Soviet tank brigade and K.G.B. security forces might wipe out human rights and fundamental freedoms of quite a number of people inside the fraternal socialist country—something that certainly happened to the Afghans, who faced up to Soviet invaders in 1979.

S.A.L.T. 2

But the great issue remained. It was vital to reduce the growing stockpile of nuclear weapons held in the arsenals of the two superpowers. On 18 June 1979 President Brezhnev met President Carter in Vienna. There they signed *S.A.L.T. 2*, designed to limit nuclear weapons until 1985. Carter promised that he would not impose any 'binding linkage' between S.A.L.T. 2 and any Soviet actions of which the U.S. might disapprove. Events soon changed his mind. Hard evidence existed to show that new Soviet medium-range missiles equipped with triple warheads—the SS-20s—were targeted on western Europe. Furthermore, Soviet troops invaded Afghanistan on 24 December 1979. The U.S. Senate refused to ratify S.A.L.T. 2 and on 4 January 1980 Carter stated that consideration of the treaty was now 'inappropriate'. Non-ratification of S.A.L.T. 2 was the great failure between 1972 and 1980, and at the time it seemed that it reduced the chances of reaching international agreement on *tactical* arms control, a subject of ever-increasing anxiety.

Arms control 1981–85

SS-20s and the invasion of Afghanistan illustrated the power and the policies of the U.S.S.R. Just before the invasion, the N.A.T.O. countries had decided to modernize their tactical weapons (i.e. weapons launched from bases in western Europe capable of hitting eastern bloc targets several hundred miles away). They agreed to base *Tomahawk* cruise and *Pershing* rocket missiles in western Europe. But when Carter's successor, President Reagan, indicated in 1981 that there was a possibility of a limited nuclear war being fought in Europe, the new missiles themselves became the target for the supporters of unilateral nuclear disarmament. The ill-health of Soviet leaders made discussions difficult: Brezhnev died in 1982; Andropov in 1984; Chernenko in 1985. Strategic Arms Limitation Talks (now called S.T.A.R.T. talks) opened in Geneva 1981, stalled over matial law in Poland and then resumed in 1983. But by 1984 NATO had deployed forty-eight Cruise missiles in Britain and Sicily. Russia's new leader, Mikhail Gorbachov, was therefore quick to oppose President Reagan's Strategic Defence Initiative, popularly known as the Star Wars programme. It was vital to update S.A.L.T. 2 but the superpowers consistently rejected each other's suggestions for balanced arms reductions.

*For a discussion of this point see Peter Summerscale, 'The Continuing Validity of the Brezhnev Doctrine' in Karen Dawisha and Philip Hanson (eds), *Soviet–East European Dilemmas* (Heinemann Educational Books, 1981).

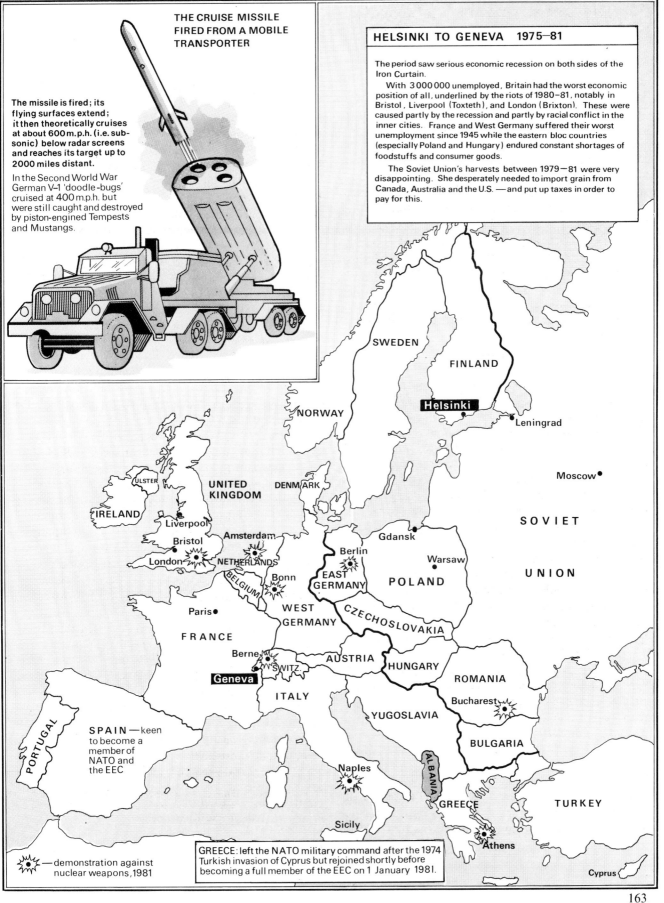

THE CRUISE MISSILE FIRED FROM A MOBILE TRANSPORTER

The missile is fired; its flying surfaces extend; it then theoretically cruises at about 600 m.p.h. (i.e. subsonic) below radar screens and reaches its target up to 2000 miles distant.

In the Second World War German V–1 'doodle-bugs' cruised at 400 m.p.h. but were still caught and destroyed by piston-engined Tempests and Mustangs.

HELSINKI TO GENEVA 1975–81

The period saw serious economic recession on both sides of the Iron Curtain.

With 3 000 000 unemployed, Britain had the worst economic position of all, underlined by the riots of 1980–81, notably in Bristol, Liverpool (Toxteth), and London (Brixton). These were caused partly by the recession and partly by racial conflict in the inner cities. France and West Germany suffered their worst unemployment since 1945 while the eastern bloc countries (especially Poland and Hungary) endured constant shortages of foodstuffs and consumer goods.

The Soviet Union's harvests between 1979–81 were very disappointing. She desperately needed to import grain from Canada, Australia and the U.S. —and put up taxes in order to pay for this.

SWEDEN

NORWAY

FINLAND

Helsinki

Leningrad

Moscow

ULSTER

UNITED KINGDOM

DENMARK

SOVIET

IRELAND

Liverpool

Bristol

Amsterdam

Berlin

Gdansk

Warsaw

UNION

London

NETHERLANDS

BELGIUM

Bonn

EAST GERMANY

POLAND

Paris

WEST GERMANY

CZECHOSLOVAKIA

FRANCE

Berne

AUSTRIA

HUNGARY

ROMANIA

SWITZ.

Geneva

ITALY

Bucharest

YUGOSLAVIA

PORTUGAL

SPAIN—keen to become a member of NATO and the EEC

BULGARIA

ALBANIA

Naples

GREECE

TURKEY

Sicily

Athens

—demonstration against nuclear weapons, 1981

GREECE: left the NATO military command after the 1974 Turkish invasion of Cyprus but rejoined shortly before becoming a full member of the EEC on 1 January 1981.

Cyprus

163

74: Afghanistan and Poland

The Soviet invasion of Afghanistan

When the Russian 105th Guards Airborne Division occupied Kabul on Christmas Eve 1979 Afghanistan was already in the grip of civil war. Prime Minister Hazifullah Amin's attempts to sweep aside Muslim traditions had enraged many Afghans in April 1979. Thousands of his opponents were in gaol. Others had fled to Pakistan. Most dangerous of all, many had joined the *Mujahideen* (Muslim guerrillas) and were waging war against Amin's communist government in Kabul. According to the Russians, Hafizullah Amin had asked the Soviet troops to come to his aid; but on 27 December 1979 Russian soldiers surrounded his headquarters and killed him. Babrak Kamal headed a new communist government, but was totally dependent upon the support of the regular Afghan army and 85,000 Soviet occupation troops.

Counter insurgency 1980–1982

Russia's precise reasons for staying on in Afghanistan remained obscure. To cope with the brave but disorganized Mujahideen she brought in all the trappings of counter-insurgency warfare—armoured personnel carriers, helicopter gunships, air-to-surface missiles and ground-attack aircraft. Yet throughout 1980-81 most of her troops and armour stayed in the vicinity of the towns and left the task of patrolling the difficult mountain areas to the regular Afghan army. By the beginning of 1982 the Mujahideen controlled 75% of the Afghan countryside.

America's attitude

America showed her hostility to the invasion by refusing to ratify S.A.L.T. 2. President Carter also boycotted the 1980 Moscow Olympic Games, stopped the export of high technology equipment (mainly computers and oil drilling gear) to the U.S.S.R. and refused to sell Russia the grain she so desperately needed to feed her livestock. But these sanctions had no effect on the Russian presence in Afghanistan.

Poland and Solidarity

In August 1980 a strike in the Lenin Shipyards of Gdansk heralded radical changes in Polish affairs. Led by Lech Walesa (pronounced *Lek Wah-lehn-sah*), the strikers became the nucleus of the Solidarity free trade union. Ten million Poles joined Solidarity, and demanded freedom of speech, freedom of assembly, freedom of movement and the right to strike. These were unprecedented demands in a communist country—but Poland wasn't a typical communist country. Poles were devout Roman Catholics and intensely nationalistic; Pope John Paul II—himself a Pole—supported them; and they had fairly recent memories of defending Polish ideas and beliefs against the German invader during 1939–44.* But they were realists. They understood the ever-present threat of a Soviet invasion; and Lech Walesa knew that conditions would not improve unless Solidarity helped to put right the chaotic Polish economy. Poland had huge overseas debts; the supermarkets offered bread and milk—and not much else; everyday goods such as jeans, soap, pop records and ball-point pens were in short supply; queues seemed endless; while the existence of a wealthy upper class ensured that there would always be a black market and privileges for a few.

Martial law 1981

Poland's communist leader, Edward Gierek, fell from power in 1980, to be succeeded by Stanislaw Kania. In July 1981 Kania held the first ever free elections in a communist satellite,** but he could not cope with the economic crisis, which was being worsened by Solidarity's brief but effective general strikes. He resigned in October 1981 in favour of General Jaruzelski. On 14 December 1981 the general imposed martial law on Poland. Polish anti-riot police, Z.O.M.O. arrested Solidarity's leaders, including Lech Walesa, and herded them into internment camps. Tanks crashed through the gates of the Lenin shipyard. Z.O.M.O. men surrounded the Fiat-Polski car factory and the Ursus tractor works in Warsaw. Polish troops took over Poland's 2,000 towns and villages. Telephones went dead. Postal services stopped and civilians found all petrol stations closed.

More American sanctions

Jaruzelski had crushed Solidarity; and Poles had killed their own countrymen in Krakow and Katowice. President Reagan's reaction was to accuse the Russians of 'a heavy and direct responsibility for the repression in Poland'. He stopped all flights to America by the Soviet airline *Aeroflot*, suspended sales of high technology materials and postponed negotiations on long-term grain agreements. Jaruzelski ended martial law in July 1983 and offered an amnesty to all Solidarity activists. He had crushed Solidarity as a political force without having to bring in Soviet troops.

---

*For an account of Nazi Kultur in Poland, see Brian Catchpole, *The Clash of Cultures* (Heinemann Educational Books, 1981).
**Seven members of the eleven-man Politburo lost their seats.

The Mil Mi-24 Hind Helicopter Gunship equipped with rocket pods and *SWATTER* missiles. It carries a four-barrel *GATLING* style machine-gun in its nose.

SOVIET UNION

CHINA

IRAN

Mazar-i-Sharif ★

Kunduz ★

Doshi ★

Herat ★
Shindand ★

Kabul ★
Jalalabad ★

Ghazni ★

Farah ★

Kandahar ★

	Soviet invasion December 1979
★	Under Russian control 1981
	Under Mujahideen control 1986
✳	Refugee camps in Pakistan
– →	Guerrilla attacks

AFGHANISTAN 1979 — 86

A huge sprawling city, divided between Afghan regulars and the Mujahideen — and a scene of constant urban warfare.

PAKISTAN

POLAND 1981

BALTIC SEA

Gdansk ●

Szczecin ●

Bydgoszcz ★

SOVIET

UNION

Berlin

Warsaw ✳ ■ ✳
✳

Poznan ★

EAST GERMANY

Legnica ★
● Wroclaw

Lech Walesa interned in a villa near Warsaw

Katowice ●
✳
● Krakow

CZECHOSLOVAKIA

★	Soviet military units already stationed in Poland as part of the Warsaw Pact defence system
✳	Internment camps
✵●	Scenes of violence when martial law was imposed

75: Indo-China since 1973

A united Viet Nam 1976

The year 1975 was a victorious one for the communists of Indo-China. The Khmer Rouge occupied Phnom Penh, capital of Cambodia; the Pathet Lao took over Laos; and the North Vietnamese Army and Viet Cong guerrillas entered Saigon. Within a year Saigon was renamed Ho Chi Minh City, and the North and South united to form the Socialist Republic of Vietnam. Over 100,000 Vietnamese had died in the twentieth century's longest war (1961–75); and the sacrifice of over 56,000 American lives between 1961 and 1973 had failed to prevent the first three 'dominoes' from falling to communism.*

Conditions in Viet Nam

Indiscriminate bombing of the countryside, systematic attacks on dams and ditches, and the constant pollution of people and plant life by chemical defoliants, such as the notorious 'agent orange', had all helped to destroy the economy of Viet Nam. Over 4,000 towns and villages lay deserted. Tens of thousands of people who had worked in the big American bases and leave centres until 1973 were now unemployed; and even more peasants were homeless. Viet Nam's new government set up 'New Economic Zones' so that the unemployed could grow urgently needed rice—but the climate was against them. Appalling rice harvests during 1975–77 led to stringent food rationing. A kilogram of rice, a few potatoes and a sack of wheat flour were supposed to last an individual a month. Rice was 10 dong (5 dollars) a kilogram on the black market—two days' supply! And this was when the average monthly wage was barely 10 dollars! in 1978 the government had to declare that all private trading was illegal—an act which led to the rapid departure of ethnic Chinese from Viet Nam.

The boat people

This extraordinary episode involved nearly 1,000,000 Vietnamese. Ever since the fall of Saigon, senior officers and middle-class business people had been slipping away to a better life in the Philippines, California and Singapore. Suddenly the exodus became a flood. Many thousands of Hoa people (ethnic Chinese) pulled up their roots in the north and crossed into China (1978–79). In the same period, tens of thousands of peasants and urban workers in the south left Viet Nam in overcrowded junks and sampans heading for destinations as far apart as Japan and Indonesia. They risked death from exposure, typhoons and Thai pirates. Half of the survivors reached Thailand or Malaysia. Others made landfalls in Macao, Hong Kong, Taiwan and Japan, while a few boats reached the northern shores of Australia. The lucky ones were those picked up by passing merchant ships or by the special U.S. and Italian task force that patrolled the South China Sea during July 1979.

Kampuchea (Cambodia)

In 1976 Pol Pot became Prime Minister of the newly proclaimed 'Democratic Republic of Kampuchea'. His mission, he said, was to create a new, purified community 'where all kinds of . . . social blemishes have been wiped out'. His methods were brutal. He emptied the cities and forced the people to work on huge collective farms and new irrigation projects. Protesters were clubbed to death. Later—in 1979—Pol Pot's Foreign Minister agreed that the Khmer Rouge had killed 3,000,000 people. In 1978 Vietnamese troops invaded Kampuchea, captured Phnom Penh and forced Pol Pot to retreat to a defence line along the Thai border. There had been frontier clashes between Viet Nam and Kampuchea for years before the invasion, e.g. over the ownership of the islands in the Gulf of Thailand where oil had been found in 1970. In 1979 China moved in to rescue her Kampuchean allies—and invaded northern Viet Nam. By 1980 all of Indo-China was involved in yet another conflict that threatened to escalate into a struggle between the People's Republic of China and the Soviet Union.

A new Indo-China conflict

The Soviet Union began supplying Viet Nam with modern tanks and a variety of sophisticated aircraft in 1979, the year in which Soviet warships first appeared in Cam Ranh Bay, the former U.S. naval base. In 1980 the Russians boosted this aid with *Katyusha* rocket launchers (the famous 'Stalin organs') and improved SAM-6 missiles. Crack Vietnamese units stationed these weapons close to the Thai border; some even attacked Khmer Rouge positions inside Thailand, only to be driven back by air strikes delivered by jets from the Royal Thai Air Force (July 1980). Simultaneously, the Chinese increased their aid to the Khmer Rouge. They had already sent some refurbished, captured U.S. bombers, now flown by Khmer Rouge crews trained in China; next, they delivered long-range artillery, anti-aircraft missiles and their latest anti-tank rockets. A 'war by proxy' was being fought in Indo-China.

*See p. 127.

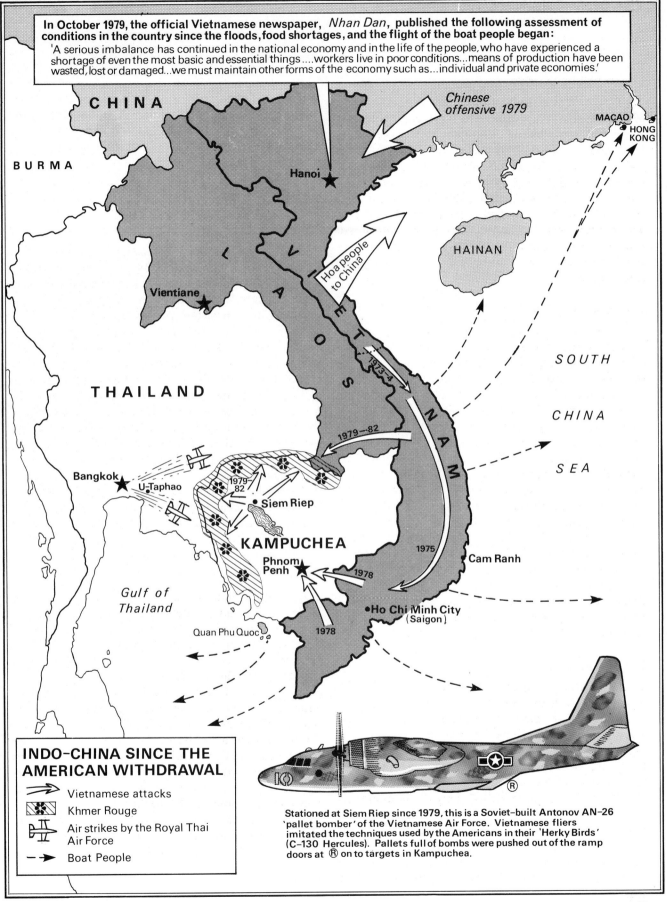

In October 1979, the official Vietnamese newspaper, *Nhan Dan*, published the following assessment of conditions in the country since the floods, food shortages, and the flight of the boat people began:

'A serious imbalance has continued in the national economy and in the life of the people, who have experienced a shortage of even the most basic and essential things....workers live in poor conditions...means of production have been wasted, lost or damaged...we must maintain other forms of the economy such as...individual and private economies.'

CHINA

Chinese offensive 1979

MACAO

HONG KONG

BURMA

Hanoi ★

HAINAN

L

A

O

S

Vientiane ★

Hoa people to China

SOUTH

THAILAND

V

I

E

T

N

A

M

1973–4

CHINA

1979–82

SEA

Bangkok ★

U-Taphao

1979–82

Siem Riep

KAMPUCHEA

1975

Cam Ranh

Phnom Penh ★

1978

Gulf of Thailand

1978

Ho Chi Minh City (Saigon)

Quan Phu Quoc

INDO-CHINA SINCE THE AMERICAN WITHDRAWAL

Vietnamese attacks

Khmer Rouge

Air strikes by the Royal Thai Air Force

Boat People

Stationed at Siem Riep since 1979, this is a Soviet-built Antonov AN–26 'pallet bomber' of the Vietnamese Air Force. Vietnamese fliers imitated the techniques used by the Americans in their 'Herky Birds' (C–130 Hercules). Pallets full of bombs were pushed out of the ramp doors at ⓡ on to targets in Kampuchea.

76: Africa: famine and violence

The famine areas 1968–85

The first sign that major environmental changes were taking place in sub-Saharan Africa came in 1968 when serious droughts hit Cape Verde, Senegal, Mauritania, Mali, Burkina (then Upper Volta), Niger, Chad, Sudan and Ethiopia. Rains failed consistently during 1968–72 and when the farmers in the Sahel (an Arab term for the agricultural zone immediately south of the desert) planted extra crops of millet and sorghum, the advancing Sahara began swamping their fields with sand. Gradually, farmers and herdspeople began moving south, and by 1972 most of the Sahelian countries had proclaimed a state of emergency. Western nations responded by sending 700,000 tons of grain in the hope of alleviating the human suffering. But poor transport facilities in former colonies that had barely 12 years experience of independent, responsible government made food distribution inefficient. In Ethiopia, for example, it is thought that 100,000 people died from starvation between 1972 and 1973. Emergency food aid, medical teams and fresh water supplies could not solve the environmental problems caused by the drought, which was at its worst in 1977. Sporadic rains eased the situation slightly, 1978–82, and then, in 1983, crisis returned to the Sahelian countries. Millions of people were at risk and African governments now faced a phenomenon quite beyond anyone's experience. Matters were worse in countries plagued by constant warfare. In Ethiopia the fighting between government and national liberation forces, particularly in Tigre, Eritrea and Wollo, interrupted the food supplies and prevented the construction and maintenance of efficient refugee camps.

The response

Television cameras alerted the world to the problems in Africa, and the people of the industrialized nations were appalled by the suffering they saw on their TV screens. Governments voted huge sums of money; private initiative collected millions of dollars. The superpowers sank their differences and sent in aid. Israel airlifted 25,000 black Ethiopian Jews (the 'Falashas') in 'Operation Moses' (1985). However, the most spectacular international effort took the form of Bob Geldof's 'Live Aid' concerts and 'Band Aid' record sales. Pop musicians freely gave their services in concerts shown on televisions around the world via the commercial satellites that now swung in synchronous orbit high above the Earth. These 'Live Aid' concerts were described as 'the largest charitable event in history',* and in January 1985 Bob Geldof arrived in Africa to supervize spending of the millions of dollars he had raised.

The condition of southern Africa

Since 1973 the U.N. had recognized S.W.A.P.O. (South West African People's Organization) as 'the sole and authentic representative of the people of Namibia'. Most S.W.A.P.O. national liberation fighters were based in Angola and the South African government had waged a long war against the forces of Angola, S.W.A.P.O. and their Soviet and Cuban advisers. Then in 1984 South Africa and Angola made their *Pretoria–Luanda Accord* in which both countries agreed to reduce the level of hostilities. Relative peace existed along the Namibia–Angolan border; but violence flared up in the Republic of South Africa, where the black majority were once again denied any form of political representation. Though the African National Congress leader, Nelson Mandela, had been in jail since 1964, his wife Winnie continued the policy of peaceful protest against apartheid. In this, she received support from the white activist Helen Suzman and from Bishop Desmond Tutu, the first African to become Bishop of Johannesburg and winner of a Nobel Peace Prize (1984). Throughout 1985 peaceful protest took the form of boycotts against schools and white-owned stores. These made little impact on President Botha's government and during 1985–6 many Africans turned to violence as their only means of opposing the government in Pretoria. During February 1985–February 1986 about 1,000 blacks died, either in conflict with security forces or in inter-ethnic battles as far afield as Durban and Alexandra.

* *The Times*, 30 December 1985.

Photographs:

Above: Famine victims in Ethiopia (*Popperfoto*).
Below: Bob Geldof is presented with a cheque ▶
to help feed the famine victims in Africa (*Popperfoto*).

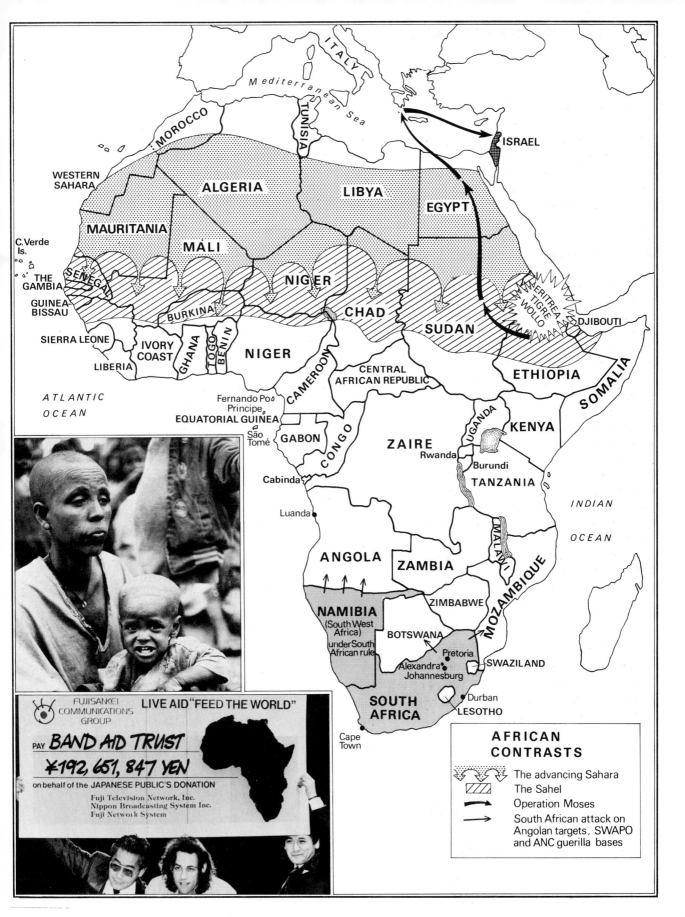

WESTERN
SAHARA

MOROCCO

ALGERIA

TUNISIA

Mediterranean Sea

ITALY

LIBYA

EGYPT

ISRAEL

MAURITANIA

MALI

C.Verde
Is.

THE
GAMBIA

SENEGAL

GUINEA
BISSAU

SIERRA LEONE

LIBERIA

IVORY
COAST

BURKINA

GHANA

TOGO

BENIN

NIGER

NIGER

CHAD

SUDAN

ERITREA

TIGRE

WOLLO

DJIBOUTI

ETHIOPIA

SOMALIA

ATLANTIC

OCEAN

CAMEROON

Fernando Po

Principe

EQUATORIAL GUINEA

São
Tomé

GABON

CONGO

CENTRAL
AFRICAN REPUBLIC

ZAIRE

Rwanda

UGANDA

Burundi

TANZANIA

KENYA

INDIAN

OCEAN

Cabinda

Luanda

ANGOLA

ZAMBIA

MALAWI

MOZAMBIQUE

NAMIBIA
(South West
Africa)
under South
African rule

ZIMBABWE

BOTSWANA

Pretoria

Alexandra

Johannesburg

SWAZILAND

Durban

SOUTH
AFRICA

LESOTHO

Cape
Town

FUJISANKEI
COMMUNICATIONS
GROUP

LIVE AID "FEED THE WORLD"

PAY BAND AID TRUST

¥192, 651, 847 YEN

on behalf of the JAPANESE PUBLIC'S DONATION

Fuji Television Network, Inc.
Nippon Broadcasting System Inc.
Fuji Network System

AFRICAN
CONTRASTS

The advancing Sahara

The Sahel

Operation Moses

South African attack on
Angolan targets, SWAPO
and ANC guerilla bases

169

Index